# What they don't tell you about

# ANGLO-SAXONS

## By Bob Fowke

Dedicated to *Thrimilci*, the Saxon month when
cows were milked three times a day

WAYLAND

Hallo, my name's Ethelfrithelfroth, and if you can say that you can say anything. I'm a Saxon woman and I'm tough as a leather garter. Come with me and I'll show you all about the Anglo-Saxons. I hope you're tough too: this book is not for the faint-hearted ...

Published in 2013 by Wayland
Text and illustrations copyright Bob Fowke 2013

Wayland
33 Euston Road
London NW1 3BH

Wayland Australia
Level 17/207 Kent Street
Sydney, NSW 2000

Produced for Wayland by Bob Fowke & Co
Cover design: Lisa Peacock
Cover illustration: Nick Hardcastle

A CIP catalogue record for this book is available from the British Library

ISBN 978 0 7502 8199 7

10 9 8 7 6 5 4 3 2 1

Printed and bound by CPI Group (UK) Ltd, Croydon, CR0 4YY

First published in 1998 by Hodder Children's Books

Wayland is a division of Hachette Children's Books, an Hachette company
www.hachette.co.uk

# THOR TEMPLAR

**Louis Theroux** went to America after graduating from Oxford University, where he wrote for the satirical magazine *Spy*. After working on Michael Moore's *TV Nation*, Louis hosted his own show, *Weird Weekends*, for the BBC. He followed this with the popular series *When Louis Met . . .* in which he spent time with, amongst others, Jimmy Savile, Neil and Christine Hamilton, and Chris Eubank. This is Louis's first book.

# LOUIS THEROUX

## THE CALL OF THE WEIRD

TRAVELS IN AMERICAN SUBCULTURES

PAN BOOKS

First published 2005 by Macmillan

First published in paperback 2006 by Pan Books
an imprint of Pan Macmillan, a division of Macmillan Publishers Limited
Pan Macmillan, 20 New Wharf Road, London N1 9RR
Basingstoke and Oxford
Associated companies throughout the world
www.panmacmillan.com

ISBN 978-0-330-43570-3

19

A CIP catalogue record for this book is available from
the British Library.

Typeset by SetSystems Ltd, Saffron Walden, Essex
Printed and bound in Great Britain by
CPI Mackays, Chatham ME5 8TD

Visit **www.panmacmillan.com** to read more about all our books and to buy
them. You will also find features, author interviews and news of any author
events, and you can sign up for e-newsletters so that you're always first to hear
about our new releases.

For Nancy

'You may lie with your mouth,
but with the mouth you make as you do
so you none the less tell the truth.'

*Friedrich Nietzsche*

# CONTENTS

# PROLOGUE

One cold December day in 1996, I met up with an elderly racist leader named Pastor Richard Butler. I was making a documentary about right-wing apocalyptic Christians who have retreated to the American North West, Idaho especially, in preparation for the end times. Butler's outfit, the Aryan Nations, represented the far end of that spectrum, a strange racist group that styled itself a Church. It was the most famous neo-Nazi organization in America at the time, much beloved of tattooed skinheads and angry convicts, and linked to at least one White Power terrorist cell that had gone on the rampage in the eighties. Its membership believed that whites were the original Israelites spoken of in the Bible. Non-whites were subhuman, no better than animals, with the exception of Jews, whom they viewed as irredeemably satanic. A race war was said to be imminent, of which the whites, needless to say, would be the eventual victors.

Butler picked me up in Hayden, Idaho, in a creaky old Cadillac, accompanied by an aide-de-camp, whom he introduced as Reverend Jerry Gruidl. I'd felt a little nervous about the encounter, worried that Butler and his followers might want to jump-start the race war by attacking an

English journalist. First impressions were reassuring, however. The pastor was then in his eighties and pretty decrepit. Jerry was in his sixties, pudgy, wearing thick glasses and a cowboy hat. I reckoned I could take them, if it came to that. But they appeared unconcerned with my racial background. The pastor hunched over the wheel of the car as we sped through the snow-covered countryside of northern Idaho. Jerry seemed more intent on sharing his love of English culture, the comedy of Benny Hill, the scenery around Cheltenham, Gloucestershire, where he'd stayed during his stint in the army in the fifties. If I was ever in Cheltenham, I should look up the Garsides, a wonderful family.

We drove up a rough driveway through a pine forest, past a sign saying 'Whites Only', into a clearing with a church and a guard tower and scattered mobile homes. The walls of the pastor's office were lined with racist leaflets in metal holders. Cold and cluttered, it was like the office of an underfunded charitable organization, albeit one dedicated to the eradication of world Jewry. A pair of German shepherds called Hans and Fritz prowled around. There was a stack of flyers with Adolf Hitler wearing a Santa Claus hat.

Butler wanted a moment to open the morning mail, so Jerry offered to take me on a tour of the rest of the compound. Icicles hung from the eaves. A sign said 'God has a plan for homosexuals. AIDS is the beginning.' The church itself was a perfect combination of mildness and menace, like a village chapel, with pews and a piano and stained glass, but with swastikas on the altar and the wall. 'There's no armed guards or anything,' Jerry said, as though I should be able to see for myself how normal this all was. 'Anybody who's white is welcome.'

We went up a ladder into the guard tower, our feet clomping on the wooden boards. And there, as we stood looking out on miles of white wilderness, me feeling as though I was at the far end of the Earth, a strange moral antipodes where Hitler stood in for Father Christmas and the halls were decked with swastikas, Jerry announced his great fondness for the TV programme, *Are You Being Served?*. This struck me as surprising on many levels – that an American neo-Nazi should have heard of a relatively obscure British sitcom from the seventies, that he should have enjoyed its broad sexual innuendo-based comedy, that he should have thought it important enough to mention at just that moment, in the Aryan Nations' guard tower, on the heels of a particularly nasty racist rant.

For a few minutes, we talked about some of the characters. Jerry mentioned liking Mrs Slocombe, the bawdy old saleswoman in the lingerie department who made frequent references to her pussy. I asked him what he thought of Mr Humphries, the effeminate sales assistant whose catchphrase 'I'm free' relied for its humour on the implication that he might be available for gay sex. Perhaps sensing this didn't sit well with the official Aryan Nations policy on homosexuality, Jerry looked confused for a moment, then said he thought he was 'disgusting'. In a playful mood, I asked Jerry to say Mr Humphries' catchphrase, and the conversation ended where it started, with Jerry saying, 'But I'm not free! Because this country's in bondage to the Jews!'

A little later, having done my interview with Pastor

Butler, I left the headquarters of the Aryan Nations, and returned to England for my own more traditional Christmas. Time passed and I moved on to other stories, but occasionally I found myself thinking about my visit to the Aryan Nations and in particular, the strangeness of that conversation with Jerry in the guard tower. I came to realize what probably should have been obvious, that Jerry mentioning a British TV show had been an attempt to bond with me, and that I'd seen him in the grip of two contradictory impulses, his loyalty to Nazism on the one hand, and on the other his desire to make a friend. I found excuses to get back in touch with him. I sent him copies of some of my documentaries, including the one he appeared in. 'I thought you did a pretty good job of making fools of people,' he said, with heavy sarcasm, when I phoned for his feedback. Hoping to get back into his good books, I looked up Sidney Garside, of the Cheltenham Garsides, the family Jerry had stayed with. Sidney was still living in Cheltenham, a retired pipe fitter of conventional political beliefs. I wrote to Jerry and let him know I'd found the family, then put them in touch.

Gradually, I fell out of contact with Jerry, but I never forgot about him. The contrast of his warm human qualities combined with the hatefulness of his beliefs set a kind of gold standard for the kind of journalism I was doing, which followed my attempts to form something more than the usual journalistic relationship with members of weird groups. As the years passed and I made more episodes of my TV series, Jerry was joined in my mental scrapbook by a handful of other characters whose fates I continued to be curious about long after the interviews were over: a UFO believer named Thor Templar who claimed to have killed ten aliens; a pimp named Mello T who was pursuing a career as a gangsta rapper; a young porn performer who worked under the name JJ Michaels. As I had with Jerry, from time to time, in the odd idle moment, sipping a cup of tea, warming my feet by the radiator in rainy London, I would phone or email and ask how everything was going. And then I'd lose touch with them, too. But my idle moments returned. After more cups of tea and more musing, my thoughts took shape in an idea.

A Reunion Tour. A six-month trip around the States catching up with ten of my most intriguing 'ex–interviewees'. (There is no satisfactory word for the people a journalist covers – his 'characters', his 'subjects' – which may say something about the oddness of the relationship itself.) An update on both them and their weird worlds. The details were vague in my mind, but the urge to do it was quite distinct. The more I thought about it, the more I liked this idea. I'd been interviewing odd people for almost exactly ten years, ever since a visit to a Christian minister in Oakland, California, in early 1994, who was predicting that the world would end later in the year. I was ready for a break. It would be a chance to work in a different way, getting closer to the people I was covering, without the sense of performance that the camera inevitably brings.

I hoped the changes in their subcultures might say something about changes in the world at large – the 'post 9/11 universe'; Clinton's America versus Bush's America; the nineties and the noughties. In hindsight, the nineties may have been a kind of golden age for strange beliefs. In that interregnum between the fall of the Berlin Wall and the attacks on the World Trade Center all kinds of bizarre heterodoxies took root: space creatures were abducting humans from Earth, a secret cabal of bankers and industrialists named the Illuminati were running the world; the approaching year 2000 heralded the Second Coming, or the arrival of a fleet of spaceships from a benevolent intergalactic federation, or at the very least some glitches on your PC.

Or it may be that the world was exactly as weird as it always was, but the media, less distracted by the spectre of a global menace like communism or terror, had time to focus on less persuasive fears. The truth was, my real motivation was less grandiose. I was just curious what became of some of the odd folk I got to know.

In early 2004, I made arrangements to move to America. I began putting things in storage, clearing out my house so I could let it while I was away. I compiled a rough list of the people I hoped to see, adding to those already mentioned: a prostitute named Hayley; a UFO cult in San Diego; a neo-Nazi childrens' folk group; a militiaman named Mike Cain; an elusive self-help guru named Marshall Sylver; and, as a wild card, the turbulent bandleader Ike Turner. I marked them on a large map of the US which I pinned to the wall of my study, taking pains to cut out little labels which I glued to the map, like a general preparing for a campaign. After an hour or so of work, I'd managed to demonstrate that most of my subjects were in the west of the US, a fact I'd been aware of before I started the exercise. But as an act of handicraft it had the virtue of taking my mind off the anxieties about the trip which, now that I'd made the decision to go, were starting to blossom inside me. And so I found myself sticking on more names, adding people and groups I had no intention of visiting, for the sheer pleasure of doing the lettering and the scissoring and seeing the labels accumulate.

My anxieties took various forms. I'd had the idea of seeing my old subjects because I was curious what had become of them. But it would also be my first visit since making the shows, which, now I thought about it, some critics had regarded as being faintly mocking in tone. Would my interviewees still be as friendly having seen the programmes? Would they feel conned? Would they mind that the series of cultural documentaries they'd participated in, *Louis Theroux's America*, had arrived on British TV screens as a light-hearted romp called *Louis Theroux's Weird Weekends*? Rather than a Reunion Tour, the trip might turn into a kind of referendum on my own methods, as voted on by my ex-subjects.

As my departure date approached, I sent out a few exploratory emails, more in an attempt to reassure myself that my collaborators were out there and available. For the most part, these emails went unacknowledged or came back address unknown. I glued some more labels to my Weirdness Map to calm my nerves. Then, in a bid to add some seriousness to my approach, I tried looking for common themes among my subjects. I drew up a Venn diagram showing the 'Four Main Sources of Weirdness' as interlocking circles, which I identified as 'Sexual', 'Racial', 'Religious', and 'Narcissistic'. Though there were some areas of overlap, I was more struck by the variety of the motivations. The militiamen of Idaho would regard gangsta rap as an end-state symptom of our godless society. People in porn generally find the idea of speaking to aliens laughable and bizarre. What, in fact, was 'weirdness'? The more I thought about it, the less clear it became.

One morning in April, I packed my last few things into the loft as a taxi waited to take me to the airport. I had a bag with a few clothes and a list of names and not much else. My plan, such as it was, was to buy a second-hand car in Las Vegas, and work outwards from there; and it was several hours later, somewhere up above the American Mid-West, that two thoughts formed in my mind. The first had to do with the nature of weirdness. I realized that the main quality uniting my subjects, be they porn performers, neo-Nazis, or UFO believers, was their alienness *to me specifically*; and that my long years of interest in their beliefs was evidence that I – in however small a way – must share those beliefs. I wondered whether taken together the weird mores of the people I'd been covering all these years might represent a negative version of myself – a shadow-map of my own most secret nature.

The second thought was about the Weirdness Map I'd made in London. In my rush to get the last things into storage, I'd left it tacked up on the wall of my study; and I imagined it there, the sole item left in that empty house, a rendering in miniature of the landscape I was flying into . . .

I was driving south from Vegas through hot flat desert in my new second-hand car, a 1993 Dodge Dynasty with 90,000 miles on the clock.

It was a week since I'd touched down, and I'd decided to ease into my Reunion Tour via the gentle and eccentric world of UFO believers. For some reason, which may have to do with the barren other-worldly landscape of the area, or the unconventional pioneer spirit of the people who move there, the vast spaces of the American West are a popular stomping ground for both extraterrestrials and the Earthlings who meet them.

In a way, it is a fitting continuation of the frontier tradition. Like the Old West, the UFO community is semi-anarchic, a wild frontier settled by adventurers, dreamers and con artists. Unlike other subcultures I've reported on, UFO belief is less a lifestyle than a vague rubric under which adherents either find spiritual sustenance or delude themselves (depending on your point of view) and where the clerical class of lecturers, authors and experts either minister to the needs of their fellow believers or rip them off.

I myself have very little affinity with the idea that there

are ongoing alien incursions into our airspace which the government, for reasons of greed and self-interest, is covering up. For me, the attraction of the UFO world is my amazement that people can spin detailed fantasies about alien civilizations out of flimsily accredited anecdotes and videos of blurry lights. I wonder what it tells us about human psychology that people are ready to believe something so unlikely and what their motivations might be.

I met many odd people during a two-week trip through the UFO subculture in 1997, but perhaps none so intriguing as Thor Templar, Lord Commander of the Earth Protectorate. His company was called the Alien Resistance Movement, and it billed itself as a kind of security agency for people either threatened by or under actual physical attack from hostile aliens. If you happened to have been abducted, Thor could remove your 'implants', the little devices put into humans by their captors while aboard alien ships. Thor had an entire catalogue of gadgets, many of them aimed at warding off space creatures: a kind of radio that crackled when aliens were near; a 'psychotronic helmet', which looked a lot like an ordinary bicycle helmet with various knobs and pipes glued on to it, to focus your 'brain energies'; an 'alien mutilator gun'.

He had come to the door wearing a quasi-military uniform – grey shirt with shoulder patches and a maroon beret. He had an RAF-style moustache, short hair and stood 'at ease' in the fashion of the army. Youngish, maybe forty, he was attended by a woman with short blonde hair, wearing a matching uniform, who I suspected was his girlfriend. He introduced her as Liz.

'One thing that we want to make perfectly clear is that these are not angels, these are not superhuman beings,' Thor said. His manner was officious, a little like a fire marshal explaining a drill. 'They have some advanced technology. They can be handled, they can be killed if necessary. So let's make that perfectly clear.' He claimed to have killed ten aliens himself – zapped them with the mutilator gun to make them materialize, then dismembered them with an edged weapon. 'There's a thick gooey substance inside,' he said, sharing the detail in an offhand way. Maybe sensing my concern, he added, 'These are creatures that make grown men cringe and soil themselves and they are no creatures to be respected.'

I tried to establish some common ground, some shared understanding of how the world is constituted, but it wasn't easy. 'You have an unusual degree of conviction that this is fact,' I said. 'Do your friends and family regard you as a little bit cracked?' No, he said, they're supportive.

You might think it would be irritating, hearing these bald claims with no back-up. But I couldn't help admiring it, almost as a piece of theatre. Later when I tried to think what it was about Thor I found so fascinating, I realized it was quite simple: despite the alien beliefs, the claims to have killed 'greys', the phantom army of earth patriots, he seemed basically quite normal.

After that first visit, we stayed in touch by phone for a few years. His interest in killing aliens waned. 'X-Files has been cancelled,' he lamented. 'Dark Skies ratings are down. Earth's basically given up the fight.' He talked about the pressing issue of predatory vampires. Then one day his contact details no longer worked. He simply disappeared.

What do you do after you've been Lord Commander of the Earth Protectorate? What is the next position on that particular CV?

✳

Before leaving London, while searching Thor on the internet, I'd made an unwelcome discovery. Among the top results were jocular comments I'd made in interviews promoting my shows, saying how bizarre I'd found him and his claims to have killed ten aliens. It was like catching a glimpse of myself in a CCTV monitor at an unflattering angle and for a moment wondering who the fellow with the big nose was – an unwelcome flash of objectivity.

There were a few references to Thor that predated our encounter. His name turned up on a couple of websites dedicated to devil worship: churchofsatan.com and puresatan.com. In the early nineties he'd published several 'grimoires' of the dark arts and a fourteen-volume collection of black-magic spells. I thought seriously about ordering one of them but they cost hundreds of dollars. The last mention of Thor's name was in 1998, the same year my UFO documentary aired. I wondered whether the fallout from the show and my own ill-considered remarks had forced him into hiding.

Chaotic and spread out as it is, the UFO world is not an easy community to dip into. But once a year, hundreds of its more colourful constituents gather at a low-budget hotel-casino called the Flamingo, in Laughlin, Nevada, for the International UFO Congress. It was here that my road now tended, through miles of empty, arid wilderness, past abandoned roadside stores, houses on the backs of lorries and signs in the middle of nowhere saying '950 acres for sale'.

Laughlin lies in the desert, on a stretch of the Colorado River. Other than the hotels – big chintzy buildings which line the bank like knickknacks on a mantlepiece – there is almost nothing there: some RV parks populated by the flock of itinerant elderly known as 'snowbirds', a few discount stores, a 'Jewelry Liquidation Center' where desperate gamblers can pawn the family heirlooms.

I arrived early in the evening, a paid-up attendee of the fourteenth gathering of the Congress. The cacophony of the casino floor hit me like a wave. The out-of-phase jingles of the slot machines and the chink-chink of the payouts mixed together, reminding me a little of a CD I once bought by the avant-garde composer Steve Reich. Waitresses in miniskirts patrolled the aisles with trays of drinks on their arms. Elderly gamblers fed coins into the machines from little plastic buckets.

The Congress is a week-long event, comprising four daily lectures, a UFO film festival and a couple of parties. I'd only paid for the last half, figuring that that would be more than enough time to spend captive to a worldview I found at best charmingly wrong-headed and, occasionally, a little irritating. I had arrived on the evening of the Meet the Speakers party. In a darkened banqueting room on the second floor, three hundred or so people in leisurewear chatted at large round tables. Oddly, the clientele was not markedly different than on the casino floor – mainly over fifty, though a few of the men sported white ponytails and UFO-themed jewellery. At one table, hearing that I was from England, the talk turned to David Icke, the Coventry

City goalkeeper who reinvented himself as a New Age prophet.

'Doesn't he believe there are twelve-foot lizard people running the planet?' I asked.

'He believes the reptilian people have an agenda here, that's correct,' said Darrell, a success coach from Las Vegas.

'But lizards?'

'Reptilians,' Darrell said.

'We're a prison planet,' said Jeanne, a grizzled-looking teacher from Colorado. 'Have you read his books? You should! He exposes the Queen of England. She's a reptile.'

On another table, a 'personal evolution trainer', Michael Telstarr, was chatting to an elderly 'space channel' named Bob Short. I knew Bob fairly well, having featured him in my UFO documentary. That time, he'd gone into a trance and tuned in to the prognostications of a spaceman named Korton. For the Meet the Speakers party, Bob was wearing a shiny gold lamé top and gold cummerbund. Around his neck was a bolo tie with a flying-saucer fastener. His white hair was pulled back in a ponytail and, though it was dark, he had sunglasses on.

Michael was also a paranormalist. He had a manic, slightly distracted air, a curly mop of hair, an overlarge suit jacket and a spherical crystal round his neck. He was forty or so, a little overweight, though later I learned he'd worked as an escape artist for some years, using the name 'Scott Free'. 'I teach people how to access cognitrons and open up neural pathways,' he said quickly, looking around the room.

I was taking notes and having trouble keeping up. 'Positrons?' I asked.

'Cognitrons. I help people access right-brain faculties. Develop psychic powers.'

'Can you tell anything about me?'

'I see good monies coming to you as a result of your direct efforts this year,' he said. 'You were restricted, hemmed-in before. You are analytical and logical but you are also creative. You're taking a chance here but you're going to do much better being on your own.'

I thought this was pretty good going, though Bob knew I'd left the BBC to write a book and I wondered if he'd told Michael. A little later, becoming excited at the idea that I was from the media, Michael offered to move a piece of paper with his mind. He asked me to fetch a pin. At the bar they had no pins but they gave me a tiny red plastic sword for cocktails. Michael stuck one end in a piece of cheese, balanced a small folded strip of paper on the other end, then put a glass over them. He twitched a few times, then made strange rotating gestures in the air with his hands. For ten or twenty seconds, nothing happened. Suddenly the paper began twisting first one way, then the other, as Michael conducted it. I put it down to some convection force inside the glass, or possibly static, but it was a good trick.

Michael brushed off my compliments. 'It should be spinning way more than that,' he said. 'The resistance of that stupid plastic thing is crazy.'

Keen to speak to someone less flighty who could give me a status report on the UFO field from a sober, though believing, perspective, I continued my circuit of the banqueting room, spotting Jim Marrs, author of *Alien Agenda* and a respected expert. Jim was short and tubby and wearing a panama hat, and working his way through a little collection of free quarter-size wine bottles.

I told him I was checking back into ufology and wondered how it had changed in the last ten years.

'Here's the problem,' he said, in a broad Texas accent, and handed me a half-dollar coin. 'Now give it back. Now ask me for it.' I did so. Then, putting on a voice of faux disingenuousness, he said: 'What? I don't know what you're talking about. I don't have a half dollar. I never did have a half dollar. How can you prove I ever had one? You can't prove it unless you empty my pockets. Maybe you can hold me upside down and shake me. *We can't empty the government's pockets.* And that's the problem.'

'How much does the government know?'

'They know a lot. In fact, *they* are the reason for the embargo on UFO information. They don't care if you know there're aliens out there. What they *don't* want you to know is that there's alternative energies that might upset their monopolies. I mean, why are we fighting in Iraq? It's not to spread freedom and democracy. It's to gain control over their oil resources.'

A soft-voiced bearded man who'd been eavesdropping said, 'And because they've got stargates there.'

Jim, picking his words carefully, said, 'And to gain ancient knowledge of futuristic technology.'

＊

The following three days I did my best to get into the swing of the Congress, attending lectures by alien abductees and supposed government whistle-blowers, interviewing experts and asking around about Thor and the Alien Resistance Movement. The field, so far as it exists as a coherent belief system (which isn't very far) seemed not to have moved on a great deal in eight years. The basic script was

still that the authorities are in contact with alien civilizations; that they allow abductions of humans in return
for help with technology; that the aliens are abducting
humans because they are having trouble breeding and need
our DNA. The one change was a subplot to do with alternative fuel sources that the aliens have shared with the
government and which the government is hiding, chiming
as it does with the supposed real reasons behind the Iraq
invasion.

I had thought abductions might be passé, but the conference held daily gatherings for so-called 'experiencers'
to interact, from which the press was banned. At the first
lecture I went to, a young man from Kent, twenty-one-
year-old Jason Andrews, claimed to go up in spaceships
three or four times a week. He went on to say he was
himself a 'walk-in', an alien in a human body. Presumably
to forestall panic, he added, in an Estuary accent, 'I do
assure you, I'm one of the good guys.' With gold rings on
every one of his fingers, snaggled teeth, gelled hair and a
surly manner, Jason made an unlikely messenger of intergalactic goodwill. At the end of his talk, he offered advice
to a few members of the audience. 'Try without trying,' he
said to one woman looking to expand her massage business. Then he appeared to run dry of New Age homilies.
Another woman asked if he was a grey. 'No, I'm a pink,' he
said.

I went up to him after his talk but found him grudging
and mistrustful. He mentioned that since he was thirteen,
he'd existed in a number of different physical locations at
the same time.

'Are you in a number of places right now?'

'Yep.'

'Can you tell me where else you are?'

'Nope.'

I asked why he didn't take a photo when he was on the spaceships. This is the kind of question you're not supposed to ask, but why not? 'If you need physical evidence,' he said, 'then you're not ready to see.'

To be fair, Jason was atypical in the baldness of his abduction claims. Others I spoke to said they'd only realized they were being abducted after undergoing hypnotic regression and that the experience wasn't strictly physical. They seemed deeply sincere about what they'd been through. A laid-back fellow from Colorado, Terry Danton, sixty or so, told me he gets picked up a couple of times a year. 'Greys,' he said. 'I see three little ones and one tall one. It's mental. It's something that comes into my mind.' Jason and his mother, also a lecturer at the Congress on the subject of her son's peculiar gifts, seemed to have a nice sideline in paranormalism. They were flogging a book about their experiences and Jason was working as an 'energy healer'. The good faith of someone like Terry was more troubling because it was harder to laugh off.

I began spending more time in the vending area where the motivations of the salespeople were reassuringly mundane. Twenty or thirty tables were set out. On sale were books with names like *Listening to Extraterrestrials*, *Healing Entities and Aliens*, *Alien Log*; DVDs of crop circles; fossils and Native-American-style 'high-spirit flutes'. You could get your 'aura' photographed or have a 'psychic body scanner' diagnose your ailments, buy Biomagnetic Health Insoles for your shoes or 'Color Therapy Eyewear' – glasses with lenses in different colours.

A skinny young man called Jeffrey was manning a table of 'advanced longevity products' invented by one Patrick Flanagan. 'He's not here,' Jeffrey said. 'He has a measurable IQ of 200. Aged twelve, he invented a guided-missile detector.'

One of the products was a supplement called 'Crystal Energy'. The bottle said it made water 'wetter'.

'Does that mean anything?' I asked Jeffrey.

'Yeah, it drops the surface tension so it feels more solvent in your mouth,' Jeffrey said. 'He learned it from the Hunza people of the Himalayas.'

A few tables along, a husband and wife team from Washington State, LeAra and Dan Clausing, were selling 'M-genic medallions' – little stone rings on cords to enhance your immune system – at the specially discounted price of forty dollars. The Clausings were followers of the rogue Croatian-born scientist Nikola Tesla. 'We made them from stone quarried in China and then put them in a black box with a Tesla coil,' LeAra said.

Dan wanted to demonstrate the effects of the medallion. He ushered me behind his desk and, as I stuck my arm out, pushed down on it with two fingers. My arm held firm. Then he handed me a small packet of artificial sweetener to hold against my chest. He pushed again and this time my arm went down easily. Was he pushing harder? It was hard to tell. But Dan had his own explanation. 'That sweetener is creating chaos in your energetic field!' he said. 'It's poison!' As the final part of the demonstration, he had me hold the sweetener *and* a medallion. My arm held firm again as Dan pantomimed a great strain of exertion (actually making groaning noises). 'The medallion is cancelling out the harmful effects!'

Feeling indebted, I bought a medallion and put it on. 'You're in your cocoon now,' Dan said.

'You can put that medallion under bad wine and it'll make it palatable,' LeAra said. 'It completely removes the bad stuff.'

Safely inside my cocoon, I attended a lecture by Charles Hall. He was a heavyset man, conservative-looking in a suit, about sixty years old. He said that from 1965 to 1967 he'd worked as a weather observer in the desert at Nellis Airforce Base in Indian Springs, Nevada. He'd had extensive contact with a community of tall white aliens, who, with the knowledge of the US military, operated a top secret 'deep-space landing area' for their craft. They spoke English and made frequent trips to Las Vegas, where CIA agents would chaperone them. 'They liked to go for entertainment in casinos,' Charles said. 'They're just like we are.'

In its favour, you could say of the Congress that it was a 'non-judgmental environment'. But there was something exhausting and ultimately futile about this community where unverifiable stories piled up, with no resolution. UFO research showed signs of being a vast database of fantasy – which I suppose I already knew, but I resented myself for spending time in a place where I was struggling to find admirable qualities. I felt cranky and intolerant. I took a break and had dinner at the casino diner, ordering halibut with a baked potato, the only item on the menu that looked vaguely healthy. I'd taken my medallion off by this time. It just didn't feel like me. But I'd left it under a bottle of wine I'd opened the day before that had tasted a little fizzy. That night, arriving back from a 'skywatch' with Michael Telstarr and a couple of others, I tried the wine. It was fractionally better, but I put this down to it 'settling down' naturally.

Several hours later, I was heaving my guts into the toilet bowl. I threw up six or seven times that night, snorting Cabernet-coloured bile through my nose. Most of the next day I lay in bed, aching all over. I felt as though I might be dying. Whether it was the halibut or the wine, or a negative reaction to my cocoon, it didn't say much for the medallion. When I finally made it back down to the Congress, I bumped into Michael Telstarr in the vending area. He speculated that I was experiencing a reaction to the collected energy of the gathering. 'That's a lot to handle if your body's not used to it.'

As for Thor, the Congress was a washout. Almost no one had heard of him or the Alien Resistance Movement. His name drew blanks everywhere. In fact, I realized, though his wild claims of encounters might seem to make Thor no different from many other UFO experts, there was an important respect in which he didn't really fit in: no one else claimed to have *killed* aliens. The very idea ran counter to one of the few points everyone else agreed on: that they *are* superhuman beings and their civilization is millions of years in advance of our own. This was the aliens' raison d'être – to make us feel like younger brothers in the cosmos. Claiming to possess the technology to decapitate greys as Thor did stretched the credulity of even these believers.

＊

With no leads on Thor, I decided to pay a visit to Bob Short, the space channel, at his home in the tiny Arizona town of Cornville. If I couldn't put Thor on the couch, I could at least have a crack at Bob.

He was one of the last survivors of the earliest generation of UFO enthusiasts, a strange crew of mystics called the 'contactees'. Their heyday was the 1950s, when they published books telling of their meetings with beautiful human-like 'space brothers' in the desert. The aliens had arrived from planets in our solar system. Speaking idiomatic English, they warned of the dangers of nuclear testing. Though couched as fact, the accounts had the flavour of an American vernacular religion. Putting a generous gloss on the phenomenon, the writer William Burroughs once commented: 'These individuals may be tuning in, with faulty radios, to a universal message.'

Forty years on Bob's story was largely the same. His space friend was named Korton, and lived in a parallel dimension in a planetary system called Koldas. This allowed him to see into the future, and for a fee Bob would channel Korton and answer questions in a booming robotic voice punctuated with lots of 'ums', a little like a fortune teller.

During my first visit, for the documentary, I'd spent a matter of hours with Bob, most of which was taken up with the channelling session. Bob's hair was teased and combed up like a sporing dandelion. He sat on a small throne in the corner of a little chapel behind his house and wheezed and gurgled and shook from side to side for several hours in the semi-darkness. For my own part, while I didn't believe that Bob was in touch with a real physical being on another planet, and I took his claims of Korton's oracular gift with a pinch of salt, I didn't view him as a con man either. It was plausible, I reasoned, that he might be in some kind of self-induced trance and really not know what was coming out of his mouth. Still,

I wondered about the exact measure of his faith. Did he ever experience doubt?

Having made an appointment by phone (he sounded a little disappointed when I said I wouldn't be bringing a TV crew with me), I drove down from Las Vegas and met him in front of a local grocery store. I'd noticed an odd-looking fellow in my rearview mirror. Then suddenly, in a vaguely paranormal fashion, he appeared by the side of my car. He was dressed head to toe in black, with a black cowboy hat and dark glasses, and his hair was pulled back in a pony-tail.

I followed him back to his house, an old, pale yellow single-storey building at the end of a red dirt road, cluttered with Egyptian statuary and pictures of Native Americans. His air-conditioning was down, so we sat in the heat in his front room. I told him I was curious about his life, how he came to be a space channel, what his family thought about it. Before I knew what was happening he had embarked on a long anecdote about the editor of the book Bob had just published. The anecdote took several sharp turns, picking up random details like a bus with no clear destination; the miracle-healing of a man with colon cancer was mentioned; somebody's mother who was a Franciscan nun; Bob's meeting with a spaceman named Sutku in 1958.

More stories followed. I was having trouble getting a toehold in the conversation, and by the time we were in his car on the way to dinner, I was starting to worry that our whole time together was going to consist of unending, unverifiable anecdotes about his close encounters of various kinds. I complimented him on his car, a sturdy Chevy utility vehicle. Bob mentioned that Korton had told his wife

Shirley what kind to get, down to the mileage and the colour. 'And my wife walked into Larry Green's Chevrolet. This was the only one on the lot.'

'Do you ever wonder if it's real?'

Bob huffed. 'Doesn't anybody? Sure, you know, I'll even ask my wife Shirley. I'll say, "Shirley, did this really happen when that . . ." She'll say, "Robert, you know it did, because we have it documented."'

'Have you ever had your confidence shaken? Have you ever thought, "Well, maybe I'm just kind of a con man?"'

'No no no no no,' Bob said. 'If you're going to set out to do that, you might as well forget it to begin with! Because what you're doing is assailing your own person with self-doubt. Okay? You're assailing! You're putting yourself down. That's what you're doing. You're assailing yourself with negative doubtful situations. Okay?'

I hadn't meant this as a provocative question. I'd thought he might say something about the inner tensions of faith, his own struggles with what he was doing, how he had resisted becoming a mouthpiece for a space prophet. It seemed obvious that anyone would doubt his sanity if called upon by unseen voices to announce himself as the bearer of a message from another dimension. But Bob felt that merely to entertain the possibility of fraudulence was self-sabotaging and dangerous. I suppose, if I'd been looking for evidence of bad faith, I'd found it here, in his defensiveness. It suggested a fragility on Bob's part that he wasn't more open to scepticism.

For dinner we drove twenty miles up the road to Sedona, a New Age haven of crystal shops and healing centres. The Mexican restaurant Bob had in mind turned out to be closed so we settled on a UFO-themed diner. Bob talked about his past lives – as a 'fisherman-philosopher in Bora Bora' and a Chinese librarian who died chasing a butterfly over a cliff. Half an hour after I'd finished my Veggie Reuben, Bob had yet to touch his chicken sandwich. 'I need to think about turning in,' I said. 'I might buy a bottle of wine if there's a liquor store on the way back.'

'Well, don't bring me with you,' Bob said. 'I don't want to go anywhere near one of those places,' and resumed a story about Steven Spielberg, whom he met around the time of 'Third Encounters', as he called *Close Encounters of the Third Kind*.

That night, I worried that Bob and I weren't getting to know one another after all. Our agendas appeared to be at loggerheads: his was to expound the many times he'd been privileged with supernatural predictions and sightings; mine was to find out about his day-to-day existence. I began to doubt my idea of a Reunion Tour. In getting to know Bob better, I found his outlook stranger and more maddening than I had on my first visit. Here and there, I'd picked up details about his life. He'd mentioned a son and a daughter, both the offspring of his wife Shirley by her first husband – and neither one keen to be interviewed, so he said. He said he used to work nine-to-five jobs, as a waiter and bartender in Joshua Tree, California, and more recently stacking shelves in a grocery. But overall, Bob seemed more interested in his life as a Chinese librarian.

The frustration, both mine at Bob's loquaciousness and Bob's at my tendency to interrupt or lose the thread of his stories, continued through the next day. By four o'clock, our appointed channelling time, Bob seemed frazzled and I was grouchy. We retreated to the chapel behind his house, furnished with folding chairs and odd bits of UFO memorabilia.

On the walls there were framed certificates and devotional paintings of angelic-looking aliens. There was a filing cabinet with the bumper sticker 'I'd rather be channeling'. In the corner of the room stood an old electric organ with switches labelled 'cornet', 'French horn', 'vox humana'.

In pride of place, in a gold frame, was a painting of an androgynous man with long blond hair and blue eyes and a large square pendant.

'That's Korton,' Bob said.

'He looks a little bit like, maybe, Jesus might look,' I said.

'I don't know,' Bob said, and laughed lightly. 'That's something I can't prove one way or the other.'

Bob put on slippers and rested his feet on a cushion. The lamps in the room were off and the only light came through the edges of the blind, which had been pulled down. Bob closed his eyes and wheezed with a sound like a car skidding on gravel. He rocked in his chair and snorted and gurgled and twitched from side to side. Bob's vocal chords gave voice to several distinct personalities, operators working a kind of interdimensional telephone exchange. One of them, called 'Addy', spoke in a tremulous old voice with his head cocked to the side. Korton, the headliner, declaimed in a booming monotone with rolled Rs and posh Yankee vowels.

'THIS IS THE HONOURABLE KORTON REPRESEN-TAH-TEEVE CALLING YOU ON BEHALF OF THE PLANET YOU CALL JUPITER!' Korton said.

'What will happen in the upcoming election?' I asked.

'MANY WHO ARE INCUMBENTS WILL, UM, BE TURNED AWAY,' Korton said.

'I was wondering about George Bush and the . . .'

'AN HONOURABLE INDIVIDU-ILL BUT THEN, UM,' Korton began, and spoke for several minutes about oil cartels and the invasion of Kuwait.

Trying a different tack, I asked about my relationship with my dad. Oddly, Korton seemed to think he was dead. I assured him he was alive and well, whereupon Korton said, as if to excuse himself, that he was 'ADVANCED IN AGE.'

'Well, he's sixty-three.'

And so it went on. Korton said he couldn't give out information about the pop star Michael Jackson because of certain 'LAW CODES', that my car's electrical system needed updating and that I should check the 'TREAD-WEAR, UM' on the 'AS YOU TERM IT, TYRES'; advised getting my eyes tested; and when asked generally about my journey said I interrupted too much in my interviews.

'IT IS VERY DIFFICULT FOR INDIVIDU-ILLS TO, UM, PROVIDE INFORMATION, UM, IN YOUR VERNACULAR, UM, IN ANY THUMBNAIL SKETCH.'

In spite of myself, and somewhat unreasonably, I found myself feeling irritated with Korton and/or Bob. Little things bothered me like his accent slipping and bouts of coughing. Intending to make it my final question, I asked whether I might have the right stuff to be a space channel myself. Korton said possibly, but that I would have to 'CHANGE A GREAT DEAL' in my 'LIFESTYLE'. He explained that at the moment I drank too much and smoked too much pot.

'WE WOULD INVITE YOU TO SEEK OUT, UM, THAT WHICH YOU TERM ALCOHOLICS ANONYMOUS AND/OR NARCOTICS ANONYMOUS, IS THAT UNDERSTOOD, UM?'

I took issue with Korton on this, and the session ended

in something close to an argument between myself and the honourable representative from Koldas.

When it was over, Bob snorted with his face in a towel. I wandered round the chapel, examining religious icons and newsletters, pamphlets by people describing their adventures in outer space. Unaccountably, I was feeling a little cheated. I say 'unaccountably', because, after all, what had I been expecting?

'Korton had me down as a pothead for some reason,' I said.

'He doesn't tell you anything unless it's really true,' Bob said. 'If it's given, it's given.'

I sensed that Bob could tell I'd been disappointed in the channelling. The subject of the paranormalist Uri Geller came up. I said I doubted his ability to bend cutlery with his mind. Bob went and got a bag of gnarled silverware and flung it on the table. The forks were so mangled that each tine was splayed out and twisted. He seemed pleased with this coup de théâtre.

'You can't sleight of hand *that*,' he said.

'You do that by twisting it.'

'No no no no,' Bob said. 'You hold it and rub it and it gradually begins to melt.'

'Well, could you do it now?' I said this softly, because I was aware I was challenging him and I didn't wish to sound rude.

'I'M NOT GOING TO DO A DEMONSTRATION FOR YOU, LEWIS! OKAY? I'm a little bit tired, getting a little bit irritated, so just be careful, okay? I've got some things I need to do here.'

※

On the way back from Arizona, driving up to Las Vegas, I reflected that there was a lesson in my encounter with Bob. Just because I wanted to know someone better didn't mean they wanted to be known better. Because I myself am literal-minded and perhaps a little self-doubting, I assume other people are happy to examine their contradictions. But it wasn't so. And in many cases those whose faith was most important to them – like Bob – were those least able to hold their beliefs up to question. (Later, I sent Bob a book about crop circles and a written apology and we patched it up.)

With Thor, I felt on safer ground. I had him pegged as hard-headed – a profiteer. This was what I'd sensed about him and liked on the first visit, I realized – there was a kind of healthy-mindedness behind Thor's bad faith. I was fairly sure he was no longer in the UFO field. He'd left so little impression on that world that I had to assume it hadn't worked out for him and he'd moved on. But to what? Then in late June, I made a breakthrough. I discovered he had once collaborated on a book by a hypnotist friend of mine named Ross Jeffries. Ross said he'd only met Thor twice, briefly both times, but that Thor sometimes went by the name James Templar. A search on that name revealed a number of books for sale on the Internet of which he was co-author. I found an email for one of his collaborators, Pat Ress, in Omaha, Nebraska.

Pat is an expert in time travel. 'I have written four books on time travel and researched it extensively,' she wrote. 'It happens! There are slippage points all around and with an electromagnetic push – walla! Off you go!' She went on to mention a mysterious secret guild of 'technoshamans' to which Thor had once belonged. She put me in touch with a man named Steve Gibbs, an inventor of a time-travel device about whom she'd written a book. Thor had apparently sold copies of Steve's pamphlet about the device. According to Pat, Steve claimed Thor was himself either a warlock or an alien. 'Don't ask me how he would know that!' She gave me Steve's number in Kansas.

Perhaps not surprisingly, Steve seemed somewhat mentally troubled when I reached him on the phone. If the believers so far fell somewhere on a spectrum that ran from fragile/sincere to hard-headed/unscrupulous, Steve was skewing heavily towards fragile. He said he'd time-travelled back to 1986, but that his friend Carl travelled to the 1600s and got thrown in jail for wearing a T-shirt. 'They thought he was making fun of the king.'

He said he'd spoken to Thor over the phone a couple of times but he stopped answering Thor's calls because he kept getting into his head and causing his nose to bleed. Thor, he said, was a 'reptilian shapeshifter' and had been sent to Hell. Or possibly he'd time-travelled and acciden-tally set up a 'paradox', erasing his own timestream. Either way, it wasn't proving a fruitful line of enquiry.

I had better luck with the organization Pat mentioned. The mysterious guild of technoshamans turned out to have a website, with pages of magical products for sale: 'Aladdin's lamps', 'spell books', 'ritual kits', 'all purpose voodoo-doll kits'. It was like an Argos for budding Harry Potters. Thor's fingerprints were all over it, phrases I'd heard him use: 'warrior monks', 'mystery schools', 'grimo-ires'. There were several books previously credited to Thor which now appeared with his name taken off. There was also a whiff of Thor's opportunism: petrol prices had recently gone up, and one of the websites was selling a disk that you could stick on to your car to improve its mileage.

'We are an ancient yet futuristic mystery school. We were the builders of Atlantis and played an important part in the leadership of that society . . . I am sure you have hundreds of questions about the above facts. Of course you do. That is your slave mind talking, questioning the real. After all, you are programmed to buy into the created history of the "well"-educated professors, the men of letters and science . . . There is only one answer: FIGHT, FIGHT, FIGHT! . . . HACK AND CUT!! THIS IS THE ONLY WAY. Let the cowards fall away! LET THE FIGHTERS SHOW THE WAY!'

I sent an email asking about Thor, and received a terse reply. It said: 'Hello, Sorry, we have no info on this person. We are a new company that bought rights to some old products and publications. Thanks.'

It was official: Thor did not want to speak to me.

My original question had been answered. What do you do after you've been Lord Commander of the Earth Protectorate? Why, you found an ancient yet futuristic mystery school that helped build Atlantis and now sells voodoo dolls.

Now what? Should I phone up? Should I pretend to be an interested customer? Should I stake out his building? Until now, I'd excused myself by imagining that Thor might actually want to get together and hang out. Not that I'd given it a great deal of thought, but I suppose I imagined meeting his family and loved ones and trying to put him in some kind of social context. I had a hunch that at some level he didn't really believe that he'd killed ten aliens, but I wanted to find out for sure, or hear how he rationalized it. I wanted to meet his mother and say, 'Do you really believe Thor killed ten aliens?' I wanted to find out his real name.

But if he didn't want to meet, where did that leave me?

One morning in Las Vegas I drove to the address listed for Thor's outfit. It was a soulless stretch of shopping plazas and franchise outlets on the west of the strip: I counted a Wendy's, a McDonald's, a 7–11, and a KFC, all within a block. The address in question turned out to be a 'postal center' where he rented a mailbox.

So I called a number on the website, putting on an American accent, and asked about the mileage disk.

'Ah, yes,' said a voice. 'You glue it on your gas tank. It works using energy rays. It changes the structure of the gas. It improves your gas mileage twenty to forty per cent. Costs one hunded and forty-nine dollars.'

It was definitely him. The same self-serious intonation, the tendency to overexplain. But speaking to him under false pretences – deceiving someone for whom I basically felt affection – didn't feel right, and I wasn't sure how to get off the phone.

'That sounds rather a lot,' I said, in my assured voice.

'You can send money orders. You can also send cash registered.'

Thor sounded ready to close the deal.

'I don't have a credit card at the moment,' I said, and rang off. A few weeks later, I called up as myself.

The first few moments were a little awkward. I explained who I was, reminded him of the TV show we made. He sounded shaky, as though he knew he'd been rumbled.

'Oh yes,' he said, recovering himself. 'I remember. I'm sorry, I spaced out a little there . . . I'm not really active in that alien area any more. It just didn't pan out for us as any kind of reality. So we've kind of stepped away from that . . . The major problem of our time is superillnesses. That's where our emphasis is. There's an amazing number of healing tools we're trying to get to people. AIDS, chronic fatigue, cancer. Who really cares if we're invaded by aliens, we'll all be dead from diseases . . .'

I told him I'd seen websites for the Alien Resistance Movement still going on the Internet.

'They're all a bunch of goofball jerks with either Christian fanatical leanings or kids that want to play army. I contacted them and told them, look, we own that name and logo, that's our organization. But it was going nowhere anyway. They're comic-book characters shooting machine guns at the sky, which doesn't even work. I think our threats are much greater from our politicians than from extraterrestrials.'

This turned out to be Thor's new theme: the disaster of the Bush presidency.

'Quite frankly, I've come to sympathize with the aliens. If they need the human crud we have on this planet to propagate, they're welcome to it. I just wish they'd start by abducting Adolf Bush and his cronies. The guy did not win the election. If he was a president in central America we would have invaded by now . . . We've got body bags coming back from a no-win war where all the people hate us. He's a stumblebum moron. I wouldn't be surprised if he's a clone because his chip ain't working right.'

He said he lived an hour or two outside Vegas, in Nevada, in 'an isolated location', still with Liz. He didn't seem averse to meeting up. We made a plan to go for coffee in September. We spoke for an hour or so, mainly about politics, finding much to agree on. That I should find so much political common ground with a one-time alien hunter struck me as curious.

At the end of the conversation, his tone changed a little.

'You know,' he said, 'I'm surprised at the number of sites you're on with your show. I wish we could get on as many sites, heh heh heh.'

'Yes,' I said.

'Interviews with you, talking about meeting the different characters. There were several different postings on our interview.'

'Yes,' I said. 'Sometimes I spoke about the show – well, I think in some interviews I crossed the line.'

'I liked your show. I watched it all the time when it was on Bravo.' He mentioned the wrestling episode. 'You looked pretty scared when you were with those wrestlers and that psycho drill instructor. He really lost it with you.'

'I may be wrong, but you changing your name, that wasn't anything to do with me and the exposure you got on the show, was it?'

'I don't really want to be connected with that area. I'm trying to step away from that stuff. It loses me credibility. I can't go in and talk to a biochemist if he says, "Oh, you're the great alien hunter, ha ha ha!"'

'Right.'

'And I wasn't in it to make money. We were a small operation. We were nobodies. If I'd wanted to get rich, I would have gone into the corporate world. But we had to make money to survive, and they were all products I believed in . . .'

'Sure.'

'So I go by a different name now.'

Then he asked if I would keep his new name to myself.

In September I called back several times to see if Thor still wanted to get together for coffee. The calls all went to a machine. The message said: 'Welcome! We're unavailable at this time. Leave a name and number and we'll get back to you when we can.' The startling thing was that the message, while recognizably Thor's voice, was delivered in a fake English accent.

＊

On the last night of the UFO Congress at Laughlin, still suffering with food poisoning or whatever it was, I made my way down to the closing banquet. The seating was at round tables, ten to a table. I spied Bob Short, in blue lamé shirt and matching shiny blue cummerbund, with a large pendant round his neck, obviously pleased because all the seats at his table were taken.

Seated across from me was Richard Boylan, a New Age educator from Sacramento, who looked a little like a jolly Irish priest, red-faced and white-haired. I recognized his name from the Congress's programme of speakers. Being ill, I'd missed his lecture that day on 'star kids' – 'hybrid children' with 'advanced abilities'. But after we'd eaten, he began testing the auras of some of those at our table to see if they might be star kids.

'Normal people's auras reach about a foot away from their bodies,' he said. 'Starseed are about twelve feet.'

He offered to test me. I was a little nervous, fairly certain that my own scepticism meant I wasn't starseed and fearful that my lack of belief would show through. I stood twenty or so feet from Richard. He walked towards me with a pair of L-shaped dowsing rods in his hands.

Suddenly, they splayed out, as though butting up against an invisible force field. 'Hombre! What's that? Fifteen feet?' he said. 'Yours is the biggest yet!'

When we sat down, he sketched out a vision of the society we star kids would one day create. Peaceful, just, egalitarian, environmentally sensitive. 'Think of a society where everybody's telepathic,' he said. 'Imagine being a used-car salesman when everyone knows what you're thinking.' I felt flattered to be a star kid. Though I had no doubt it was folderol (shortly afterwards Richard handed out business cards, explaining we could attend his seminars to develop our starseed potential: learn telekinesis and so on), my being included in the club inclined me to be charitable towards his unlikely vision. Later I thought how ironic it was that Richard should use the example of a used-car dealer, there amidst the mountebanks and latter-day snake-oil salesmen of the UFO world. But at the time, I didn't think that. I was just happy to feel part of the team.

How odd, I thought, that even though I don't believe, it still feels nice to be included. What does that prove? I wondered. That even something untrue can produce an effect; that sometimes a con is also an act of kindness.

# JJ MICHAELS

The corridors outside Jim South's World Modeling were clogged with porn performers. A closed casting call was in progress. For Jim's stable of talent, it was a chance to schmooze with directors, producers, photographers. The director Henri Pachard was there, supposedly the real-life model for the Burt Reynolds character in *Boogie Nights*. Oyster-eyed behind thick glasses, a tasteful diamond in his ear, his hair was still bouffant. Looking good for sixty-five, I thought. I'd interviewed him eight years before. 'Sure, you did the bondage thing,' he said. 'No,' I said, 'that wasn't me.' Max Hardcore was there, the legendarily vile maven of degradation and rough sex, recognizable by his trademark cowboy hat. I'd interviewed him briefly, too. Real name Paul Little, he was sitting in his office with his cowboy boots on the desk, looking like the sheriff of Cock County. His door was open. No women were going in there, though. His reputation preceded him.

Twelve directors in all. All men, all looking creepy to various degrees. I spotted myself reflected in a dark window. Lank-haired, unshaven, I looked creepy too.

It was one of the pitfalls of being back in this world, I reflected, that you felt creepy. I'd had the same sensation –

of being compromised and distracted by the images, of cutting a faintly ludicrous figure as a semi-serious journalist covering the porn industry – on my last visit seven years earlier.

On that occasion, I'd been making a documentary about JJ Michaels, a young performer who was then new to the game. JJ was out now, working a straight job in Missouri. While I was here in the San Fernando Valley, California (the capital of the US porn industry), I was keen to find out what I could about the business in 2004, and how it had changed.

Outside I'd been speaking to a farmboy from Georgia. His working name was Mac Turner. He was fresh-faced, twenty-one years old, brand new to porn. He looked like he'd walked off a production of *Oklahoma!*. 'Sometimes I'll work five days, sometimes I'll work a couple. Which is why I'm here today, to meet some more people so I can try to work every day.' He used to manage a training company for gyms, but said it was 'stressful and boring'. His grandparents raised him. They still didn't know about his change of career.

Jim Jr was standing by, guarding the entrance to World Modeling with a clipboard, making sure no unaccredited producers wandered in – no scavengers or pimps. Jim Jr was in his early twenties, the son of the boss and founder, Jim Sr. I'd met him before, too. The faces of the performers change, I thought, but the behind-the-scenes people, they stayed the same.

I asked what he knew about JJ.

'Oh yeah, he was a nice guy,' Jim Jr said. 'He got married to an Australian girl called Astrid. Then they got divorced. Then he got married again. A girl from Russia, I think.'

'Was he working a lot?'

'Yeah, he was doing pretty good. He was working consistently.'

The women were all shapes and sizes. Tall, short, busty, flat-chested. Raven-haired pale goth girls, bottle-blonde girls. Generally the older the woman, the bigger the bust, almost as though they were compensating for their age by shooting for more volume. The male performers were fewer – buffed and groomed in tight sleeveless T-shirts.

The atmosphere was charged, a little giddy, like market day. I began chatting to the performers as they waited to be called into the offices of the producers. A Hispanic woman, mid twenties, wearing bright red lipstick and a beige business suit, gave her name as Catalina. She'd been in the business four years, she said, and had done more than a hundred films with Max Hardcore. 'I like his stuff because it's very different and it stands out like a sore thumb in the industry. It's my career. It's not just fun and games.'

A twenty-three-year-old Asian woman, Paris Waters, from southern California, whose T-shirt bore the legend 'I make my own money', said she'd seen an ad in a newspaper. That was how Jim got many of his walk-ins. His sign and his ads generally said: 'Figure Models Wanted'. You went up thinking, catalogues, boat shows, maybe glamour magazines. Then he told you how much you could make if you had sex in a movie. 'I went ahead anyway, 'cause I'll try anything once.'

Holly Wellin, from Manchester, England. Eighteen

years old. She was wearing white stiletto boots, a denim miniskirt, giggling. 'I don't know how many scenes, I've done loads,' she said. 'I love it over 'ere. The weather, the people, everything. It's so different. It's like a different culture.'

I asked her to be a little more specific.

'It's like there's loads of different fast-food places,' she said. 'I actually had my butt torn a few weeks ago. But it's like any job. You have good days and bad days.'

Still thinking about this piece of wisdom, I wandered into a dark little office where a curly-haired, walrus-moustached man in his late fifties was sitting with two female performers – one a veteran named Anita Cannibal, who was on his sofa, the other an aspirant named Donielle Dare. Donielle Dare was stark naked in a desk chair. 'Because it's easier than putting my clothes on and taking them off again,' she explained – meaning for photographers and directors, I assume. Thirty-two, she'd grown up in the Central African Republic, the daughter of missionaries.

The man was Bill Margold. An ex-performer and now the head of a support group for people who work in the industry, he describes himself as the 'most knowledgeable person in the world about this business.' I'd interviewed him on my first visit, too, an encounter that stayed with me because, out of prankishness, and also to test his assertion that there was nothing intimate about the human genitals, I'd asked to see *his* and without much cajoling he'd taken out his penis and begun rubbing it. But he couldn't remember me.

'Has the business changed much?' I asked.

'I think there's less creativity,' Margold said. 'There's more attempt to shock than to arouse. They can't really put the time into creating eroticism because, hell, most of them don't know how to *spell* eroticism.'

'We're getting into circus tricks now,' Anita Cannibal said. 'Who can stick what up their ass. It didn't used to be like that.'

'There's no suspense left in sex any more,' Margold said. 'It's all just right in the face. This industry has choked on its own freedom. We found ourselves so free that we thought we could get away with anything. It reminds me of Rome at the end of the Empire, the worst excesses at the Colosseum . . . If Bush gets re-elected, the next four years in this business will give us a chance to grow up.'

I told Bill about my book, that I was curious about JJ and what kind of dimple he had left on the waters of adult entertainment.

'Little short kid?' Margold said. 'Don't know . . .'

'What happens to the perfomers? They just disappear and no one knows where they go to?'

'They eventually grow weary of doing this. They sometimes get some external pressure on them not to do it. And they disappear into the real world. There are some people who stay, because they're accepted into it, and they don't want to leave. There's no reason to go looking for these people. You don't really want to find them. There's no reason to dig them out of the anonymity they've escaped into.'

'I'm surprised you don't remember more about JJ. He made hundreds of films.'

'A minor note in the history of this business,' Margold said, in a lordly way. 'I don't even remember what his last name was. Didn't it start with an M? Or an L?'

'Michaels.'

'There wasn't much there. He wasn't a great stud. He just did his job. Plus he was short. Short guys don't get a whole lot of attention.'

Out in the corridor, the ranks of the performers were thinning. I bumped into a director named Robert Herrera. A soft-spoken Hispanic man, he said that according to the trade magazine *Adult Video News*, the porn business now produces four hundred films a week. 'There's too much product,' he said.

'People say it's becoming more extreme,' I said.

He agreed, and cited the influence of reality TV shows where members of the public ate live grubs and pig rectums and dangled from helicopters. 'The majority of people who buy our product, our DVDs and tapes, and take them home and watch them – I call them raincoaters – I believe they're lonely people. They don't like women, so they want to see them degraded. I love women and I will quit the industry before I shoot them the way they're being shot today.'

✳

Though I'd only been in the Valley a few days, I already felt lightyears away from the UFO believers. I remembered my conversation at the Congress about 'star kids'. In this world, star kids meant eighteen-year-olds from Manchester willing to risk tissue damage for a few thousand dollars and a moment in the spotlight.

And yet, looking beyond the strange rummage sale of sex and occasional injury, there was at least an openness and honesty about the business. No euphemisms or flim-flam here. No claims to be changing the world. Porn was porn. Herrera had mentioned reality TV, meaning it disparagingly, but porn also shared some of the democratic ethos of that genre. And it spoke of a touching kind of humility in the industry that, despite its huge profits and the global reach of its images, a thinly credentialed reporter like myself could still wander with impunity at a casting call for the leading talent agent.

I'd driven west from Las Vegas and, after the desert, the landscape of the San Fernando Valley was like crashing back to Earth – an anonymous sprawl of chain stores and strip malls and low-rise housing, where dusty banners advertised special offers on rent. Though there are, allegedly, separate cities with names – Van Nuys, Sherman Oaks, Chatsworth – you get no sense of them as distinct places, no recognizable high streets and downtowns, no squares or parks.

I thought back to my first visit. It was only the second episode of my series, and, because I was sensitive to the creep factor, I'd sought out a male performer who was as unsleazy as possible. In the production office, we referred to him as our 'hungry young male' – someone just starting out, dewy-eyed and unjaded, with a good attitude and a nice personality. Jim South had put us onto JJ.

He was twenty-three at that time. He'd done four years in the airforce – they'd taught him Chinese and computing – but he'd dropped out to work in porn. He'd been in the business five weeks and done thirteen movies, including *Anal Witness 4* and *Bottom Dweller*. He'd proven himself in one of his first scenes, pulling off a tricky 'double penetration', or 'DP', which is, as it sounds, two men inside one woman, one by the back door and one by the front. (Surprisingly, I'd heard that some women preferred this to straight anal, the front entry being the 'spoonful of sugar' that helped the medicine go down.) JJ was aiming to make 'a nice career' out of porn, as he put it.

His apartment, in a two-storey building round a swimming pool, was unusually tidy for a young bachelor, with racks of Heavy Metal CDs, John Carpenter movies and Godzilla toys, all neatly organized. His fridge was stocked with low-fat yoghurt and tins of tuna and not much else. He took me down to the gym where we worked out together. 'Can you get wood? That's the most important thing right there,' he said. 'Can you keep a hard-on the entire time? And believe it or not, it's not easy like it seems it should be. I don't care how beautiful she is, how turned on you are. Sometimes it's not happening.'

The next day I followed him to the set of a movie called *Twisted*. Shot on film, on a soundstage, *Twisted* was the kind of movie that became a rarity soon afterwards, when 'gonzo', the unscripted quasi-documentary style of pornmaking, took over. It had lines for the actors to learn, dramatic situations, proper sets. The scenario was based on the short stories of Edgar Allan Poe. JJ's scene was adapted from 'The Masque of the Red Death': the world had been overtaken by plague. Left with nothing better to do, four workers in a laboratory, played by JJ and the male veteran Peter North, and the female performers Johnni Black and Kaitlyn Ashley, dropped their white lab coats and had romping sex.

In hindsight, I think JJ probably didn't want me on set with him. And whether because of my presence, or because my questions about 'wood problems' at the gym had jinxed him, or for some other reason, he struggled to stay hard for the scene. I loitered in the background, chatting to Johnni Black's boyfriend who, bizarrely, was on hand to watch his wife in action. As the shoot overran, I could see the crew becoming impatient. 'Woodless wonders,' the soundman grumbled. 'Whatever drives people to do this for a living, perhaps some people shouldn't.'

JJ was a little downcast after it was over. 'Well, I didn't do as good as I'd like,' he said. 'It's just so many people. And I was nervous, kinda, working for Shanahan 'cause he's a big director. You get nervous, it's hard to work. But yeah. Near the end, it was fine.' As I walked him to his car in the dark parking lot, I asked his thoughts on a recent HIV scare – an industry stalwart, John Stagliano, better known as Buttman, had tested HIV positive.

'I've got a death wish,' JJ said. 'So I don't really care.'

After that the plan had been to visit JJ on the set of a film called *Forced Entry*, a rape-themed film which was being shot by Rob Black, a young director who was carving out a niche as a maker of 'horror porn'. In the end, JJ didn't appear in the movie because his paperwork from the clinic vouching that he was free of HIV or venereal disease, which performers in porn have to keep updated on a monthly basis, hadn't been processed in time. Still, I went along to the shoot. Though not exactly shocking, the artless, willed offensiveness of the action seemed out of key with the light-hearted documentary we were trying to make. My director filmed me leaving the set.

The next day I had a final conversation with JJ about his choices. We bought lemonades at the mall. On the way back to his apartment, in the van, I said, 'Porno seems like a dark brooding place to us in the outside world.'

'For me it's not,' he said. 'It's the opposite . . . I finally found somewhere where I like being, where the people like me being there and where I am appreciated. I am happy and it makes me happy so why should I leave this?'

∗

In subsequent years, I watched as porn drifted mainstream. The Clinton era was good to the industry. The number of federal obscenity investigations plummeted. New technologies – smaller cameras, the Internet, Viagra – led to increased production. It cost nothing to shoot a porn film. Meanwhile, respectable newspapers and magazines began taking note of how big the industry was. Estimates varied but the annual profits were always put in the billions of dollars. Stories about porn appeared in such august journals as the *New York Times Magazine* and the *New Yorker*. The performers turned up in pop videos, advertising campaigns, supermarket tabloids, and became semi-celebrities.

It is possible that the increasing strangeness of the sex acts was a response to its new respectability, a way of keeping its outlaw edge. It is also, I suspect, the natural tendency of capitalism to innovate constantly, to find new niches in the market, to stimulate the jaded palates of its consumers.

'Back in 1998, I made a joke. "Short of driving a train up someone's ass, I don't see where they can go with it",' an industry veteran, Sharon Mitchell, told me. 'But the kink factor has just gone through the roof! It's almost like, we have a show here in the States called *Fear Factor* where they have secretaries and members of the public jumping off fucking buildings, you know? Think of that "Can you top this?" in the porn world and that's an idea of the changes I've seen. It's just – shocking. Ejaculating in women's eyes – that's a series. Where people ejaculate in each other's eyes!'

'Because that stings, doesn't it?' I said.

'Yeah, it stings. It's a very good way to get HIV or gonorrhea of the eyes, too.'

Indeed, the higher health risk associated with the new weird sex acts was being blamed for an HIV outbreak that had taken place just a couple of weeks before I arrived back in Los Angeles. Five performers had tested positive, prompting an industry shutdown, a 'moratorium', which had been observed by all the big companies.

But there were signs of an end to the ascendancy of porn. In addition to his 'war on terror', George Bush was gearing up for a fight on obscenity. There had already been two skirmishes in this confrontation. The first, widely publicized, was an aggressive clampdown on Viacom, the parent company of CBS, after Janet Jackson had her breast bared by Justin Timberlake during a half-time Superbowl dance routine. 'Until then, we were flying. We were cooking,' the head of publicity for Vivid, one of the high-end porn companies, told me. Within a week of the furore, a cable network had cancelled plans to air a documentary about the Vivid girls.

The second, less well-known theatre in the war against indecency was a case the Attorney General was pursuing against a young porn director. If carried through to trial, it would be the first major federal obscenity case in more than ten years. The target of the case: none other than Rob Black, the 'horror porn' maker who'd appeared in my documentary.

Rob Black works out of offices in Chatsworth, in the far north of the San Fernando Valley, on a quiet semi-industrial street of single-storey brick buildings and warehouses.

Late one afternoon, soon after I arrived back in Pornworld, I found him sitting at his desk at the back of his new premises, writing an email to his general manager. Since I'd last seen him, in addition to being investigated by the government, he'd started his own company, Extreme Associates, been crowned Best New Director at the 1998 Adult Video News Awards (the porn equivalent of the Oscars), then lost all his money in an ill-advised attempt to launch a wrestling league, Extreme Pro Wrestling. In the wake of the obscenity case, he folded XPW and returned to porn. But where before he'd been one of the innovators, now he found himself outflanked by directors even more willing to stage outrageous stunts.

On the plus side, he did remember me. 'What do you do?' he said. 'What the fuck do you do?'

'Make documentaries about offbeat subjects,' I said. 'Try to get involved. Now I'm doing a book.'

'Kind of like that Plimpton guy that died, huh?'

'George Plimpton, exactly.'

It was odd hearing him mention Plimpton. Stocky and hirsute, thirty-one years old, Rob affects a goombah mafioso persona. (His real name is, in fact, Rob Zicari.) He was wearing a Sean John velour tracksuit and had a wad of chewing tobacco in his mouth – from time to time he spat brown juice into a large coffee tin which stood on his desk. All in all, he seemed an unlikely audience for the New York writer and doyen of 'participatory journalism'.

He offered to take me on a tour of his premises. We walked back into a large, high-ceilinged stockroom, where shelves were stacked with boxes and boxes of videos with titles like *Squirmin' Germans*, *Planet of the Gapes*, *Anal Blitzkrieg*. He said he'd made over 450 movies since my last visit. When I mentioned that I was curious about JJ, he looked vague and said, 'Yeah, that little prick! I don't think he's around anymore.' He talked about changes in the industry. 'You've got your puking, choking, slapping. Everyone does everything now. What I started eight years ago, everybody does now.'

'Do you ever worry that what you do is degrading to women?'

'You know what? We're in the year 2004. Nobody's kidnapped off the street. And in our business, the girls get most of the money. And the thing is, why are our movies judged differently than Hollywood movies? A girl is degraded in a Hollywood movie, what happens? That's acting. And they get a fucking Academy Award. A girl is degraded in porn and for some reason that's more extreme than a real movie.'

'Isn't it because it involves things like spitting and pissing? It's kind of a self-evident thing that that's degrading.'

'Being degraded is a sense of one's own mind,' Rob said. 'You're only degraded if you let something happen. If you perceive that what's going on is degrading to you, then that's that. But if you don't perceive that you're being degraded, then it's not degrading.'

I asked how he'd feel if he had kids (which he hasn't, but was hoping to) and his daughter wanted to be in a porno.

'Nah, I wouldn't *want* her to . . . Just because you do something, doesn't necessarily mean you would like your loved ones to do it. I'm not saying that there's anything *wrong* necessarily, but, you know, we can support things that we wouldn't want.'

Rob picked a garish box off a shelf. 'Here's a movie I did a couple of weeks ago, *Creampie Milkshakes*,' he said.

I looked at the cover and said: 'Jesus.'

'You like that, huh? Fucking filthy.'

The names of five tapes had appeared on the search warrant the government used during its raid in 2003. Rob was now selling these at a bulk discount, as the 'federal five'.

Rob had a specific take on the case against him. To him, his films were no different than any other films. His performers were actors, acting out fictional scenarios. He was a kind of relativist – he saw no intrinsic moral or emotional value to the acts themselves. The performers consented to have weird sex, so what was the problem? He didn't seem to see that, irrespective of the legal case, it might be questionable to pay people, some of them, presumably, penurious and confused, to take part in degrading sex. Rob also mentioned the indignities suffered by the contestants on reality TV shows. How was it different just because sex was involved? he asked.

For my own part, I had mixed feelings about the case. I could see the argument that it was an infringement of civil liberties to prosecute someone for making a movie. If the acts themselves weren't illegal and all the participants were consenting adults, then what was the problem? It was also true that, notwithstanding the recent HIV outbreak, the rate of infection in the industry was quite low. But – I also had a sense that the porn industry, with its ever more grotesque provocations, was spinning out of control, and I wondered whether a successful case against someone like Rob might help to rein it in again.

We walked outside.

'Do you think you'll go down?' I asked.

'Nah, because Bush isn't going to get re-elected, and if he doesn't get re-elected then all the charges go away. Remember, it wasn't a local bust, it was a federal bust.'

'How long a stretch are you facing?' I asked.

'Fifty years.' He paused. Blew a raspberry. 'Fifty years. Five years per count.' Another pause. Then Rob said softly, as a strange kind of joke, 'It's your fault.'

'In a way, it is, because I can vote in the US and I didn't vote in that election. But I don't live in Florida.'

'See? You were that one swing!'

'I was the dangling chad.'

'Dangling Chad,' I realized, would be quite a good porn name.

❉

Since arriving in the Valley I'd been looking for clues on JJ, but he seemed somewhat forgotten. One of the few facts I was able to glean was that towards the end he'd been working mainly for a director called Jim Lane.

Jim Lane, like Rob Black, specialized in the new brand of disturbing, freaky films. I found him in the phonebook, and arranged to meet him in the far north of the Valley on the set of *The Violation of Missy*. A spiky-haired forty-two-year-old, an ex-stockbroker, Jim remembered JJ in characteristic porn terms. 'He was a guy, he got his dick hard,' he said. 'He was a good kid.'

He told me JJ had left because his then-wife, Astrid the Australian, was getting into the business, and he couldn't handle her being with other guys. JJ was working in computers now; and his new wife wasn't Russian but Ukrainian. A 'mail-order bride', Jim said.

A few days later, I returned to Jim South's office. With no JJ, as a way of understanding the business as it was now, I'd decided to meet up with another young performer – a 2004 version of the 'hungry young male'.

Up a flight of narrow stairs, in a dingy two-storey building with blinds over the windows, Jim's office feels raffish in a faintly old-school way, like a private detective's office in a movie from the forties. There was him, Jim Jr, and a young Asian woman called Envy Mi. Even though, by Jim's standards, it wasn't busy, the phone still rang frequently. Sitting at his desk, in western-wear shirt and Wranglers, with pompadour hair, Jim would say, in his Texan drawl, 'Hello, my darling. Bobby at Wildlife wants five girls. Single girl masturbation and a handjob.' Or, 'It's a boy-boy-girl anal.' Or, 'It's a BJ, I don't know if it's two different girls giving different blowjobs or two different girls giving the same blowjob.'

I stayed several hours, parked on his sofa, trying not to stare at the many glossy posters of porn stars with large breasts.

'So what was the thing you did?' Jim asked me during a lull.

'A documentary for the BBC,' I said. 'I followed JJ Michaels around. You took my Polaroid.'

'And we gave you your photo back at the end. Yeah, you were the crazy guy!'

'Do you still keep up with JJ at all?'

Jim looked vague, as though he didn't remember JJ too clearly.

'He's no longer with us, I believe,' he said. 'I think he even left the state, got remarried.'

'To a Russian woman,' I said.

I had a vision of Jim as a schoolteacher with generations of young talent passing through his profane cloisters, all remembering him and his shaping influence, him remembering them less clearly.

'I get people through here now who say, "You used to be my mother's agent,"' Jim said. 'I've been in this more than twenty years.'

'Has the industry changed a lot?'

'Oh yeah. More directors. More producers. Everyone's an agent or a manager now.'

'What about Viagra?'

'Since Viagra, everybody's a stud,' he said. Then, citing two of the most stalwart male performers he said: 'Let me tell you something. There's no more Peter Norths or TT Boys out there who can do two, three scenes a day without assistance. And I mean without assistance.'

Through the afternoon, female performers breezed in and out – Tiffany James, Barbii Buxxx, Desire Moore. They gossiped and traded war stories. I saw only one male performer, a young man in wraparound dark glasses and baseball cap who gave his name as Tommy X. He had an odd, over-stimulated air. He walked in and out of the offices in a restless way, like a figurine going in and out of a mechanical clock. Each time he entered, the bill of his cap was pointing in a different direction. 'Tommy Boy!' Jim would sing, with over-the-top bonhomie. There was something faintly off-putting about his constant moving around and his dark glasses and his rotating cap. Nevertheless, I took his phone number, and a few days later I visited him at home.

His house was beige, single-storied, in Reseda, another anonymous spread of tract homes and wide streets in the far west of the Valley. It was set back from the road, a little decrepit, but large – five bedrooms – with a decent-sized swimming pool in the back, strewn with twigs. It had smudged yellow walls and stained green sofas.

Tommy is an all-American-looking kid, with blue eyes and a dyed blond mohawk. His forearms are tattooed with flowers. He was wearing a blue hooded top, baggy shorts, and a ballcap.

I explained about my documentary. 'I'm doing a kind of update,' I said. 'Did you ever hear of a performer called JJ Michaels?'

Tommy looked blank. 'I've definitely heard the name before,' he said.

'Well, thanks for making time for me.'

'No problem. I'm taking today off anyway because I'm about to shoot three days straight.'

He'd grown up Chris Thomas Essex in a suburb north of Los Angeles. He'd been a fan of porn since early adolescence. 'I used to take pictures of my girlfriends. Then I had this freaky girlfriend. We were both between jobs and between places to live. She saw the newspaper ad for [Jim South's] World Modeling. She went up there and shot her first scene the next day, and then she took me up to World, and that was in February 2002.' He'd been working bagging groceries at Gelson's supermarket at the time.

He'd done some high-end shoots, *Hustler Young Girl Fantasies 4*, *Real College Girls 12*. Plus a lot of Internet work. Bangboat.com., Backseatbangers.com.

'How have you been doing "wood-wise"?' I said.

'For me it all depends on my chemistry with the girl,' he said. 'Any problem I've had is because I've been doing too much recreational partying, you know what I mean? It's just how much confidence you have. Any second-guessing might affect my performance. But I don't have that any more. Sometimes if I need to I'll take Viagra. I'm not against that at all. Because it's my job to have good wood to do a scene.'

'It's all about the wood, isn't it?'

'Yeah, if you don't have good wood, you're not going to get another job. And you can get a bad reputation really fast,' Tommy said.

I asked him whether the HIV scare and the moratorium had given him pause.

'I was *way* freaked out,' he said. 'I wasn't on any of the lists but it was like *dang*!'

'Why do you do it?'

'I do it for the money, but also because I want to be a porn star. I want to be famous for what I do. The fast times. The meeting a lot of people every day. Like, every day you meet someone and you have sex with them and you don't ever have to see them again after that if you don't want to.'

Most of Tommy's friends were people he'd met during a stint at a fast-food restaurant called In-N-Out Burger. 'But I'm the only one who's in showbusiness,' he said.

The truth is, I was starting to regret my choice of hungry young male. He didn't have the focus and drive which had made JJ unusual. Tommy was a little lost, and he seemed to regard my interview as confirmation of the status he was looking for, as though I was a sports writer profiling an athlete. 'I'm ready to be the next big thing in porn,' he said.

The following morning, I picked him up and we drove to a smart private house on a leafy street in the far west of the Valley. The film was being directed by a jovial, vaguely Hispanic-looking fellow who gave his name as 'Andre Madness', for a company called Kick-Ass Pictures. Andre Madness was thirty or so, a graduate of a Christian University in San Diego, so he said, with a BA in literature.

I asked what they were shooting.

'It's a series called *Ten Man Cum Slam*,' he said.

'Sounds weird.'

'It's a niche.' He pronounced it the American way, 'nitch'. 'And it's popular. It's very popular. Believe it or not, this is very mainstream for the porn industry now. Everyone's trying to do something more over the top than the others.'

The female performer was eating a bagel in the kitchen, having just had her hair and make-up done. Her porn name was Summer Rain; she was from Cornwall. Short blonde hair, a friendly face, tanned freckled shoulders, she'd been in the States a little more than two weeks and had done seven movies. She was due back in England in another two weeks. Rather bizarrely, she'd worked in the security department of the BBC documentaries building in London where I used to have my office. She'd seen an ad in the *Stage*. 'If you'd like to earn $25,000 a month . . .' She was getting a thousand dollars for this film.

I asked why she was doing porn.

'To get more of an impression of sex,' she said. 'Because I've never really had an exciting sex life. The money's a bonus, really.'

But she didn't seem to know what she'd signed on for. A little later, I found her sunbathing outside.

'How are you feeling?' I asked.

'Yeah, fine. I'll take the lead. I take control.' She sounded as though she was trying to convince herself. 'I don't stand for any nonsense. What's this project called?' she asked.

'*Ten Man Cum Slam*,' I said.

The filming started with Andre Madness interviewing Summer Rain on camera about herself and the shoot, to give the scene a quasi-documentary feel. He asked about her sex life, how old she was when she gave her first blowjob, how many men she'd given blowjobs to at one time. Summer tried to enter into the spirit of it but she'd had a puff of a joint in the backyard and she was struggling to find the right tone between man-crazy porn chick and normal person. She said she'd only given a blowjob to one person at a time, then upped the number to two, seeming to think that was what was required of her. 'After knowing what I'm about to do now, it's a bit different from what I was expecting but I'm sure I'll cope with it,' she said.

The guys got undressed and started playing with themselves. Summer gave a little speech. 'I just wanted to say, I'm not into rough sex. I don't mind you deepthroating me but treat me right.'

'Guys, look for me when you're about to come,' Andre Madness said. 'Don't come without a sign from me.'

The scene commenced. There were so many male performers I scribbled notes: 'Brad Boldman (slightly weird, big nose, beefy, late thirties); Tony Tedeschi (fifteen-year veteran, quietly intense); Johnny Fender (Hispanic dude?); Carlton Banks (black guy, braids, kept his woolly hat on); Rob Longshot (surly goth-geek, kept his boots on); Rod Fontana (older guy, jolly, manic, overweight); Jim Beam (Gen-X dude, tousled hair)'. There was also, of course, Tommy X, who kept his baseball cap on sideways, and two others whose names I didn't get.

Summer did her best to be enthusiastic, issuing bawdy come-ons and blandishments, but there was no disguising that her heart wasn't really in it. I went outside and stood by the pool until it was over.

One by one, after they finished, the men went outside and stood by the pool or chatted about the upcoming presidential election in a little huddle. 'Two to four supreme court appointments are open,' someone said, mentioning the name of Chief Justice Rehnquist. 'Unemployment is out of control,' someone else said. Then, referring to Republican voters, a third said: 'You get away from the coasts and this is just a very backward country. It's scary.'

The scene took maybe an hour. Afterwards, Summer came outside looking dazed and bleary. 'It was great,' she said, without much conviction. 'I just got it in my eye a bit.' A little later she added: 'It is hard work, though.' Her manager arrived, a bald, gnomish man in his fifties, Mark Spiegler. 'You done?' he said, and whisked her away.

The whole experience was profoundly depressing. I wondered if I'd been unlucky with my choice of sets to visit or people to follow. 'I would like for you to see a scene that's not so much work,' Andre Madness said, referring to Summer Rain's lack of enthusiasm. 'Honestly, I don't know if I'd work with her again.' I asked Tommy how he'd found it. 'It was excellent,' he said. 'We had good chemistry.'

＊

JJ now lives in the outer suburbs, in a town outside St Louis, Missouri, called Florissant. Like his old apartment, his house, a single-storey building in a new subdivision, remains a temple consecrated to his fan-boy enthusiasms: John Carpenter, Heavy Metal, comic books, all still neatly stowed on shelves. On his coffee table is a row of six remote controls. He has massive free-standing stereo speakers in the front room and a TV screen that is five or six feet across. His work has something to do with computers at Boeing. 'I could explain exactly but it probably wouldn't make any sense,' he said.

I arrived at his house late one day in August, having driven across country. His door was answered by Viktoriya, the Ukrainian girl he married two years earlier. Blonde, pretty, twenty-two years old, she works at Walgreens, a chain of chemists. She dreams of being an actress. She was wearing tiny white hot pants, which looked all the more incongruous while she was cooking, preparing a Ukrainian dish of chicken broth followed by chicken cutlets and a potato salad with ham and peas in it. European dance music was playing. JJ looked much the same, hair parted and gelled, big mouth and lips; animated, demonstrative. He's about five feet five and muscular, a little bundle of personal passions and weird bugbears – that online comics fans are petty or 'negative'; that certain movies are overrated; that people are 'flaky'.

I'd brought some wine, a couple of bottles, and some beer.

'I don't drink anything except water,' JJ said. 'And coffee in the mornings. That way I can save on calories for food.' He uncorked the wine and very gingerly filled my glass. 'This is the first time I've ever poured wine,' he said.

'You'd never know,' I said.

We talked a little about how he and Viktoriya had met, through an online dating agency. 'They've got about twenty different URLs, but I think I went through get-marriednow.com,' JJ said. At first they corresponded by email. JJ had learned a little Russian. Viktoriya knew no English so she used a translator programme. 'It translate word, not sentence, so meaning is not always correct,' she said. Then they'd telephone, using an interpreter whom they conferenced in. JJ visited Viktoriya in her hometown of Kherson, three hours from Odessa. JJ said she was a little less tall than he expected. Viktoriya said he was 'much shorter' than she expected.

In May 2002, Viktoriya moved to the US. They married three months later.

'What do you think of St Louis?' I asked Viktoriya.

'There's nothing. Like it's supposed to be at night city is booming. But it's empty. It's so boring here. Two horses running. That's it. I was shocked. When I first arrived, I was like, "OK, show me the city." He said, "Let me call my friend and ask how we get there."'

'I don't need to go out, I got my DVDs,' JJ said.

'Would you like to go back to porn?'

'I would like to direct again,' JJ said. 'I would quit my job if I could get a solid enough career.'

'How would you feel?' I asked Viktoriya.

'I want to make him happy, you know? Because it's not cool when you come home and you see your husband depressed. It's like he want it but he don't want it.'

'It's a risk,' I said.

'But you don't risk, you don't drink champagne,' Viktoriya said.

I was happy to see JJ again, and pleased that he seemed happy to see me. Our relationship was friendly and straightforward. He was putting me up while I was in St Louis, and this simple act of hospitality touched me. This was how I'd hoped my journey among my old subjects would be.

The next day, after JJ got back from work, he took me into his utility room in the basement. There, next to the boiler, was a cardboard box containing JJ's films. These movies represent three-and-a-half years of his life.

'I made a movie in November 1996. The next one was in February 1997, and that's when I got in full-time. I always watched porn, of course. I guess I wanted to be like those guys I watched: Marc Wallice, Joey Silvera, Tom Byron. What a great job! Be a porn star! The idea of saying: "I'm a porn star." But the reaction I got is something else. Internet dorks *despise* you.

'So I called Jim South and for some reason they let me come in. And while I was there they told me about a casting call. I met Todd and Terri Diver. They hired me to do an orgy thing. I got paid $100.'

JJ started pulling out videotapes in battered covers. *Ho in the Haystack*. 'It was an Amish movie.' *Austin Prowler. Chamber of Whores. White Trash Whores 12.*

He showed me some of the films he made at the end

of his career with Jim Lane. He played a leprechaun in *Perverted Stories 20*. A gorilla in *Perverted Stories 23*. For *Perverted Stories 25*, he covered himself in butter and sang a song about being 'the butter boy' while masturbating.

I scanned the back of the box of *Perverted Stories 20* for a still of JJ's scene, as though nothing could be more normal than to scrutinize a photo of a friend in the throes of a bizarre sex act. There he was, all in green, dressed as a leprechaun, receiving a blowjob. 'This looks like a good one,' I found myself saying. Then I asked, 'Did you get sick of the sex?'

'Oh yeah,' JJ said. 'It's just work. I mean, think about it. Doing it all the time, it becomes work.'

He said he got around $300 a scene from Jim Lane. 'I had fun working with him so I'd take a little below standard. At the time, full rate was $500. I was always happy with the money. If I didn't want to stay married I would probably have never quit, 'cause I was making fine money. I make less cash-wise now, but I have a pension plan, I have insurance.

'I just really want to make movies. Working at Boeing is fine, it's a great paycheck. I could do it till retirement. But it's not fulfilling. I'm sure it's the same with a lot of people, they have those frustrations. But with me it's slightly worse, because I've had a taste of it.'

JJ offered to show me the movies he directed.

'Are you sure it won't be weird for Viktoriya?'

'She doesn't mind.'

Viktoriya was watching a documentary about Jennifer Lopez on the E! Channel. She went into the bathroom and spoke in Ukrainian on the phone to a friend in Boston.

We watched *Pornworld* first, fast-forwarding through the sex. The plot was hard to follow. It had something to do with a magic crystal that could transport its holder to a realm where his every sexual fantasy was fulfilled. For some reason – maybe, as JJ claimed, because the sound recordist was on cocaine – you could hear the pssshht! of the smoke machine with perfect clarity but none of the words. '*Hustler* gave it a four out of five,' JJ said.

*In Search of Awesome Pussy* was a James Bond spoof starring JJ as Jimmy Bone, a secret agent who bonked his way across the Czech Republic. Most of the Czech women couldn't speak English, so JJ had to teach them their lines phonetically. 'You thowt you could fule us, Mr Bone' was one of the few lines I could make out.

Viktoriya wandered back in and sat down on the sofa. JJ kept fast-forwarding through the sex, then rewinding to the end of the sex scene, so we wouldn't miss any of the dialogue. As a result, we got to see virtually all his pop shots. I was trying to read Viktoriya's expression – whether it was strange for her to be watching her husband have anal sex with Czech porn stars in fast-forward.

'You don't like us making fun of accents; I know what you're thinking,' JJ said.

'No, you don't,' Viktoriya said.

*

'It's an industry of lonely people in a crowd,' Bill Margold was saying. 'They're scared to get close to each other. You're far better off having someone to sleep next to than having someone to sleep with, because you have to trust someone you sleep next to. I don't think these people can maintain relationships. They don't want to let their guards down long enough to get to know the people they're having sex with, so they keep avoiding getting to know them by fucking them.'

It was late afternoon, a few months later, and his room was dark.

I thought about JJ. For most of us, sex brings with it some kind of intimacy, a kind of mutual ownership that we share as couples. If you have sex for a living on camera, that intimacy is lost. The glue that binds person to person dissolves. This was something almost everyone I'd spoken to in porn agreed on, that it was impossible to have a long-term relationship and be a performer. For some performers – the most sturdy, the most driven, the most detached – that loss of intimacy was worth it, for the fame or the money it brought. But not for most.

JJ had no regrets about his porn career. His only ruefulness seemed to be that it had ended, and that now he had to face the normal suburban challenges of keeping down a boring job and making a relationship work. His most difficult adjustment was anonymity. And I suspected that it was because he felt so positive about porn that my own journalistic relationship with him was so uncomplicated. He was happy about the documentary I made, happy to update it for the book, too – both of them were testaments to the modest celebrity he had once enjoyed.

I was running out of questions for Margold, and so, for old time's sake, I asked to see his penis. He stood up, pulled down his trousers and boxer shorts, and out it came, like a pork sausage. Hanging several inches lower than the end of his penis were two of the biggest, dangliest balls I'd ever seen.

We stayed like that for a moment, me looking at his genitals in the darkened room. Then I said: 'Okay, you can put them away now.'

# IKE TURNER

One Friday night, not long after my encounter with Bill Margold's penis, while I was still in Los Angeles, I drove up to the ritzy clifftop town of Malibu, to a club called the Malibu Inn.

For weeks – since before I'd left Britain, in fact – I'd been calling and sending letters to the famous and famously temperamental bandleader Ike Turner. In 2000, I'd spent ten days with Ike, filming a documentary which was never completed. I'd hoped the Reunion Tour would be a chance to see him again and sift through the wreckage of the project. But I'd heard nothing back, and so, having read that he was playing not far away, I had decided – in the nicest possible way – to ambush him at the gig.

Unlike his ex-wife, Tina, who went on to multi-platinum success, Ike spiralled downwards after their split in 1976, settling into a debilitating regimen of cocaine and 'orgy-ing', as he calls it. At his lowest ebb, according to legend, he would travel Los Angeles dressed as a policeman so he could confiscate drugs from crack dealers for his personal use. But he cleaned up during a stretch in prison in 1989, and these days he makes his living gigging with his seven-piece band, the Kings of Rhythm, playing a mix of barnstorming blues and boogie-woogie, along with some of the old hits.

I arrived at the Malibu Inn early and ordered a large glass of red wine. The truth is, I had a feeling of trepidation about seeing Ike again. Though he's mellowed with age, I had witnessed his 'artistic temperament' first-hand when we were filming together, and I was worried he might be annoyed with me for never finishing the documentary.

The Malibu Inn was a road-house type joint. It had a raised stage on one side, a place for the audience to stand, a bar at the other side. It looked like it could comfortably take two hundred people, but because of heavy rains only eighty or so were there – older, white, affluent husbands and wives who had grown up with Ike and Tina's music.

The stage itself was barely big enough for Ike's band. The three members of the brass section stood in front of the second keyboardist, and they had to shuffle to one side during his solos so the audience could see. But the music was raucous and soulful, and the crowd was happy, no one more so than Ike himself. He's seventy-three now, and his voice, deep and bluesy, still carries the stamp of his native Mississippi. Dressed in a long shiny gold jacket with an upright collar, eyes shining with pleasure, he sang raspily, played his piano with unselfconscious virtuosity, and told lewd jokes – even, during one song, miming cunnilingus and making slurping noises.

Halfway through, Ike's lead singer Audrey Madison took the stage, picking her way past the other musicians like someone trying to cross a crowded pub. I'd met her while filming the documentary – a full-figured black woman, forty or so, she is also the lady in Ike's life. She wears a shaggy brown wig which makes her look more

The Call of the Weird

than a touch Tina Turnerish. 'You know Ike Turner sure know how to pick singers,' Ike said. 'Men, get your hands out of your pockets. I know some of you got holes in there.'

Afterwards, I found Ike backstage. He looked delighted when I said hello, hugging me and saying, 'Louis, Louis!' Then he seemed to say 'The madman!' but, with my face in the lapel of his gold coat I may have misheard.

'How are you doing?' I said.

'Yeah! Getting older!' 'You livin' out here, now? Give me a call!'

I called the next day and set up a lunch date near his home in southern California.

＊

Though he's a musical pioneer, an inductee into the Rock and Roll Hall of Fame, and credited with writing the first ever rock and roll single ('Rocket 88' in 1951), it's for his stormy relationship with his ex-wife Tina that Ike is chiefly known nowadays. Her memoir, *I, Tina*, and the hit Hollywood film it inspired, *What's Love Got To Do With It?*, have turned Ike into an international byword for spousal abuse. His image as a svengali-like figure is so well-established that in some anti-cult literature he is cited as an exemplar of a certain kind of psychological manipulation.

Partly it was this notoriety that had attracted me to the idea of doing a documentary in 2001 – how Ike handled his strange status as a media bogeyman. But I was also curious about his personality: what had driven him to mistreat Tina and, at the same time, how he had kept her loyalty all those years. I had an idea that spending time with him might help me understand the self-destructive lifestyles pursued by some of the more obviously 'weird' people I've interviewed.

It had seemed a good time for the project. Ike was releasing his first solo album in twenty years, *Here and Now*, the title itself an announcement of Ike's intention to turn his back on the past and remind the world that he is a soulful performer and musical pioneer, and not just Tina's volatile ex-husband. The music was blues of the type that Ike was playing before he met Tina, and for the first time in his career, Ike was singing lead – coming out front and centre and making his voice heard.

We had begun filming at his house a few days before the album was due out – the idea was for me to spend a little time getting to know him, then ride along with Ike and his band on a cross-country tour. His son answered the door, and Ike came out from his bedroom – slight and dark-skinned, with his trademark Van Dyke beard and moustache. Like millions of others, I'd seen the movie when it came out, and I'd been expecting someone a little like the suave, self-assured character played by Laurence Fishburne. But Ike was quite different, the opposite of suave – high-spirited and playful and slightly silly.

He took me on a tour of his house, which was decorated with awards and mementoes from his fifty-year music career. Ike spoke about how scared he was about the upcoming tour. I tried to reassure him, and later thought how odd it was, my attempting to soothe the performance anxieties of a rock legend whom I had met just an hour or two before.

For most of that first day Ike and I seemed to be hitting it off. He was warm and friendly, and so it came as a shock every now and again when I sensed that something I'd said had offended him – mentioning Tina, or spending too long looking at one of the many photos of Tina on the walls, or even, at one point, using the word 'anabolic', which Ike mistook for Tina's real name, Anna Bullock.

At the end of the afternoon, heading out to a karaoke club near his house, he gave me a stack of publicity photos to carry. One of Ike's foibles is that he likes to hand out smiling headshots of himself wherever he goes, almost as though, having been typecast in the mind of the public as Diabolical Husband, he is now engaged in an ongoing audition for the new role of Loveable Ageing Rocker. At the bottom of the photos was printed the contact information for Ike's fanclub, which was called 'I Still Like Ike!'

Seeing an opening for a run at the Tina question, I asked, 'Why do they say "I *Still* Like Ike"? It sounds a little defensive.' Ike grumbled that it was a reference to 'all the bullshit'. Then with faint irritation he added, of the slogan, 'I didn't do that.'

Inside the club, the clientele was a mix of well-scrubbed suburban families in shorts and open-neck shirts and older couples drinking cocktails. Ike looked a little incongruous in reflecting sunglasses with gold chains round his neck, but he seemed to be known as a local figure and several times he was approached for his autograph. Afterwards, I said, 'You signed a lot of photos.' And then added lightly, 'Are people always friendly?'

'Yeah, why would they be otherwise?' Ike said.

I wasn't sure how to respond, so I said, 'I dunno.' Then, remembering Ike's remark about 'all the bullshit', I said, 'Maybe that thing you were referring to earlier.'

We went back to watching the karaoke, waiting for Audrey's turn to sing Tina's hit, *River Deep Mountain High*, and I thought about Ike's remark – 'Why would they be otherwise?' – reflecting that it was going to be hard to get to the subject of Tina and the movie if Ike didn't even care to acknowledge that a negative perception *exists*. Still, I thought, at least I had approached the subject delicately. Then, with a chill, I heard Ike say to Audrey, 'If he asks one more question like that I'm outta here.'

I didn't know quite what to say or do. I flatter myself I can usually tell when people are upset but Ike had given nothing away. Shaken, I went out to the men's room. Later, back at my motel, I became gloomy, thinking I would have to spend the next week with someone whose emotions were at once so raw and yet so difficult to read.

✳

Perhaps I should have pulled the plug on the documentary then, but I didn't, I decided to persevere, hoping, against the evidence, that with time Ike might relax and be happy to discuss his past and how he felt about his behaviour.

For a while it seemed as though that might happen. I stopped trying to ask questions about Tina, figuring he'd broach the subject himself when he was ready. I learned how to be around him, how to maintain eye contact, and be encouraging and supportive; which subjects to avoid. In truth, I began feeling a little like Tina, which may be the fate of everyone who spends time with Ike. I came to appreciate that a great part of Ike's control of people comes from his excessive sensitivity: that the vulnerability I'd noticed on the first day was also the source of his power, because those around him can feel his sensitivity and they feel protective. I felt it too and wondered if I was falling under his spell.

Ike's spirits rallied as we left San Marcos for the first few dates of the tour. Laid over in St Louis, he reminisced about his tomcatting days in the fifties, when he had the keys to thirty-two women's apartments. I asked him for the secret of his success. 'Stay handsome and hard to get,' he said. 'Keep 'em wonderin'' all the time what you gonna do and wonderin'' how you feel about 'em. *Do* you love 'em? 'Cause once they are sure that you do, you got a problem.' This struck me as an interesting piece of wisdom, and probably quite true.

But as his first gig drew near his nerves kicked in. The pressure of performing up front, and having to do interviews to promote the album, and organize the band – all of it piled up. He felt ill; his voice went and he literally turned a dark shade of green; he fired his drummer, then became so exasperated with the replacement, a man named Bugsy, that after one unsatisfactory show, seeing Bugsy in the parking lot, Ike shouted at his driver, 'That's the nigger right there! Run him over!' Oddly, though, Ike never lost his temper to Bugsy's face. The following day, when he was honoured with a star on the St Louis Walk of Fame, Ike broke down in tears and had to leave the stage. 'I'm too emotional for this stuff, man,' he said.

My access shrivelled by slow degrees, a protracted diminuendo in the key of Ike. I could film with him but ask no questions; I could travel with him but not film; and then one day in New York word came that he'd had enough.

And yet Ike's rawness and his anxiety were so palpable, I found it hard to blame him for no longer wanting to do the documentary. It wasn't arrogance on his part – he was just too sensitive. He was a walking spider's web of nerves.

Back in London, a few weeks later, I got a plaintive stammering call of apology. 'I don't want you to never feel I mistreated you,' he said. 'I want you to please forgive me, man. If you can find it in your heart. I wouldn't abuse our relationship for anything in the world. I value it too much. I just had too much pressure, you know? And I just couldn't take no mo'.' He'd finished the tour, and was now back in his home town of San Marcos. The call seemed in part a tacit plea for me to continue filming, to pick up where we left off. I had that same sense of Ike trying to secure his legacy.

The following year I heard that Ike's album, *Here and Now*, had been nominated for a Grammy for Best Traditional Blues Album. He also did some sell-out dates at Ronnie Scott's jazz club in Soho. I was pleased to feel that even if the documentary hadn't worked out, Ike had made his comeback.

✳

In the days before I was due to see him again, I reread both Tina's memoir and the book Ike wrote as a rebuttal to her version, *Taking Back My Name*. I also watched the movie. This was a strange experience, as I was rocked back and forth by contradictory blasts of indignation. One moment I was shocked at the liberties the filmmakers had taken with Ike's life; the next I was shocked at what Tina suffered at Ike's hands.

At times harrowing, at times ludicrous, the film's depiction of the brutality of the Ike character seems to rise in proportion to the strangeness of his wardrobe. He becomes most savage around the time he begins wearing a little pudding-bowl wig, almost as though the hairstyle itself is exerting a malign influence. At one point, he crams a slice of cake into Tina's face in a restaurant, then beats up one of Tina's girlfriends, before tucking into the cake himself and saying, 'Damn, this frosting tastes good!' According to Ike, at least two of the most shocking episodes never happened, and it's true that they are nowhere mentioned in Tina's book: the notorious scene in which, upset over the way she's singing *Nutbush City Limits*, Ike beats and then rapes Tina; and their last encounter, where Ike turns up at one of Tina's shows after she's left him and threatens her with a gun. Indeed, there are some suggestions that Tina herself may regard the movie as exaggerated.

And yet there are whuppings aplenty in Tina's written account – whuppings of Tina, of Ike's other lovers, of his son, Ike Jr., whom Ike once pistol-whipped so badly he needed more than thirty stitches. According to Tina's book, Ike would use whatever household object was at hand – phones, shoes, twisted-up coat hangers – breaking her jaw on one occasion. In his version, Ike takes a semantic approach to his defence. 'Sure, I've slapped Tina. We had fights and there have been times when I punched her without thinking. But I never beat her.'

Later, he recalls a time he 'spanked' her with a coat-hanger. Overall, Ike seems to feel that the relationship was no more physical than most people's, and where he expresses remorse, it's over his womanizing, which he scores in the three figures. If he had his life to live over, he writes, he'd still sleep around but 'be more discreet about it'.

I arrived at his house one spring morning, driving down from Los Angeles. Though he grew up in Clarksdale, Mississippi, Ike now lives in a smart development of ranch-style homes not far from San Diego. This time the door was answered by Ike's agent, a jumpy, slightly frazzled little guy named Dennis Rubenstein. Dennis ushered me into a bedroom he was using as an office where he booked dates for Ike's band.

Dennis made conversation in an over-caffeinated way about his long association with Ike and Tina. I asked his impression of their relationship. He said he'd never seen Ike be physical with anyone. Then he said, 'Let me tell you something. She used to push his buttons. I was around them twelve hours a day, okay? She knew what she was doing.'

Something in Dennis's manner reminded me of someone. Later I realized it was the Dennis Hopper character in *Apocalypse Now*, the spaced-out photographer who buzzes around the deranged Colonel Kurtz, played by Marlon Brando. Not that he was as crazed as that, but the situation felt similar: the vague sense of waiting for a kind of royal audience, and being chaperoned by a zany hanger-on.

Ike emerged a few minutes later, wearing a zebra-patterned shirt, and colourful patent-leather shoes. He took me into his back room where he has a small home studio – several synthesizers, a mixing desk, expensive-looking guitars on stands. As a party piece, Ike threw together a short blues instrumental. Because he's shy, this is his way of playing host, and he does it with the casual panache of a chef cooking up a dish, adding instruments like ingredients. First the drum machine, then layers of keyboards, then bass. When he was done, he erased it without ceremony.

As he worked, I concentrated on smiling and maintaining eye contact, concerned that Ike should understand how much I appreciated being there and that I didn't do anything to cause offence. I felt privileged to see him making music; I also felt a little afraid.

＊

We went out for lunch, he, Audrey and I, riding in Ike's smart Mercedes with its IKE TNR licence plate. I sat in the back with a new stack of Ike's latest publicity shots, which showed Ike smiling broadly, the tip of his tongue poking between his teeth, the ill-named fan club now omitted in favour of his website. Ike was in a good mood and he reminisced about losing his virginity to a middle-aged next-door neighbour, named Miss Boozie, when he was just six years old.

'You know, man, today you guys talk about starting sex at that age.' Ike put on a prissy voice. '"Oh! That's child moles-" What's the word?'

'Child molestation,' Audrey said.

'Child molestation. Man, that's crazy! I was enjoying myself! Miss Boozie was somewhere between forty-five and fifty years old. And, man, she would show me how to move and stuff.' Ike raised his arms. 'How to roll my stomach.' Ike rolled his stomach. 'And then say, "Hit it! Hit it! Hit it!"' Ike said 'Hit it!' in a high-pitched voice – I wasn't sure if it was meant to be Miss Boozie or possibly a man whose voice had gone up in a moment of passion. Ike laughed and then yelped, 'Yrowgh! Aigh! But everything today is all screwed up, you know?'

Over lunch, he shared stories about his days 'orgying' in the seventies. One of the hazards of being a Don Juan, Ike said, was that you couldn't always remember the people you'd orgied *with*. 'It's not that you're being snotty. It's just they change . . . One girl walked up to me and said, "You don't remember me?" She did this on Geraldo's show. I said, "No." She said, "I orgied you for three days!"'

'You "orgied" with her – what does that *mean*?' I asked.

With glee, Ike said, 'That, man, it were her and a lot more girls and I was doing them *all*.'

'Have you ever orgied, Louis?' Audrey asked innocently, and pressed her wig with her hands.

'I don't think I ever have orgied,' I said.

'You never had five or six women at one time?' Ike asked. 'Hey, life passin' you by!'

I remarked that I could see maybe orgying with two women at the same time, but that five or six seemed excessive.

'Yeah! I'm excessive with everything. That's why I don't do dope no mo'. I was excessive with it. I don't do a lot of women no mo' because I was excessive with it. I don't gamble any mo' because I was excessive with it. I go to the extreme with everything. Now I'm a good guy.'

Seeing Ike so relaxed and expansive, I thought I'd hazard a Tina question. I knew from Ike's book that one of Ike's mistakes during his drug addiction was to sign away his rights to sue Disney, the studio that made the movie, over his portrayal. I asked about this. 'That's how they did it,' he said. He chewed his lamb chop. 'Forty-five lousy thousand dollars. To assassinate my career.' He forked some vegetables into his mouth. 'But that's in the pahst now. So let's go forward.'

* * *

Back at his house, Audrey made tea, and Ike and I went into his little studio.

I asked about *Here and Now*, the record I'd seen him promoting. I was surprised to hear that, despite winning critical acclaim, it had sold poorly. 'It really wasn't played,' Ike said. His recording contract had lapsed now, but he was excited about his new music, which he described as 'blues with a twist'. One song went, 'Gimme back that wig I bought you and let your head – your head go bald!' 'This is Tina!' Ike said. In another track, he sang, 'They made a movie 'bout me and what they said in some parts ain't true.' The last verse talked about people turning up their noses at him, ending, 'I can't live forever, and how long do you think I'm gonna wait?' – the music dropped out – 'For forgiveness!'

During a break in the music, I asked, 'For people who only know you from the movie, what would you say to them?' I'd already asked one Tina question and to ask another was pushing it. Ike's eyes flicked to the side, and he took a very long pause, sixteen seconds when I counted it on my tape. I couldn't tell if he was irritated or just considering the question carefully. Then he said, 'I'm sorry that they didn't get to know me themselves, rather than know me through a movie, where they had to make some-body the demon and somebody the god. I ain't the demon that I've been portrayed to be.'

He cued up a last track. He pointed at the CD player.

'This song here tell you my real feelings.' He hit pause and called Dennis in from the bedroom. The song was the tortured thoughts of an addict in the depths of his addiction. 'It's a crime and a shame that I call myself a man!' it went. 'I'm down on my knees beggin' please!'

Dennis swivelled back and forth on his chair holding his spectacles. The song put Ike in mind of all the time he'd wasted on drugs, all the money, all the lost relationships and after it was finished he let loose about his wilderness years. 'I done slept on damn near floors in Los Angeles. I went from riches to rags. And then when I got ready to come out from under it, here come a movie to stomp me further back down in it. People look at me and *hate* me, man. And they don't know how much love in my body. Like what I got from you and you?' He pointed at Dennis and me. 'They don't know! And I can feel the hate from them. And they don't know what this soul has got and how I am inside. All they know is how I've been portrayed to be. And the me that they portrayed me to be, that's not me. *This* is me.'

I felt moved by Ike's crie de coeur. I was no longer thinking about what he might or might not have done to Tina, or how he felt about it. I was encloaked in his world and his pain.

Ike's tale of ill use had made Dennis excited. He stood up and pointed at me. 'Ike, he asked me today about that. And I said to him, "I was there *all* these years, ten years." I said, "Look, Tina *knew* how to push your buttons!" He'd be in the studio recording with a *roooom* full of musicians, okay? And Tina wants to go shopping and has got to come in in the middle and stop everything and he'd say, "Just a minute, just a minute." And she'd go outside and she'd stomp around. I *watched* it and—'

Ike broke in. 'You know, but I don't even talk about it, man. I never said nothing about whether she good or whether she bad. 'Cause let me tell you something. I could let go on her and I could do a movie about Ike and Tina, a *true* one. But I wouldn't do that. Because like I said today, man, I feel like a powerful – you name it, if I want it, I can get it. And man, let me tell you, this is the Jesus Christ. I ain't lookin' for shit. I got no pressures, none, nowhere. I'm just free. I just release myself to God. I say, "Take me where you will." And that's me.'

'That's beautiful,' Dennis said.

'That's great, man,' I said, and, without really knowing what I meant by it, I applauded.

MIKE CAIN

I was a world away from Ike's suburban bungalow, stand-ing outside a ramshackle old house in Northern Idaho.

Seven years earlier I'd stayed here when I'd been mak-ing a programme about the patriot movement – that fierce and paranoid sect of self-styled freedom fighters who believe that the end times are imminent and that the world is being taken over by a shadowy cabal of evil-doers.

Back then it had belonged to Mike Cain and his family. Mike had been one of those dedicated to resisting the onslaught. He'd moved up to Idaho to be part of a patriot community called Almost Heaven, stopped paying his taxes, and awaited the armed showdown with the govern-ment which he regarded as inevitable.

But Almost Heaven was little more than a memory now. Mike and his family were gone, and the house was in the hands of Mike's ex-neighbour John Moore, another Almost Heaven pioneer, though of a less radical stripe.

'We turned it into a gymnasium and a community home,' John said, with a trace of defensiveness, per-haps wary of being seen to capitalize on another man's misfortune. 'It's called the Woodland Acres Community Center.'

The metal frame of a trampoline I'd once jumped on was rusting in the yard. The plywood porch looked dirty and weather-beaten. Inside the house it was dark. The blinds were down over the windows, and in one corner were a drum kit and some gym equipment. The kitchen was full of stacked boxes. In the old master bedroom mats were laid down for wrestling. It seemed less a community building than a storage area for John and his wife Michelle, and a clubhouse for their kids. 'We replaced that stove,' John said, as if to assert his rights over the place.

I looked in on the bedroom I'd stayed in nearly eight years earlier, when the community was still full of idealism. I felt oddly moved being back. Of all the shows I'd made about weird people, this one had been my favourite. I'd assumed that was partly because it was the first I did, when I was fresh and excited. But coming back, I realized there was more to it than that. There was something deeply romantic about these strange bearded renegades who carried guns and quoted the seventeenth-century English philosophers John Locke and James Harrington, and were willing to lay down their lives for their vision of correct living, even if it came to nothing. 'It's a little sad,' I said. 'Thinking this was his dream.'

'It coulda worked out right for them if Mike hadn't got involved with the wrong people,' John said. 'I think he wanted to be the guy who made that stand. I think he wanted to be the guy that *did it*. I think he wanted to be famous . . . He was supposed to be the guy who died in his house trying to keep his home from the nasty government. That was the philosophy of these people. They really thought this would make a nationwide show of how bad the government was, to take this man's home.'

I tried to think why I felt sad. The community had been founded by gun nuts and Bible thumpers. When they talked about the slide into immorality they meant people like me and my friends: drug takers and fornicators, supporters of welfare programmes and socialized medicine. George W. Bush, the born-again president, who to me seemed far right, to them was another socialist, a puppet of the New World Order. But they also spoke for intransigence; idealism; a refusal to take the world on the world's terms. There was clarity in their simple notions of discipline and justice. In a childish way, I'd like my world to be a story with goodies and baddies. Every time I used to read about a patriot group declaring themselves a sovereign country, as they sometimes did, my heart gladdened. Though undoubtedly weird, it's also a kind of maverick statement to ask a notary to witness your own personal declaration of independence. A little part of me would have liked to be the sovereign state of Louis.

※

On a frosty morning eight years earlier, Colonel Bo Gritz unfurled a map and explained his concept for the community. A highly decorated Special Forces commander, supposedly the real-life model for Rambo, he'd run for president in 1992 and found many Christians were paranoid and fearful. They believed America was off-track and needed to return to the core ideals of the Constitution and the Ten Commandments. This was at the end of Clinton's first term, at the height of paranoia about gun control. 'Billary' was hatching plans to take everyone's firearms away so the government could impose martial law. UN peacekeepers would be in charge; it was all part of the

New World Order promoted by the first George Bush and masterminded by a shadowy cabal of bankers and industrialists. Many thought we might be close to the 'end of days'.

The same evidence tended to get circulated, often at gun shows and 'preparedness expos': supposed sightings of black helicopters conducting surveillance; signs of concentration camps being built; Soviet tanks on manoeuvres; markings on the back of roadside signs that would direct the foreign-born troops during the takeover. One militiaman in Florida spotted government plans in a map on a Trix cereal box. Doubters were directed to consider Waco, the government's heavy-handed siege of a religious community in Texas which ended in the deaths of about eighty congregants; or Ruby Ridge, another federal stand-off that resulted in several fatalities.

Now, Bo's idea was to go further, found a whole community dedicated to mutual support and safety, a place to sit out Armageddon. Using data from FEMA, the Federal Emergency Management Agency, he'd figured out that north central Idaho was the safest place in America. He and a partner had bought up 200 acres there on the mountaintop. They'd subdivided it and called it Almost Heaven. It was as though, having failed in his bid for the presidency, he'd decided to be chief executive of his own little republic, a secessionist state within a state.

Bo had only recently moved up there full-time when I arrived. We spent the day chatting at his house, which was some way from being the frontier redoubt I'd expected, more like a spacious suburban home, sitting on a bluff with a beautiful view over a sheer snowy valley. He drove me down to one of the lots that was available. He was a thick, sturdy man, with snowy hair, and a deep growling voice –

warm and friendly enough, though I suspected he was just happy to have an audience and anyone might do.

But even then, there were ominous signs for the community. I got the sense Bo didn't like it up there. He complained about the cold. He seemed to have misgivings about being the leader, perhaps rattled by the hostile media coverage. After the bombing of the federal building in Oklahoma City by far-right anti-government terrorists, the climate was even less friendly towards people viewed as 'militia types'. Where before he'd bragged about the military advantages of his mountaintop position, and written in his memoir, *Called to Serve*, 'It is exciting to be Americans during this time of prophetic reality,' now he downplayed the idea of any confrontation or the imminence of the apocalypse. He sounded offhand when he said Mikhail Gorbachev might be the Antichrist. He was exasperated with some of the more volatile personalities he'd attracted up there, a handful of radical 'noodles' who were looking forward to an armed stand-off with the government.

Mike Cain was one of the 'noodles'. Bo warned me he might try to shoot me if I went and saw him. I went anyway, finding him rolling out insulation with his friend Pat Johnson for a house they were building up on the hill. A tall, thin man, aged fifty or so, a heavy smoker, he'd been a building contractor in Las Vegas. He'd sold everything to be part of Almost Heaven, bringing his family with him. He'd bought an acre and built a house in 1996.

He spoke about wanting to 'take America back under the law'. 'I'm not opposed to taxes, I'm opposed to forced taxes,' Mike said, as though there were another kind. He objected to paying for services he didn't use, like upkeep of the cemetery. Like some others up there, he'd signed a 'covenant' agreeing to stand firm and protect his neighbours should the government ever try to invade and enslave them.

He told me about Almost Heaven, how they wouldn't use money, preferring a barter system. 'We're aiming for total self-sufficiency, so we need all skills. We need everybody up here.' I asked whether they might need a TV presenter.

He invited me back to his ramshackle cement-block homestead, with its free-standing stove, gun rack, log-cabin extension, and I met his Mexican-born wife, Chacha, and two of their daughters, Vanessa and Tamara. The media had depicted the militia movement as racist, so Mike's being married to Chacha seemed a good sign. He told me he was an old hippy. I pointed out that hippies put flowers in the ends of guns.

'See that's when you're young and dumb. When you get to be my age you learn that it's better to put bullets in guns.' Over a Mexican dinner, I asked him to explain as simply as he could what he was doing up there. 'There has been a conspiracy for some years by a group of people that has become known as the New World Order,' he said. 'The problem with the New World Order and the one-world government is it requires a benevolent dictator. You show me in history anytime that there's been a benevolent dictator. Ever. And if you don't have a benevolent dictator then you have a tyrant.'

I spent two days under his roof. I liked him more than I ever expected. He was friendly, modest and, only occasionally, when he had a glint in his eye speaking about the government, scary. He told me he no longer paid taxes. He didn't register his pickup, didn't carry a driver's licence. 'Those are all New World Order items,' he said. It was only a matter of time before the government came looking for him.

On my last afternoon at Almost Heaven, he took time off from his house-building for some target practice. I'd been planning to have a conversation discouraging him from provoking a confrontation. In the event, he brought it up himself, saying, when I asked about earmuffs, 'You don't wear earmuffs in a war.' It was as though he'd been waiting for his moment to declare himself. He got that strange look in his eye and said: 'It's all-out war . . . maybe before the year 2000.'

I told him how sad I'd be if I heard he'd got into a shoot-out. 'Louis, I appreciate what you say, I really do,' he said, hoisting his gun on to his shoulder. 'I guarantee, if you hear anything, it won't be because we started it. My refusal to pay taxes is my right as an American. It's the out-of-control government that wants to put me in jail for that or take my home or harm my children. It isn't correct that because I refuse to pay my taxes I am sentenced to die. I should have my day in court . . .

'And it's not just me saying it. There's tens of thousands of Americans just like me all across this country. I'm not in any way unique. Perhaps even millions of Americans that are ready for the war. We're *ready*. We pray daily that it doesn't take place. We lift a banner of peace always. But if they would have a war, then let it begin here.'

As I left Mike for the last time, I said: 'Don't do anything silly.'

*

A year or so after my filming trip, in 1997, I received a letter from Mike. 'It's been a long year for us and very busy. There have been legal battles; some won, some lost, as the NWO continues in its efforts to control us . . . I was arrested and jailed on Nov 8 for the crime of asserting my rights as secured by the Constitution for the united [sic] States of America. My brothers acting under inspiration from our Lord were able to secure my quick release. The dragon is now showing his teeth, and I feel an armed assault against us is imminent. If it takes place, please remember us as a people who feared and loved our God, our country, and our families.'

An officer had pulled him over for driving without plates. Asked for his driver's licence, and not recognizing his authority, Mike said: 'I neither admit nor deny but leave you to your proofs.' He was charged with resisting and obstructing justice.

Hearings followed. One of the beliefs of the patriots is that because the flags in US courtrooms have decorative gold fringes on them, it means they are illegal admiralty or martial-law courts. Mike showed up to the hearing with a US flag sewn on to his shirt, with no gold fringe. 'This is the flag of my country,' he said. To all the judge's questions, he replied: 'Sir, I do not understand a foreign language.'

Around that time, I spoke to Mike on the phone. It was a little odd. There's a part of me that half expects contributors to 'become normal' after we've finished filming. Conversely, Mike seemed to expect me to 'become weird'. 'We're not on film now, Louis,' he said. 'You know what's going on. You're a journalist. You know what the New World Order's about.' I assured him that I was aware of no satanic globalist conspiracy. I urged him to work through the courts. 'I don't care to be arrested, Louis. I've broken no law! . . . I cannot and will not compromise with the Devil. And that's who we're dealing with here . . . The compromise is that they should acknowledge the law. And by their own law they're treasonous.'

In September 2001, I emailed Mike, wondering if the attacks on the World Trade Center might have caused him to realign his priorities. He wrote back: '"Perhaps it is a universal truth that the loss of liberty at home is to be charged to provisions against danger, real or pretended, from abroad." James Madison, 1798. Louis, Bin Laden didn't do it!' He viewed the attacks as a kind of Reichstag fire, to justify a suspension of civil liberties.

Meanwhile, Mike hadn't been paying his property taxes. The county had sold his house, valued at more than $30,000, for $3,500 at auction. Mike, who didn't recognize the county's right to levy 'forced' taxes in the first place, also regarded property ownership as absolute: the way he saw it, no government had the authority to take his home, tax bill or not. So he was still living there, but the new owner wished to take possession, and the county authorities were rumoured to be poised for a SWAT-style attack.

'If they want to come up here and make war I guess that's what they'll have to decide to do,' he was quoted as saying in a newspaper article. 'But I'm not leaving. Not unless I'm in a body bag.'

After that, I heard nothing. I sent letters and emails to the addresses I had. Nothing came back.

※

When I arrived back in America in 2004, at a loss as to how to reach Mike, I paid another visit to Colonel Bo Gritz.

He'd had his own troubles since I last saw him. In 1998,

distraught over his wife leaving him, he'd shot himself in the chest. Strangely, he survived with only minor wounds. Cynics maintained that a highly decorated green beret would know how to kill himself if he was serious about it. They concluded it had been either a plea for sympathy or a publicity stunt. Since then, he'd moved back to his old house in Sandy Valley, Nevada, an hour outside Vegas in the middle of the desert.

In other news, the failure of the apocalypse to take place as planned seemed to have taken some of the wind out of the patriot movement. The preparedness expos were no more. On the Internet, the only event that featured Bo as a speaker was the Esoteric World News Convention. Here the real-life Rambo was listed between Catheann Fronda, 'astrologer and Reiki healer', and Michelle 'Shelly' Hanson, 'a seashell reader'. From a high of 858 in 1996, patriot and militia groups had dwindled to 194 in 2000. Some militia sympathizers rallied to the government after 9/11, seeing the federal government as a lesser evil than Arab terrorism. Some were imprisoned on firearms charges. Stricter laws were passed against the time-wasting legal actions favoured by many patriots.

I drove down to see Bo one hot spring day. Sandy Valley isn't on the way to anywhere: on the map it lies at the end of two different roads, not far from the California border. Like many named places in Nevada, it's not so much a town as a grouping of mobile homes and beached RVs, served by a grid of bright sandy streets. Bo's house was a triple-wide trailer, prettified into a big suburban-style ranch house. To one side, where you might expect a garage, was an airplane hangar with a small prop plane inside. I'd had difficulty with Bo's directions and I was about twenty minutes late.

Possibly because of this, he did not shake my hand. His two Alsatians were padding around with Stars and Stripes neckerchiefs. The dogs were called Hartzall and Shmily. 'Shmily. That's See How Much I Love You,' Bo said. I didn't catch his meaning. I asked him how to spell the name. '*See How Much I Love You*,' he said sharply.

The house was cool and shady and full of military and patriotic kitsch: paintings of wounded Confederate soldiers, dolls in bridal gowns, teddies in Confederate uniforms. Bo was wearing cowboy boots and a Special Forces T-shirt. We sat in his office where he was due to broadcast his shortwave radio show after lunch. I was there to talk about Mike Cain but Bo was preoccupied with matters of the heart. His new wife Judy had gone into Vegas for the day. He still pined for Claudia, his ex. He'd married her when she was sixteen and he was thirty-five. 'I can't help that I think about her every day,' he said. 'Twenty-four years wasn't long enough . . . but I'm married to Judy, and I would like to fall in love with her, but it's awful hard.'

Claudia had run off with a handyman. I asked the handyman's name. Bo paused. 'Why would I even want to remember? I was going to kill him just for the principle, because the bastard stole my wife . . . And he needed to be killed 'cause he's a no-good son of a bitch. And if I was a normal person I would have killed him, 'cause that's what I do best.'

When he told me the name, I asked for the spelling. This was pushing it. Bo's tone changed. 'I don't know, I don't give a damn, and, you know, God knows my limitations. Prayerfully, I'll never be in his presence, because I am a weak man, and I am a six-degree-martial art black belt and I've learned to control myself, 'cause I've wanted to take the throat out of a couple of media people, but usually they can tell that so I've been lucky. I haven't killed anybody that wasn't a communist so far.'

I took this as a veiled warning and changed the subject to Mike Cain.

He remembered Mike as one of a small group of paranoid 'knots'. 'You ever been fishing? Or you ever got up a line to try to tie something in the back of your car or whatever? And you're pulling out nice smooth line and there's always a knot somewhere that you gotta go back and fish out. There were about five or six of those guys that thought that Almost Heaven was gonna be Armageddon. But the *reason* you go to Almost Heaven is so that nothing happens. You got to *make* something happen. You got to entertain yourself by watching the elk or driving along the Clearwater River, because there's no crime up there . . .

'I built that community up there so that people wouldn't have to be paranoid,' he went on. 'They don't have to worry about house invasions or crime. They don't have to worry about the FBI getting the wrong address and breaking in their doors. The children would go to home school where they don't have to be taught alternative lifestyles and sexual education in an explicit way. So it gave them a choice and two hundred and twenty-five families are now living up there . . .'

He wasn't sure where Mike was now. He spoke vaguely of the house being taken over by a motorcycle gang, some problems Mike had had with the law. From the way he talked, Almost Heaven was still thriving. I hadn't really thought through the implications of Bo's not being there: that for many in the community his presence had been the big draw, and how upset they'd be, having dragged their families up there and invested in his idea, when he upped and left. No wonder there was discord. But at this stage, I didn't know.

A few weeks later, in July, with a few phone numbers Bo had given me, I drove up to Idaho, hoping to find out what had happened to Mike.

※

Kamiah is a small farming and logging town. It sits on the bank of the Clearwater River, green mountains on all sides. With the town's population at around a thousand you can do all your research just going from shop to shop on Main Street, the sheriff's office (never open), the tiny town hall. The local weekly newspaper, the *Clearwater Progress*, 'Serving the upper Clearwater Valley since 1905', looks like it hasn't been redesigned since it was first published. The week I was there the features included 'Tips For Keeping Black Bears Away' and 'Cellphones Are As Entertaining As They Are Practical'.

I checked into a motel in town and spent several days on the mountain chatting to the patriots still up there. Driving to Almost Heaven from Kamiah, you cross the Clearwater River, take a hard left, then weave up the side of a mountain for half an hour, enjoying a view clear across a broad fertile flatland, the Camas Prairie.

News travels fast on the hill. Visitors stand out. As I drove up in the morning and down in the afternoon, the driver of each passing pickup would lift his fingers from the steering wheel in a wave, wondering, presumably, who that was in the town car with Nevada plates. I had the same sense I'd had before of people buzzing and excited. Everyone helpful, going out of their way to set up interviews.

Maybe because of their exaggerated sense of the conspiracy at work in the world and the dark intelligences machinating against them, they have a commensurate gratitude and naive faith in what a well-disposed journalist can achieve.

One of those I saw was Mike's old friend Pat Johnson, whom I'd met that first day, eight years before, when they were laying out insulation for the house they were building. Unusually for Almost Heaven, Pat's property had a fence round it. There were two No Trespassing signs, another one saying: 'UN Free Zone'. Though I'd set up the appointment by phone, I approached cautiously.

'We're still morally bankrupt! Even worse than before!' Pat said, by way of a hello. A slight man, bearded, with a deep smoker's voice, he was sixty-two. He wore round glasses, a workmen's shirt and boots. He looked a little shrunken, but still had a warm manner, a friendly face and a ready laugh.

We sat in his modest mobile home, the Ten Commandments on the wall, a Confederate flag over his bookcase, and on the door a quotation from John Locke about a person's right to defend himself by killing if necessary. He had a TV in one corner, a free-standing stove in another, and on one bookshelf *Strong's Exhaustive Concordance of the Bible*, *Webster's Dictionary*, *Black's Law Dictionary*, automotive books and books on car paint – his trade. I sipped water from a jam jar.

He'd been talking about Bo's divorce. 'He was fooling around, too. He got into fornicating. I'm not poking the finger. I'm single now . . . It's hard for the ladyfolk living up here. Lots of stress. We've got a lot of bachelors.'

'Why is it stressful for the women?' I asked.

'I know what mine would say to me. She'd say, "I never know if you're coming back alive!"'

'Coming back from where?'

'We would police the police. If there was trouble, we'd go where the trouble was, for righteousness's sake . . . That's what happened to Cain. Chacha left first. Then he pulled out and joined her, I guess. Been a lot of that. Families breaking up. Divorces . . . I've changed from where I was when you were here. I thought I could do it with a gun. I believed a good man armed could make a difference. Now I don't see that and I haven't for a while. The system is so far gone, we've gone so far into unrighteousness, there's nothing we can do. We've got the aborticide of fifty million children since 1970. The marrying of sodomites, allowing that. And it goes on and on. There is a curse on us. God has put a curse on us, I believe.'

Pat had been among those who thought a concentration camp was being built nearby. 'There was a light patch in the sky over there at night, but no town, no stadium. So we thought the UN might be setting up a facility.' He said he'd like to see a return to the biblical law outlined in Isaiah and Jeremiah.

'Stonings? Things like that?' I asked.

'You bet! There would be no more adultery. It would put our people back in God's order . . .'

'You'd agree that I have the liberty to do what I like as long as it doesn't impinge on someone else's liberty?' I asked. 'We can all go to Hell in our own fashion?'

'Oh, sure,' Pat said. 'Unless your conduct hurts me. As a nation, when people become morally bankrupt, it hurts me. Your conduct damages me.'

He talked wistfully of a time when some state constitutions called for blasphemers to be branded with a 'B' on their forehead. 'And I bet there was very little of it done. Can you imagine walking around with a "B" branded on your forehead?'

'Seems a little extreme,' I said.

Pat reminisced about the good old days, when he and twenty or so others went down to the courthouse to spring Mike Cain out of jail after his traffic infraction, all carrying guns ('running heavy' he called it). Now most of those patriots were gone. Some in prison, some fled to Costa Rica or lying low in other states. 'When you see your friends leave and go back into Babylon, it's disheartening. I've seen a lot of them come and go, and they profess and believe the same things I believe.' He seemed a little lonely; but his strict adherence to scripture meant he couldn't think about getting divorced or taking a girlfriend.

Like Mike, Pat stopped paying his property taxes and had his house sold from under him. But Pat bought back his house at auction, at the bargain price of $110. After that a distance came between him and Mike. 'Because mine went away and he was still in a stand-off. He said, "Patrick, don't you see? If we can get enough people in the same situation . . ." I sensed he was angry with me because it turned out that way.'

One afternoon, Pat took me down to the Clearwater River for some target practice. We loaded the gun rack in the back of Pat's battered Ram Charger. 'This is a forty calibre semi-automatic Smith & Wesson. This is a Ruger 10–22 semi-automatic. Just a fun little gun. It's a good starter gun.' Then we crept down the hairpin bends of a long winding gravel road, to the bottom of the canyon. We chatted about conspiracies. Naturally, Pat thought 9/11 was the work of the New World Order. He didn't think we'd been to the Moon and had serious doubts whether we'd been to outer space.

'I did not have sex with that woman,' Pat said, quoting Clinton. 'What kind of world is it where our president lies – under oath! You asked about stoning. I'd stone him!'

'Wouldn't that be "cruel and unusual punishment"?'

'Nope. Short and quick. One big boulder. Squash him.'

'What about Bush?'

'He's the same. Clinton did us a lot of favours. He was so blatant with his Monica Lewinsky. They've been a lot more able to keep stuff hidden with Bush. So a lot more people are deceived.'

We took turns pinging a can, shooting uphill towards the sheer sides of the valley. Yellow and purple wildflowers were in bloom, the river idled at our backs. It was a beautiful clear day. We picked some yellow cherry plums and blackberries. If civilization collapsed at this time of year, if the beast system took over, I'd be okay for a few days, I reflected, as long as I could find my way back to this plum tree. 'It's like Paradise,' I said. 'It really is almost Heaven.'

✳

Maybe a little naively, I'd thought the election of Bush Jr. might placate the patriots at Almost Heaven. But they hated the Patriot Act with a passion and they opposed the invasion of Iraq, not on humanitarian grounds so much as an example of the federal government overreaching its lawful powers. If anything, the patriots were more pessimistic now. During the Clinton years, they'd managed to cross over and win converts among mainstream right-wingers. But those mainstream right-wingers liked Bush. The so-called war on terror, which was proving so effective in intimidating the majority of the public, was regarded by patriots as a ruse, a pretext for the suspension of more liberties.

One night, down in Kamiah, in the back dining room of the Lolo Cafe, I attended a meeting of a local constitutionalist group, the Watchmen on the Wall. The moderate edge of the extremist fringe, WOTW pride themselves on being law-abiding citizens, whether or not they view those laws as legitimate. They believe in working through the system. There were about thirty-two people present, of whom, I was told, eight or nine were from up on the mountain. Most were in their sixties and seventies. The MC, Tom Simmons, was one of the younger ones. Dressed like a cowboy, with a big white hat and jeans and a big belt buckle, he was, in fact, a web designer who'd moved to Idaho in 1996.

'Welcome global citizens!' he began. 'Okay! Let's get back to doom and gloom here!'

The first item was an initiative to preserve local wildlife habitats by curbing public land grazing. 'Environmental extremists,' Tom said.

Next up, a newspaper story about microchipping pets at a local animal shelter. 'If they know where the dog is, they know where you are,' one of the matrons commented.

Then federal funding of schools. On this issue, Tom the web designer took a surprising neo-Luddite line. 'Why is it that Abraham Lincoln didn't have a computer and he succeeded?' Tom asked. 'Why is it that Albert Einstein didn't have a computer and he succeeded? Why is it that *the man who created most of the computers we have today, Bill*

*Gates*, he didn't have a computer and *he* succeeded? It's a string that attaches us to the federal umbilical cord.'

A bald, gnomish old guy in dungarees, with baggy cheeks and wild eyebrows, said that if the sheriff didn't obey the constitution then he should be 'eliminated'.

This was greeted with nervous laughter. 'Wait a minute,' Tom Simmons said.

'I'm talking about *removed*,' the old-timer said, backtracking.

'Agreed,' Tom said. 'The problem that we have, and you well know this, Dave, is that we are *not* the majority in this county. I think we have to be prepared to be patient. It's like the swirling commode. It gets faster and faster. As we get closer to the bottom, more and more people are going to wake up.'

At the end, Jack McLamb, one of the community leaders from Almost Heaven, stood up and said a prayer. 'You've given us a commandment, Lord, to occupy the institutions of this land until you return. Let us focus on that and remember that's a commandment from you, oh Lord.'

❋

I pieced together a picture of Mike's last few years. After the run-in over the driver's licence and the missed court date, the judge issued a warrant for Mike's arrest. After that, Mike rarely left the house. To earn some money, Chacha qualified as a nurse's assistant, got a social security number, joined the 'Antichrist system'.

Mike had become well-known in patriot circles, from the interviews he'd done and for his stand on property taxes. Not paying income tax, sure, who did? But not paying property taxes? That was hardcore. Mike's house became a gathering place for anti-government types. One called Dave Roach would drive down most weekends. Another, a 'legal expert' named Larry Raugust, moved in with Mike. They put plywood over the windows, with little slits to shoot through in anticipation of the showdown.

'Chacha used to cry at people's houses,' John Moore said. John was the next-door neighbour, an air-conditioning salesman who'd moved up there in 1997 with his wife, Michelle, and their two sons. 'When we cleaned the house up, I found a note from Chacha saying "I can't live like this anymore."'

Around the time of Mike's trouble over his driver's licence, he asked people to send in their licences to Idaho County in a mass protest. John refused. 'I said, "You're kidding. I've got a job! I've got to go to work!"' After that, they fell out.

John became convinced there would be a shoot-out. He built a concrete wall between his house and Mike's, to protect himself and his family from the crossfire. By early 2002, the local biker who'd bought the house from the county was suing to get possession. Supposedly, he wanted to turn it into a clubhouse for his outlaw biker gang, 'The Highwaymen'. In John's account, the sheriff was only waiting for some bomb sniffer dogs from the 2002 Winter Olympics in Utah before making his move: he thought he might need them after the shoot-out if the house was booby-trapped.

In the end, without telling Mike, John stepped in and bought the house on behalf of a 'trust'. John seemed a little sheepish talking about the trust. Who was in it wasn't clear. 'We saved it from becoming a biker hang-out,' he said. 'I just let Mike think it was still going to happen, that the cops were still coming up to get 'em.' Mike left in the middle of the night, got a lift down to the bus station and hopped on a bus. He left everything behind, furniture, mementoes, family photos and went to ground, hiding out from the authorities and from his fellow patriots who felt let down that he hadn't martyred himself. 'So many of his followers were disgusted with him for leaving like that,' John said, ''cause they all had confidence in him.'

No one was sure where he was.

Unlike Mike, John was a fan of Bo's. He used to listen to Bo's radio show, bought his book, even paid for military-style training for himself and his family.

'I liked being around Bo because he had such a good character. It wasn't like we were looking for a guru or some kind of cult leader. Here's a guy who's been exposed to so many things in his life. I want to say he was *wise*.'

But even John seemed a little disillusioned with Almost Heaven. Now people were leaving, he said. Property values were going down. His lot lost $2,000 in value the previous year. There was no work. Many of those who left sold their property to people who weren't patriots. 'So now it's like a regular old community.'

John is a moderate by old Almost Heaven standards. Still, he believes the New World Order and its shock troops, the UN peacekeepers, are on course to take over and annihilate anyone who isn't cooperative. 'America is going down a course right now that's destined, through immorality and lack of faith in God, that we can't turn back from . . . I feel we're going to see Christians treated as terrorists.

I don't think I'd be safe up here but I'd probably be one of the last to die. After they mopped up the cities they might come after these teeny communities.'

John and Michelle walked me to my car. I was struck by something John said: 'Mike Cain didn't participate. He wanted everyone to participate in his thing.' Mike had his cause; John started a 'neighbourhood watch', which he coordinated with the sheriff; down in Kamiah there were the meetings of the Watchmen on the Wall. Everyone wanted their own outfit. Everyone was looking for community, but on their own strict terms. A cooperative of rabid individualists, it was oxymoronic in its very conception, like a social club for hermits.

Patriots are ornery and paranoid by their very nature. They don't mix well. Many of the pilgrims up on the mountain were so mistrustful of government, so resigned to the triumph of evil and the globalist octopus, that the only options were total withdrawal (waiting for Armageddon) or to go down in a hail of bullets. Bo's leaving obviously didn't help. Nor did the priorities of the original sales pitch, which were to do with safety and defensiveness and immunity from natural disasters, and not civic-mindedness and how to influence local government. Maybe if there had been work in the area they might have muddled through, but there wasn't even that. As the saying goes, the Devil has the best tunes; and the satanic system has the best jobs. This was the ultimate irony, in a way. It's all very well to crave independence, but what are you going to do for a job? Running out of money's fine if civilization is about to collapse. But what if the end never comes?

Not long after Mike disappeared, his old patriot brothers-in-arms started getting rounded up. Mike's friend and frequent guest, Dave Roach, was revealed to be a government informant. Larry Raugust, the live-in legal advisor, was arrested in late 2002. He was charged with manufacturing and possessing 'a destructive device' – seven counts. They'd been removed from Mike's property, as it turned out. ('They were flash-bang things,' Pat said. 'You can buy them in *Soldier of Fortune* magazine.') At his trial, according to an article in the *Lewiston Tribune*, he referred to himself as 'Larry Eugene of the House of Raugust'. He was sentenced to seventy-seven months in prison.

Another who lived with Mike, James Newmeyer, nicknamed 'Snake', was arrested and charged with eight felony weapons charges.

Thanks to Dave Roach, federal authorities have 600 hours of recordings of meetings of Mike and Larry's group, 'Idaho County Unincorporated Posse'. Pat was at many of those meetings, speaking unguardedly. He has good reason to think he might be the next to be arrested. He said he pays his property taxes now. He's got a hole in the yard where he sleeps when he wants to be extra low-profile. 'Like Saddam Hussein,' I said.

I asked him if he thought they'd come after him.

'Uh-huh. I think they're coming after me right now. Because I've been a thorn in their side. I think they're going to put me away for a while. But that's in God's hands. I'm not going to change my beliefs. I haven't used a social security number in over ten years, and I'm not going to start now. I won't be part of that Luciferian system.'

✳

Some weeks later, after a series of phone calls to people who knew people, followed by a letter, and more phone calls, I got a call from Chacha. We met for coffee in Las Vegas, where she was living. Forty-eight now, she looked younger and more glamorous than I remembered, like a dainty gypsy lady.

'I don't know what happened,' she said, unasked. 'I don't know what stuff they planted or anything. They didn't tell me anything. You know how they felt about women.'

Now the woman who'd once denounced 'international banksters' and hosted a cavalcade of guvmint-hating right-wing groupies was hymning the daily miracles of the suburban shopping experience: Starbucks and Borders; the apartment she shared with Mike, its swimming pool and jacuzzi; her new job caring for Alzheimer's patients. 'And when they get cancer, they don't die. Because they don't know they have it. We have one old man, he was supposed to die two years ago, but he didn't, because he doesn't know.'

She'd been in Vegas three years, driving through the night from Idaho to get there. Mike had left Almost Heaven seven months after her. In that time, they spoke every day. Now he was working as a truck driver, registered, back on the books of the beast system. 'He was off the grid for a while, wasn't he?' I said. 'I don't want to talk about that,' Chacha replied.

She was upbeat and in tune with her surroundings in a way she never was in Almost Heaven. Her face clouded over when she spoke about it. 'The worst mistake we ever made was going up to Idaho,' she said.

They live in a gated community of apartments. Mike was still asleep, so we crept around and whispered. Cream carpet and walls, cute furnishings, flowers, mirrors: as feminine in decor as their house in Almost Heaven had been masculine. Mike was living on Chacha's terms now. He came out of the bedroom, bleary-eyed, wearing a T-shirt that said 'Bum'. He'd been working nights but looked well, still lean and weathered. It was odd seeing him in those circumstances.

We chatted over coffee. I had thought he might have mellowed in his beliefs, but his obsession with the illegitimacy of most laws, his fixation on weird legal niceties (the difference between 'Nevada State' and 'the State of Nevada' and so on) was as strong as ever. The only difference was Chacha didn't participate. Now she disapproved. 'She's had her bellyful. She's saturated. She doesn't want to hear about any apocalyptic views on end times. She's done with it.'

I explained how I'd wanted to find out what happened to the patriots, him especially. 'A rise and fall kind of thing?' he said, a little sardonically. 'I chose to challenge the system, and the system just wears you down. It's not that it comes after you directly; the delays just go on and on and on.'

'How do you feel about the whole experience?

Mike paused and said 'Hmm. Chacha and I spoke about it. Sense of loss, I guess. It's not the property, you can always get that back. I guess my sense of loss is that I'm no longer surprised at the cunning and contrivances of men. And I'm sorry I lost that, because I'd always like to remain a little surprised when I encounter evil . . . Something Goethe said, and it impressed me deeply: "At the moment of commitment, the universe conspires to assist you." I have great admiration for Goethe, but in this case it didn't turn out to be true.

'I have good feelings about it because I feel like I've become more spiritually in tune than I was before, and

I'm terribly, terribly sad that I missed out on so many years of my daughter's life, years that I can never regain. That's what I'm saddest about. I couldn't participate as she was growing up from twelve to eighteen.'

'Has she forgiven you?'

'I asked her about that. She said, "I was angry about that for a long time, Daddy, but I'm not any more." But I don't think that trust can ever be totally rebuilt.' Mike's eyes were welling up. 'It was hard to leave there. It was a lot harder to leave than it was arriving. At this stage of my life, leaving there was the best thing that ever happened to me.' He paused and said: 'What did they say about me up there?'

I explained that different people said different things; that people had liked him but they wondered why he'd been so inflexible, puzzled that he would make a stand on the issue of property taxes. I also said they speculated that Mike had ended up feeling it was more important to be with Chacha than to make a stand.

'I lost six years with my daughter. I didn't want to lose my wife too. Sure, they're right. I left to be with Chacha. And I'm glad I did.'

# HAYLEY

A Wednesday night in July 2004, and in the saloon of the Wild Horse Resort and Spa, Nevada's newest legal brothel, the working girls sat perched on barstools like mermaids or lounged on comfy chairs and chatted among themselves. Men came in, singly or in pairs, looking around shiftily. They had a beer at the bar. One of the women might go over and make conversation, offer them a tour of the premises. Then they'd pass through a green door at the back of the saloon into the main brothel.

A year earlier, I'd spent several weeks getting to know the women who work here in the run-up to the brothel's grand re-opening in lavish new premises. On coming back, I'd expected the place to be buzzing, but it was quiet. Windowless, dark, with a small stage in one corner, a pole for pole dancing, a buffet down one side, the atmosphere was somewhere between honky-tonk and a doctor's waiting room: you found yourself looking round wondering what the other men were there to have done. But then, my experience of legal brothels was that they could be busy without feeling busy. Men might be entering through the side door, bypassing the saloon, going straight into the parlour for a 'line-up' – a beauty-pageant-style parade of the available ladies, in which they filed out from the wings and said their names.

I'd been back a few hours, looking round the house. The old interviewee of mine that I was hoping to see again, a working girl called Hayley, was long gone. She'd taken off one night amid a swirl of rumours. But I'd come, figuring one of the other women or the management might know something. And I was curious about the progress of the establishment, having seen it open with such fanfare and high hopes on my first visit.

There were several new faces. Cicely, a twenty-three-year-old black woman who was studying criminal psychology at a State University she didn't want named. She'd been a part-time prostitute for two years. Her parents thought she was working at the Mac counter at Macy's in Las Vegas. Jane, forties, an Englishwoman from West London – she'd seen my documentary and flown out. She couldn't get used to being in the desert. 'It's like being on Mars, innit,' she said. 'The Yanks don't get my sense of humour. They're not on the same mental level.' Debbie, also twenty-three, with dark hair, who'd grown up in North Dakota with an abusive father. 'When I'm here I just switch my brain off,' she said. 'I make myself stupid . . . Honestly, and I don't mean this in a bad way, but I don't really regard men as human.'

In the parlour I chatted to Kris, who works in the cashier's cage, handing out clean sheets and condoms, listening in on the negotiations over the intercom. Since the working girls are all, technically, independent contractors, they set their own prices, which they negotiate with the customers in one of the small negotiation rooms. The house takes a 50 per cent cut; the cashier eavesdrops on the bargaining to prevent the girls from skimming. After the negotiation, the women check the men's penises for signs of disease. Then they grab a stack of sheets – a 'set-up' as it's called – and escort the clients back to their rooms.

The cage was better stocked than I remembered: sheets stacked behind the fax machine, boxes of condoms, bottles of lotion, massage cream, gargle, toothpaste, shampoo, furry cuffs, dildos called 'Big Tool' and 'Wild Stallion', a strap-on called 'Purple Delight'. Monique, a tall black woman in a blonde wig, forty or so, came past with an older guy she'd been chatting up in the bar. He was swigging a beer, dressed in a T-shirt, ballcap and baggy shorts. Her overalls had a smily face badge and one strap was off the shoulder. She went in one of the three negotiation rooms, came out, took her sheets, told Kris to put the timer on half an hour, then said to the guy: 'Okay, hon, follow my butt.'

＊

The Wild Horse was the brainchild of a couple called Susan Austin and Lance Gilman. Susan, the madam, is a former working girl herself, having 'turned out' (as the expression has it), aged forty-nine, after a divorce. Before that, she was a successful rep for a jewellery company, and she still has the polished manner of a saleswoman. Lance, the owner, is a high-powered real-estate developer and local business leader of some celebrity. They met as courtesan and customer, when Susan was working out of another Nevada brothel in Moundhouse, near Carson City.

When they opened the Wild Horse in 2002 it was the first new brothel in Nevada in eighteen years and one of the most ambitious in state history. For a year it operated out of a small prefab house at the back of the property, while Lance and Susan built and furnished its eventual home, splashing out four million dollars of Lance's money on twenty-nine bedrooms, each with its own en suite bathroom (one with wheelchair access), three themed VIP suites (the Marilyn Monroe suite, the Retro Suite and the Jungle Suite), a small gym for the women, a jacuzzi room, a swimming pool and a Hemingwayesque parlour appointed with the heads of African wildlife.

A few weeks before they were due to re-open in their new premises, Lance and Susan took me on a tour. As I trailed after her, Susan, elegant, petite, her blonde hair nicely coiffed, spoke about her ambition of providing 'a quality experience' for their clientele, 'Something that they can take back in their memory banks and replay over and over again.' Lance, who is tall, late fifties, used the well-thumbed phrases of his business life. The women would follow 'proven success procedures,' he said, adding, of Susan, 'She has the compassionate knowledge to interface with people who do a very difficult job.'

They spoke about wanting to make a healthy environment for the women who worked there. 'I had all boys,' Susan said, meaning her four sons. 'I have a house full of girls now. I've finally got the opportunity to guide a few ladies and get them to a better place in life.' She arranged regular appointments with a financial adviser to help the women manage their money; she ran a programme agreeing to pay half the tuition fees of anyone who attended college locally. The high standard of the premises were part of this vision, too: unlike most other houses, here the bedrooms would be furnished for the women, 'like a lovely hotel' as Lance put it.

The Call of the Weird

Lance's and Susan's enthusiasm was clear, as too was their affection for each other – the new premises were in part a testament to their autumn romance, and their finding each other in such circumstances seemed a good omen for the house. Ultimately, the signature of the house would be the quality of the 'parties' the women provided. 'We've coined a phrase here,' Lance said. 'And it's called the "boyfriend experience". I mean, you would enter the world yourself looking to meet someone who would treat you with respect and kindness and love as a boyfriend. And our customers who come here to the Wild Horse – we expect them to get a boyfriend experience.'

'Knowing that he may never see the lady again,' said Susan, 'and she may never see him again. But while he is here he has those same feelings of warmth, of companionship, of not being rushed, that it's not just a sexual game, that he matters. That's the type of party I'd like to see the ladies give.'

For several weeks I lived in Reno and visited the Wild Horse every day. There were twenty or so women working at that time; each had a different story. Some were brand new to the business, others were veterans of ten or fifteen years standing. Some saved their money, some spent it. Their ages ran from twenty to fifty. Many worked straight jobs too, or they attended college and did shifts at the Wild Horse in their spare time. Some stayed at the brothel for months on end. Others came for a few days and then disappeared. Some were married, to husbands who they said didn't mind, others said they couldn't see combining their jobs with relationships. One thing they did have in common: they were doing it for the money. In some cases, this might be upwards of $3,000 a night.

It reminded me, in some ways, of being part of a theatrical troupe. When the girls got ready for work, putting on their skimpy outfits and their make-up, it was as though they were about to take the stage. The areas where the clients weren't allowed unattended – the kitchen, the corridors and bedrooms – I came to think of as 'backstage'. The 'front of house' was the saloon and the parlour, where the women acted for the customers – hustled them at the bar, or faced the audience in the line-ups, playing the roles they thought the clients wanted them to play.

Not knowing much about brothels before I came to the Wild Horse, to begin with I viewed the line-up as a kind of paradigm of the commercial nature of the relationship between the women and their customers. I assumed the brothel was like porn in three dimensions – emotionless and voyeuristic. But the relationships between the working girls and their customers could be surprisingly human and well rounded. They liked many of the men who visited them. Occasionally they would get crushes. As I stayed longer, it was the naturalness that existed between the women and the customers that struck me. Many of the women had 'regulars' who they might continue seeing for many years. Rather than libertines or satyrs, the men were mostly people who for various reasons – because they were shy, or ugly, or disabled, or because they didn't want commitment – had difficulty finding girlfriends in the outside world.

Again, like actors, the women's roles leaked over into their real lives, even more so, since they were impersonating versions of themselves, working in a weird grey area between sincerity and insincerity. They were self-impersonators – paid to be the people their clients couldn't

**The Call of the Weird**

find in life. Comfortable, poised, sometimes deceptive. For me, this brought its own set of challenges. They could be glib, their answers a little too ready. In my conversations with the women, I was aware that I, as a man, was in a small way being hustled, and in none more so than with Hayley.

She'd had no hesitation about being interviewed. This in itself was unusual. Most of the women avoided publicity. But Hayley liked it, even telling me her real name, which was Tammy.

She seemed to enjoy flouting the many conventions of brothel life. She said she sometimes kissed the guys in her parties, a big taboo for many of the women, and where the others made a point of separating the business from their outside emotional lives, Hayley talked about how 'real' the job was. 'Your masks come off when you're asking for sex,' she said. 'People see this as a very phony profession. It can get real emotional sometimes.' She said she loved her job, but it didn't seem quite that simple.

Tall, athletic, faintly Native American-looking, she was in her late twenties. She'd grown up in northern California, a few hours west of Reno over the Sierra mountains. She'd been working as a prostitute for four or five years, having made the transition from dancing in clubs.

One afternoon, as she got ready for the night's work, I asked her why she became a prostitute. 'I was very wild,' she said. 'At first, I had a lot of issues. I felt, "Oh my God, I should have gone back to school." But now I'm lazy and I make great money and I'm not ready to do that. I may at some point in my life, if I meet someone that's worth it, but now, no.'

She professed that working girls have a 'sixth sense' that allows them to size up customers. I pressed her on this. I asked her to size me up. 'But to be honest the only way that you would really be able to embrace that or understand that is if you were a customer and you've never been a customer. Would you ever be a customer? Would you ever be with a working girl? Would you ever pay someone for sex?'

'I like the idea that if I was with a woman that she wouldn't have to be paid to enjoy my company,' I said, perhaps a little primly.

But this suggestion, which had been thrown out lightly, took root and in the subsequent days grew into a standing challenge: Hayley would only allow me to continue interviewing her if I booked a party.

I talked to Lance about it, mentioning that she'd set terms. 'Oh, only for today,' he said. 'Hayley is the essence of a manipulator. She plays, she grandstands, she titillates, and she'll have a great deal of fun at your expense and mine, because she's a very attractive, alluring, devilish little lady.'

But more days went by and Hayley didn't back down. If anything, her behaviour towards me grew more unpredictable. Some days she would be friendly and talk engagingly about brothel life; others she refused to answer questions, flashing her breasts if I didn't stop. For my part, I began to see some merit in the idea of a massage. I hadn't found it easy to meet clients of the brothel. If I'm honest, I was struggling a little for material for my documentary. By paying for a massage I could be the client myself and enact what happens during a party, albeit a chaste one. In other stories I'd done, I'd been a 'participant reporter'; booking a party seemed a reasonable and possibly revealing way to enter into the spirit of life at a brothel.

We agreed a price of $200. In her bedroom, I stripped down to my boxer shorts and lay face down with a towel round my waist. The massage itself was fairly embarrassing, which I suppose was half the point. She seemed to regard it as a coup to have snared me, the visiting reporter, into doing business with her. 'I'm having a blast,' she said. Hoping to get my money's worth, I peppered her with questions. Did she ever enjoy the physical side of it? Did she really kiss the guys? Did she tell guys she went out with in the 'square world' what she did for a living?

She said she enjoyed the sex sometimes. 'Yes. Of course! I'm human. You know, the body is alive. A feeling is a feeling. A sensation is a sensation. I would hope that I wasn't totally shut off and I couldn't feel any kind of thing. That wouldn't be good, right?' As for kissing the guys: 'Oh well, rarely. Only if they're really good-looking. Like cowboys. I'm a sucker for a good-looking cowboy with a nice smile. And if he's got a sense of humour, it's a date.' She said she didn't see many men outside work; that if she was in love, as she hoped to be one day, she wouldn't be working in a brothel. And if the guy didn't mind her working: 'Then I probably wouldn't be with that guy.'

After the massage, something changed between Hayley and me. Perhaps I no longer held any challenge for her. She was distant. She became unruly around the house. A few weeks later, she was thrown out. Several offences were mentioned. The saloon in the new premises had recently opened and she'd been binge drinking. She'd been rude to one of the other women and made her cry. She'd got one of the security guards fired, tricking him into bringing her drinks in her room by pretending she was partying with a high-rolling customer. She'd also sassed a client in the saloon, a dark-skinned man from Fiji who was rude to one of the other women – she'd shouted out 'Bye, Bin Laden!' as he left.

But Hayley was back a few weeks later, having promised to keep her drinking under control. 'This place is going to make lots of money,' she said, as I helped her unpack her things and move back into her room.

*

A year later, when I was back in America meeting up with my old subjects, I called the Wild Horse from Las Vegas, and wasn't terribly surprised to learn that Hayley had been thrown out again. 'This time I don't think she's coming back,' Kris the office manager told me, with an air of finality. I drove eight hours through hundreds of miles of empty desert, and arrived back at the brothel early one evening, with a dinner date with Lance and Susan and some business friends of theirs.

A table had been laid, banquet-style, in the saloon. Above us, an extra-large TV showed softcore pornography, frolicking nude models in artistic locations (desert gas station, old-fashioned corner store), which made it difficult to focus on what anyone was saying. I felt as though I was dining in a film by Luis Buñuel. The genteel accoutrements of the meal, the napkins, the arsenal of silverware, the discreet waiters in black suits, all of it seemed rather surreal as around us the sirens of the Wild Horse waited for business – Onyx in her see-through body stocking; Monique in her platinum-blonde wig and cocktail dress; Cicely in her fishnet top and lace choker . . .

The next few days I spent loitering at the Wild Horse. As before, I felt oddly vulnerable speaking to the women. Unlike other worlds I've spent time in, populated by evangelists and pitchmen and people looking to make a name, here the women stood to gain nothing from publicity. The only possible benefit I could offer them was if I booked a party. Knowing this, I sometimes sensed that idea hovering unspoken, which added to the complications of my being there. I found that with no camera present, only my notebook, I began to doubt my own good faith. I felt fraudulent, sitting around in the brothel kitchen all day or propping up the bar, jotting down notes. 'Do you want some more cock?' the Hispanic bartender would ask. What exactly was I doing there? Did they believe me when I said I was writing a book? Did I believe myself? I worried I was becoming a 'PT' – a 'professional trick'.

I never knew exactly where I stood with the women. One of the new courtesans was called Scarlett. She was thirty-two, tall, slender, with long red hair, brown eyes – she was also a registered nurse. She'd got in after watching a documentary about prostitution with her husband Mike. 'I don't remember if it was his idea or my idea. It just came out, "Well, that looks like fun!" On my own I'd thought about it, because I was interested in the money . . . So when I figured out it was legal and it wouldn't affect my nursing, I just thought, "Go for it!" It's a kick-in-the-pants job. I can't think of a better one.

'Mike is awesome. Very open-minded and not caught up in that jealousy . . . And he likes that I get to explore my sexuality. I'll be like, "Honey, I got a new position for you!" He has a field day!' She shrugged and added, 'Everybody has their quirk for sex. Mine is I like sex with strangers. I don't like dating. I don't like playing hard to get. So this keeps me out of trouble.' But the next day, killing time at the bar, I chatted to Scarlett some more, and this time she said she *didn't* enjoy the sex that much, that for her the appeal of the work was that it was like nursing, answering people's emotional needs.

I'd been hoping that if I stayed long enough I might learn where Hayley was. Certainly, there was no shortage of stories about her behaviour, which everyone agreed had been obnoxious: she'd been drinking heavily; she had a boyfriend who'd supposedly got her mixed up with drugs; she'd insulted Susan's masseuse, who had a legbrace from a motorcycle injury, calling him either a 'fucking cripple' or a 'handicapped fuck'. In another account, Hayley had been drinking so much and getting so little sleep that she began to think she was having an attack of some kind.

'She got worse and worse,' Susan said. 'I'd let her go. Then she'd promise to be good. She'd come back. But it would happen again. Before, even when she was bad, there used to be a little part of her that I could reach. But that went.'

On the third day, I bumped into a working girl called Ricky, who I knew to be talkative and indiscreet. According to her, Hayley had been strung out on 'crank' – the street name for crystal meth, a particularly toxic form of speed – 'talking all this Bible stuff . . . how she thinks she's figured it all out.' She also said Hayley had had sex in one of the negotiating rooms.

'Is that such a big deal, having sex in the negotiating room?' I asked.

'No condoms? No money? Yeah!'

Hayley had either retired, started dancing in Sacramento, or was working out of another brothel. It was evidence of the loose attachments this business fostered that no one seemed too sure where she was or what she was doing.

Even knowing the strange, alternate existence of brothel life, with its assumed identities, I'd thought there would be enough professional camaraderie between the women that one of them would have an email address or a way of leaving a message. It was a testament to the shame that was still so deeply embedded in the business of sex, I reflected. Everything at the Wild Horse was sequestered: the relationships between the working girls and customers; friendships between the women. No one even seemed to know Hayley's real last name, or perhaps they were wary of giving it to me. I hesitated to ask Susan, sensing I might be crossing a line by poking my nose into their non-brothel lives.

In one of my last conversations with Susan she mentioned she thought Hayley might be working out of a brothel in Elko. I knew Elko only as a name on the map – a town in the east of Nevada, towards Utah, out in the middle of nowhere. I called round a few of the bordellos listed in the phone book and two said they recognized the name: a man at Sharon's, who sounded drunk, and a woman at Sue's Fantasy Club, who said: 'She won't be working here again.' If nothing else, I figured it would be a chance to see some of the old-style cathouses.

✳

The road was straight highway for 280 miles, through a landscape of distant suede-brown hills and flat, treeless semi-desert.

Twenty miles from Elko, I hit Carlin. Sharon's lies a few miles out of town, within sight of the interstate – a weathered old double-wide trailer, its eaves strung with Christmas lights, white walls and bright red trim, with neon beer signs in the window. It's set down on a rumpled blanket of bare brown hills with no other buildings in sight.

The sky was broad and blue with wisps of cloud as I pulled up on the gravel parking lot. The owner and manager, Charlie, came to the door. Late forties, he had a moustache and a faintly camp manner and was dressed as though for athletics in a white T-shirt, a pair of sweat shorts and trainers. He was smoking a cigarette, and his voice was dark brown and boozy-sounding, even though it wasn't yet lunchtime.

Inside the front room was a small bar, the walls pasted with dollar bills signed in magic marker by truckers with their CB handles – Poker, Deuce, Snoopy – many of them old and peeling off. 'Mother says it looks tacky,' Charlie said. 'Tacky it may be, but I'll never have to paint it again!' A row of workmen's helmets, also signed, hung on the wall. A ceiling fan spun slowly. A Rock-o-la jukebox stood silent. An old woman – not Charlie's mother, who was away for the day – sat knitting in the corner.

Charlie took me on a tour, down the narrow, low-ceilinged corridors, past the bedrooms. 'I have seen a hundred and thirty-two women in sixteen years,' he said. 'The shortest one worked for fifteen minutes, the longest for seven years.' There were stuffed bunny decorations on the bedroom doors, little signs saying 'Welcome'. 'This is one of the girls' rooms,' he said, slurring so that 'girls' sounded like 'girlziziz'. I peeked inside. The room was homey, furnished with lots of cushions on the beds and chintzy oddments, bits of needlework, teddy bears, a TV, a VCR, mirrors on the walls and cheap wood panelling.

'I have two on the floor right now,' Charlie said, 'Crystal and Suzanne.' In a back room, a conservatory, Crystal was giving directions to a trucker on a CB radio. 'I love movies,' she was saying. 'Ask for Baby Doll when you get here.'

Back at the bar, Charlie poured me a Coke. I asked about Hayley.

'I remember her but I do not know where she's at. I do not know what working name she's under, because the girls will change their working names, and that's the reason some of 'em rotate around from place to place. They get tired of seeing the same customers day after day. Mother will say to these girls, if you don't get a marriage proposal a day, there's something wrong. So that wears on them, hearing that week after week. If they wanted to get married, they'd go out and get married. They wouldn't be in here working.'

Something in Charlie's manner made me suspect that Hayley had never worked at Sharon's – maybe he'd claimed to know her on the phone just to get me down there, to generate some business or for publicity. But I asked if I could leave a message for her anyway. Then, thinking about what he'd just said and my own experience of the women, I said, 'They're not looking for love?'

'I don't think so. But, in our sixteen years we have married five girls out of here and two of 'em are still married. I don't consider that bad, 'cause the national average is fifty per cent divorce rate.'

'Lance at the Wild Horse said some of the working girls come from abusive backgrounds,' I said.

'I used to have a sign that said, "Six o'clock – the psychiatric hour is over." They want to hear a sad story? I'll give them a sad story *if I have to make it up*!' Suddenly, from nowhere, Charlie sounded annoyed. 'I don't want to *hear* their sad stories! They're supposed to be here to laugh and joke around!'

He paused and said, 'Some people go in bars to say the world's shit upon them. Usually they've shit upon themselves.'

I tried Sue's Fantasy Club in Elko. A little old cattle and mining town, Elko's grid of streets is slung like a net between the interstate and the railroad. Unusually for Nevada, instead of lying outside the city, the brothels are downtown, four of them in a small cluster on Third Street where it ends at the train tracks. Sue's is a nondescript two-storey building, with an L-shaped bar in one corner, and a sofa and comfy chairs in another. If the bar were a reception desk, you could imagine the layout as the lobby of a budget motel, with a corridor of rooms leading off, where the women do their entertaining.

The place was quiet when I arrived. A cork board behind the bar said 'Meet Our Ladies'. On three-by-four index cards were the names Frenchy, Dee and Marie. Dee was at the bar, smoking a cigarette. She was fifty or so, with short red hair, wearing a figure-hugging stretch black lace outfit. Like some other prostitutes I'd met, she'd got into the business via swinging. Before that, she'd worked in 'medical management' on the East Coast; she didn't care to be specific. She was well spoken and educated. She'd been the editor of various newsletters, and had two sons, who didn't know what she was doing. One was graduating from college in a few weeks.

'How have you been finding it so far?' I asked

'Tedious at times. Frustrating at times,' Dee said. 'I actually had more sex at home with a close circle of friends.

And unfortunately so many of the guys who come for sex at the brothel are very basic. They don't tend to play. And then you get the guys who come in like guys at the fish market, looking at you. Occasionally it can be hard on the ego. A lot of them are in the brothels because they have difficulty in relationships.'

I asked about Hayley. Dee said she wasn't sure – she'd only been at Sue's a week. Before that she'd been working at a brothel in Wells, an even more remote town an hour east. 'There was a $100 minimum there but business was getting so bad we were doing $60 truckers' specials.'

She took me on a tour. A computer sat in the corner. Internet access had been cut off because the bill hadn't been paid. There was a jacuzzi room with wood panelling and decking for clients paying $500 and above. Dee's bedroom was small, with painted brick walls – a little like a prison cell, I couldn't help thinking. She'd thrown a scarf over the lamp, put some pictures on the walls. There was a bookshelf with ten or fifteen books: literary novels by Isabel Allende, James Carroll, two books about Katharine Graham, the publisher of the *Washington Post*, including her memoir *Personal History*.

We sat on her bed. I thought about booking a party – a massage or just giving her some money to talk. I felt bad for her – this intelligent, seemingly kind woman who was spending her golden years giving 'truckers' specials' in desert brothels on two-month shifts.

On the way back out, we passed a bedroom where a tall woman with a big mane of dark brown hair was lounging on her bed in a Chinese gown, watching TV.

'That's Marie. She's the manager,' Dee said.

I said hello. I mentioned I'd called a few days earlier asking about Hayley.

'Yeah, Hayley left about a week and a half ago.'

She came out to the bar, sipping a glass of wine, smoking a cigarette. 'She said she was getting out of the business,' Marie said. 'But I don't think she really is. I think she might be working at Sheri's' – a brothel an hour out of Vegas, in Pahrump. 'She had a lot of bills. She supports her whole family. I know she needs money, so I bet she's working in one of the houses.'

With nothing better to do, I sat at the bar until late in the evening. No customers came in. 'Wednesday is no-hump day,' Marie said. A TV in the corner of the bar was showing a cable channel – an eighties thriller with actors I half recognized. It was muted but from time to time as we sat there at the bar our eyes flicked over at it. The quiet, almost mausolean atmosphere; the gloomy decorations. I couldn't work out if it was depressing or cosy; a little outpost of humanity or one of the most desolate places I'd been in my life.

Back in Vegas, I called Sheri's and a couple of the other big brothels in Pahrump, asking for Hayley. No luck. I thought about driving up there, but I'd already spent longer than I intended creeping around brothels, and I was keen to move on to other stories. I called Marie in Elko a few time to see if she'd managed to leave a message for Hayley but I assumed it was the end of the line.

And then, in mid August, she called.

✳

She was at Sheri's – she'd got my message from Marie. 'I can't believe you went all the way to Elko,' she said, sounding a little drunk. 'What did they say about me at the Wild Horse?' I wasn't sure whether to tell her about the rumours of her throwing fits and taking crank. Then she asked if I believed in God. I said no. 'You're going to have real hot feet one day,' she said. 'What about the connection with the infinite?'

She was now going by her real name, Tammy. She lived in Marysville, northern California, a small agricultural town a few hours east of San Francisco and west of Reno. She had a boyfriend, Walter, who was twenty-five and a mechanic. They met as room-mates in Sacramento. She was happy to meet up, but circumstances were such that it was October before I was anywhere close. One afternoon, having made an arrangement to see her, I drove up from Los Angeles and booked into a cheap motel patronized by Hispanic field labourers who slept seven or eight to a room.

I called her at around seven. Walter answered. He sounded friendly enough, though Tammy had told me he'd watched the documentary and been a little bothered by the massage scene. He had a slow voice; Tammy had said he was a hippy and I imagined a sleepy, bearded dude with long hair. I could hear her in the background, saying in an English accent: 'Is that Louis? Is he getting cold feet?' She was on her way out, Walter said, then put the phone down.

I called back but got no response. I tried not to worry too much about it. I went into town, got something to eat, and an hour or two later, I was writing my notes at the motel when there was a knock. I peered through the window. It was Tammy. Her hair was tied up in a ponytail. She was wearing make-up and a skimpy top.

'You look bushed,' she said. 'Why are you staying here? This place is a fleapit!'

'I'm trying to save money,' I said.

She said she'd been on her way to a strip club when I called, as a last minute thing to make money. 'Girls are supposed to book but usually I can just show up because I'm the hottest one there and they'll let me dance. But tonight they had eleven girls there and would've had to bump one and they didn't want to do that.'

I asked about Walter disconnecting me.

'No, no, he's fine. I mean, yeah, he's a little threatened. He's never lived outside this little town. I think he meant to put you on hold and he disconnected you by accident. But I said to him, "He's a BBC journalist, for God's sake! Why would he be interested in someone like me?" This place is a *dive*.'

I looked around, seeing it through her eyes. I had my notebook on the table and a glass of red wine in a little plastic cup. It looked a little depressing. Lonely journalist on the road. Sad empty little life. I felt unmasked. She reached for my cup of wine. I remembered her problems with alcohol and became nervous that she was going to drink it. She brought it over to me.

'Do you want to go out to the strip club?' she asked. I said I wasn't keen. The truth is, I didn't want to go out at all very much: I wanted to sip my wine and watch TV and recover from the long drive. But I thought I'd better seize my chance with Tammy.

We went instead to a diner called Lyon's, just outside the town centre. As we waited in line to be seated, I asked how she'd wound up in Elko.

'I was kind of enjoying mixing with the dregs. Maybe part of it was self-abuse. I wanted to hit rock bottom so I could see that this was what my life could be.'

Our waitress seated us in a booth. I asked about Hayley's new life. She said that she danced occasionally, waited tables and volunteered at an animal sanctuary. Then she said, 'I might go back into it but I don't know. Especially with my commitment to God. I just wish I'd saved more money. I think how lucky I am. There's not too many people in the world who have the option of making $3,000 in one night.'

'So that's still there as an option for you?'

'No, I shouldn't have said that. It doesn't exist. No. Because I made a commitment to God.'

God had come into her life not long after I left the year before. She was back in Marysville, 'feeling low, emotionally bankrupt, not fulfilled'. She went to the New Life Assembly Church. 'I had an experience, and it felt right, and I prayed, and that motivated me to go to church.' She asked what I'd been doing and I told her about meeting the porn people and the UFO believers, and my plans to meet up with a pimp in Mississippi and a self-help guru.

'You want to be careful with all that negativity. I couldn't do that. You must either be really strong mentally or else you're just very cold and you view it in a voyeuristic way.'

This surprised me. I don't think of the stories I cover as particularly dark or negative. But later, I wondered if she might be right, and whether I was a little detached. It suggested sensitivity on her part that she picked up on it – the sixth sense she'd claimed she possessed. And at the same time, how strange, I thought, that she would regard doing stories on subjects like prostitution as requiring more mental strength than actually being a prostitute.

'Do I seem weird to you?' she asked a little later.

'No, not really,' I said. 'Maybe a little chaotic. I guess you like to party too much. But you probably knew that.'

We took a drive round downtown. It looked like a lot of old town centres in the West, with a few blocks of red-brick buildings, some posh little businesses, a store selling musical instruments, a craft shop, a barber's. 'It's nice, isn't it?' she said. 'Before, I hated it. But since I straightened out, all the things I didn't like, I like now: how quaint it is, and little, and old.'

On the way back to my motel, I told her what they were saying about her at the Wild Horse, being on drugs, having sex in the negotiating room, calling one of the staff a cripple.

'That's a lie. I hate drugs. I'm totally opposed to drugs. And that guy, I never called him a cripple. And I challenged Susan to find that on the security camera where I said that and they didn't even look for it. I didn't have a fit. I'd been drinking lemon drops and B-52s and my eyes were going in and out of focus. The person at the hospital said, "It looks like you're having a stroke." She had me panicking. It's because I'm borderline diabetic.'

The next day, we met at a little alternative coffee shop with bare brick walls. It was hot out, in the nineties. I'd been hoping to meet Walter, but that didn't seem to be on the cards. We had lunch at an upscale eatery of her choosing in the neighbouring town of Yuba City. By now, some of the air had gone out of my attempts to interview her, and our time together was starting to feel uncomfortably close to a date. I realized that she didn't particularly want to talk about her life and her background, and while I was happy to make conversation and compare ideas about the world, it was with the basic assumption I was there for a book I was writing.

At three or so, we headed back to the coffee shop. I bought her an expensive novelty coffee and we read out Trivial Pursuit questions. 'Was the first note broadcast by Sputnik 1 a B flat, C flat, or D flat?' 'Who was the first US president to visit all fifty states while in office?' An attractive young woman, Bohemian-looking in a long skirt, mid-twenties, came in with a little boy. 'That's Natalie,' Tammy said. 'Walter had sex with her when I was in Vegas. I wanted to come and see if he was meeting up with her.'

I knew 'When I was in Vegas' meant 'When I was working as a prostitute at Sheri's.' An act of revenge on Walter's part, presumably. Either way, it was time to go. We walked out back where a Volkswagen camper van pulled up. 'There he is, that fuck!' Tammy shouted, and flung a handful of Trivial Pursuit cards through the driver's window. 'I can't fucking believe you!'

I'd been expecting a long-haired dude, but he was short-haired and skinny. He looked a little like a student – mid-twenties, in a western-wear shirt of a kind I sometimes wear. Though we hadn't exchanged a word, I immediately felt I liked him. He seemed perfectly friendly, and I wondered if Tammy had exaggerated the sensitivities of my meeting him, and if so, why? To keep us apart, to make him more insecure?

'Hi, Walter,' I said.

'Hi, Louis,' he said.

But Tammy's sudden rage was embarrassing, and I didn't want to watch an argument unfold. So I drove off.

That evening, the phone rang. 'I just wanted to make

sure you got what you needed with the interview,' Tammy said. She and Walter had talked it through. She'd apologized to him. Apparently he'd only stopped off because he'd thought we might be there, and he wanted to meet me. Nothing to do with Natalie. 'I have a number of issues I have to work on. My big one is trust.'

'What was it that got you out? Was it meeting Walter? Was it quitting drinking? Was it finding God?' I asked.

'All three.'

She said she wouldn't be dancing tonight. 'I can't do that anymore. It's one of the things we agreed.'

It had been a strange encounter, revealing in some ways, in other ways a non-event. She had wanted to keep it on terms she understood – sexual – and I had wanted to keep it on terms I understood – journalistic. Two professional manipulators, I thought, trying to manipulate each other. Several stories I was chasing dealt with deceivers and con artists, but only in this one was the con difficult to see through, and only in this one did my own enquiries feel like grappling with air. But perhaps this said less about Tammy's subtlety than it did about the more persuasive forms of influence peddled by working women, where the sales job was a facsimile of affection, and, from time to time, the real thing.

On the last night of my return visit to the Wild Horse, Susan had told me, 'Once you've stayed in this business a few years, you don't get out.' This fatalism was surprising coming from the person who'd planned to help women get an education and move on. But she seemed a little chastened by her first year of business in the new premises. In general, Susan's ambitions for the women to change their lives hadn't borne much fruit. The house pledge to pay half the college tuition of the women had found few takers. 'I still offer the same programme to everybody but I have to be realistic that most of them won't take it,' she said. 'I have had some success stories. It's just that they're few and far between.'

Still, business was great, she had said. 'I always said, to run the house we'd need a pool of three hundred ladies. Right now we're at two hundred.' And they were expanding. A clump of new pink buildings, the carcass of the long-closed Mustang Ranch, a historic Nevada brothel, had been helicoptered on to the property. Lance had bought it on eBay. They would be using it as the premises of a brothel museum and adding another thirty rooms.

When I left that night, the working women were in the saloon killing time between customers by taking turns at karaoke. There was something touching about how uncomfortable they were in the spotlight. It spoke of a modesty, a decorousness, that, not knowing better, one might hesitate to ascribe to the profession. Shyly shuffling on the spot, giggling, singing softly and out of tune, they took turns at the microphone. 'Private Dancer'. 'Natural Woman'. A country song about an angel flying with a broken wing. All songs of romance and heartbreak, I thought. All love songs.

# JERRY GRUIDL

Before leaving London, I'd read that Pastor Richard Butler, the aging führer of the Aryan Nations, would be hosting a World Congress for his fellow Aryans later in the year. It was over seven years since my visit to the headquarters and my conversation with Jerry Gruidl about his fondness for *Are You Being Served?*. Since then, the bits of news I heard suggested the organization was on the skids. Hate groups as a whole were being clamped down on in the post-9/11 anti-terrorism climate. In 2000 Butler had lost his compound, bankrupted by a court judgment after his bodyguards attacked a woman and her son at his gates, allegedly mistaking the sound of their car backfiring for a gunshot. Given how doddery he'd been, I kept expecting to hear that Butler had expired. He appointed a successor, a neo-Nazi called Neumann Britton, but Britton pre-deceased him. Butler found another candidate, Harold Ray Red-feairn. Then Redfeairn died too. Perhaps fearing a jinx, Butler stopped appointing successors. 'Rasputin's got nothing on this guy,' one hate-group expert commented.

The latest news concerned a trip Butler made to Phoenix in 2003, when a young female partisan he'd been travelling with was arrested at Spokane airport on an outstanding forgery warrant, and unmasked as 'Bianca Trump', veteran of more than 180 hardcore adult movies, including *Barely Legal Latinas, Brassiere to Eternity*, and *Little White Girl, Big Black Man*. In a group for whom 'race mixing' was the ultimate no-no, it was a spectacular own goal. Aryan Nations Chief of Security Rick Spring issued a press release quashing the idea that Butler's relationship with the woman whose porno nickname had been 'the Latin Princess' was anything more than platonic: 'She had only been staying in Idaho a few days, helping around the house,' he said. 'Nothing more, nothing less; and if anyone wants to make jokes about anything else, then they do not know Pastor Butler.'

Perhaps because of his poor health, Butler had held no World Congress in 2003, and so the 2004 event was being thought of as a last hurrah.

I found Jerry in the phone book. I called him up from Las Vegas, reaching him by coincidence on his seventy-first birthday. He sounded a little frail. 'Barbara?' he said, to someone I hoped was in the room with him, ''bout how long was it that I came down from Aryan Nations? It's been a while. Uggh! It's close to five years.' Barbara was his daughter, he said. I told him I was following up on stories I'd covered over the years. 'Well, can I be on your list of people to visit?' Jerry said. 'It's good to hear your voice. There's been a lot of changes at Aryan Nations. Pastor Butler was sued and lost his crown . . . Have you ever had another contact with the Garsides?'

I visited him some weeks later, driving east from Reno, where I was staying at the time, turning north at Winnemucca, into Oregon. The high desert softened into prairie. Flat and empty, the land stretched on for miles to the pale brown hills in the distance, with no trees or houses in sight. Farm towns appeared, with John Deere dealerships and feed stores. After the clamorous hoard-ings and hotels of gambling country, these towns seemed spooky and aloof.

No longer in Hayden with Pastor Butler, Jerry lived 400 miles south, in lower Idaho in a town called Payette. I arrived late in the evening. He seemed pleased to see me: he looked as though he'd made an effort, in a smart pin-stripe shirt. He still wore thick glasses, and he'd put on quite a bit of weight round the middle, quite literally 'going pear-shaped'. He'd swapped his home in a neo-Nazi com-pound for a one-bedroom suite in Louise Garden Apart-ments, a single-storey motel-shaped building, where the main corridor was decorated with cute rustic ornaments, Raggedy Ann dolls, scarecrows in dungarees sitting on chairs. The residents were mainly elderly. 'The lady next door is dead. She just hasn't laid still yet,' Jerry said.

I'd never seen inside Jerry's home before. I'd been expecting swastikas and pictures of Hitler, but the apart-ment was mostly bare. There was a computer on one side, a table serving as a desk with medication on it, a bookshelf with videos, and photos of loved ones on the wall. A TV, muted, showed the History Channel. He had a couple of fish tanks with guppies in them. 'They're quite small, aren't they?' I remarked. 'Well, they're only fifteen-cent fish,' Jerry said.

I sat on the sofa. Jerry sat at his desk. 'I enjoyed the shows you sent me,' he said. 'I bring them out if I have visitors. I was kinda shocked by the one where you were in the porno thing. I laughed my ass off. I thought that was really gutsy.'

He showed me photos of his family. Then he said, 'I thought you were going to have your crew with you.'

'No, just me. I'm taking a break from TV.'

Jerry looked concerned. 'But are you still connected?'

'I still know people in TV, sure.'

'Good, good.'

It was a little like talking to an elderly relative. I'd told Jerry I was heading up to Hayden for the World Congress. He'd been in two minds about going too, deciding against it in the end. Money was tight and he was undergoing regular treatment with his doctor for some scars from burns he'd sustained on his legs as a child and didn't want to miss an appointment. 'Oh, while you're here, have you seen the Aryan Nations homepage?'

He woke up his computer. The background on his screen said: 'I'm out of bed and I made it to the keyboard. What more do you want?' We read the line-up of speakers: Tom Metzger, the leader of White Aryan Resistance; Billy Roper, the leader of White Revolution; some other names I didn't recognize. 'If you do go up there, plan on getting a hotel. I wouldn't stay in a tent in the campsite with all the idiots up there. I wouldn't trust 'em. See, these people's mindsets: newsmedia; Jew. They'd be suspicious from the get-go. There's nothing you could do to stop it.'

'You think they might be hostile?'

'I don't know the people that are up there. Oh, I've got an email!'

I could see it had something to do with a high-school reunion.

'Friends Reunited?' I asked.

'Supposedly,' Jerry said.

Five minutes' drive away, on Payette's main street, a

quiet few blocks of independently owned stores, we got a tuna melt and a glass of wine each at a local bar. We made chit-chat.

'You think Rodham's not a Jew? Wake up and smell the roses!' Jerry said. 'They've been hardcore communists since their school days, both Rodham and Clinton. And communism is Jewish. You show me a commie, I'll show you a Jew.'

'Stalin?'

'His wife was.'

'Castro?'

'He's one of their puppets. He's got to be a kiss-ass to keep his job.'

'What if I was Jewish?'

'*Shit!* Are ya?'

'I'm not saying yes or no. Would it change your attitude?'

'Yeah, it would.'

'I bet you've had friends in your life that were Jewish.'

'Not that I know of. But Prince Philip has Jewish ancestry. So Prince Charles does and little Harry. And I think that's why God's working it around so they can't become king . . . Are you Jewish? Tell me please you're not. Lie to me if you have to. Please.'

I changed the subject.

※

Through the next couple of days, I got to know Jerry a little, finding myself in the slightly uncomfortable position of being treated in a grandfatherly way by an unabashed neo-Nazi and anti-Semite.

He had grown up in East Oakland, where his father had

a neon-sign company. The second of three boys, with a younger sister, Jerry had been the black sheep of the family. He'd worked as an Electrolux vacuum-cleaner salesman for twelve years, delivered Winnebagos, driving them across country, and installed neon signs. Like many on the neo-Nazi fringe, he'd started out a member of the John Birch society, a right-wing anti-communist group that wasn't explicitly racist, then drifted into the Klan, then into the Aryan Nations. He married four times ('number two and number three were the same one: I had to go back for seconds') though his wives hadn't shared his beliefs. He had four children, a son and three daughters, only one of whom, Barbara, he was still in touch with.

Now he was retired, he said, having been drummed out of the Aryan Nations amid a vicious hate campaign, orchestrated by unnamed enemies within the organization. Ousted as chief of staff, he worked for a while on their web outreach. 'But that wasn't enough for them. They wanted me out of there.' One of the new members of staff put sugar in his gas tank, then challenged him to a pistol duel. 'Pastor Butler can't have that crap around the place!'

Rumours spread – that Jerry was gay, that he was a child molester. 'I was being attacked from all sides. I was being smeared *so bad*. And I couldn't figure out *where* it was coming from. They'd make up anything. They had Pastor Butler hire a private investigator to do a background check on me. And he never did that to anyone else I know of. I had to sign consent slips to let the investigator do the investigation. But it didn't stop the rumours and the Pastor finally gave in to the pressure.'

Now, with no hate group to help run, Jerry spent his

days playing mah-jong on his computer with only the guppies for company. 'I'm still waiting for Pastor Butler to have a change of heart and call me back to work.'

On our first morning, Jerry gave me a tutorial in the strange racist religious faith which underpins the Aryan Nations.

Called Christian Identity, it holds that white people are the real Israelites spoken of in the Bible and that modern-day Jews are impostors, 'Edomites', descendants of a sexual encounter between Eve and Satan. It was all there in Genesis, if you knew how to read it. The cosmic story of humanity was a kind of *Star Wars* saga, with Anglo-Saxon whites as Jedis, and Jews collectively standing for the Empire. Non-whites were inferiors, 'mud people', dupes of the Jews, used to keep the white man down. But the Jews weren't inferior: they were diabolically cunning. There was a kind of negative flattery of Jewish people in the cosmology of Christian Identity.

On his wall, Jerry had a colour poster showing the supposed descent of Jews and Anglo-Saxons on different coloured lines, with the relevant biblical verses. There were also predictions for the end-time, around the year 2000: growing United Nations influence, out-of-control immigration, concentration camps all over the US for the purposes of imprisoning the true Israelites.

'We've got the United Nations already, but we're not totally enslaved yet,' Jerry said. 'America has the most prisoners incarcerated anywhere in the world. And those prisons are going to be for us. They're not building them for the blacks. They're telling the poor blacks, "You've been picked on too long! You go out there and take what you want from the white man that's persecuted you!" They're going to turn 'em on us. And we'll have to fight 'em. And if we do, then we'll go to jail.'

I asked Jerry about non-whites. To my surprise, he said it was possible they might be able to get into heaven. 'God says that anybody that believes and obeys, can.' I asked about Jews. No, they were irredeemable. Their ultimate fate: to be vanquished by Jesus at the Battle of Armageddon. 'They'll be totally eliminated. There won't be any left. Maybe God'll send rattlesnakes to do it. In many cases it's an earthquake, a flood, all kind of things that do the job. But God gets it done.'

'So you haven't changed your beliefs since I interviewed you in 1996?'

'No, the only thing I've changed is some of the people that I was around.' He paused. 'Where did all these Jews come from that are running our government? Every school's full of Jews. Every college is full of Jews. Our medical profession is full of Jews! Our legal profession is full of Jews! Our politicians are almost all Jews! The Jews are occupying this country. Now if Hitler killed 'em all—'

'Jerry, Jerry, Jerry,' I interrupted. 'Jerry, Jerry, Jerry, Jerry, Jerry, Jerry, Jerry, Jerry, Jerry, Jerry, Jerry, Jerry.'

'Listen to this point! Listen to this point!'

'Something weird happens to you when you talk about this.'

Jerry chuckled. 'May-*bee*.'

'What is that?'

'Well, ah.' Jerry fumbled and looked away. Then his manner became sinuous and knowing. 'You wanted to find out about me. I guess you're finding *out* about me, huh?'

'Where does that come from? What are you thinking about when you think about Jewish people?'

Jerry paused. He looked down. 'The Devil. Satan. That's where Jews *come* from. They're the ones that are oppressing us. They're our *enemy.*'

'They're just people, Jerry. Just like anyone else.'

'Not true.'

When he spoke about Jews, it was as though a sickness came over him. His whole manner changed. We went back and forth on this several times. Had Jerry ever actually met any Jews? What did Jews mean to him?

'It's so obvious!' he said, pointing at the chart. 'Jews are those people following the red line! It's the *opposite* of those following the blue line!'

And yet, as hateful as they were, his views somehow didn't shock me as much as they should have, maybe because they were couched in religious terms – it was all about what God was going to do, not what Jerry was going to do – maybe because it was hard to imagine Jerry himself physically hurting anyone. None of it seemed quite real. A little later, he started foraging in a small storeroom in the back of his apartment. He dug out some of his old certificates of rank from his Klan and Aryan Nations days. On being made a 'Kleagle'. An 'Exalted Cyclops'. Photos of Jerry receiving a trophy for his work as a door-to-door salesman of Electrolux vacuum cleaners. In his younger days, Jerry wasn't bad-looking. Finally, he came out holding some sacks.

'You know, since you're going to Aryan Nations,' he said, 'would you do me a favour and give these to Pastor Butler?'

'Okay. What are they?'

'Burlap sacks.'

'Okay.

'They'll use them for the cross-lighting ceremony. I never got around to mailing them. And I never had the opportunity to go up there.'

'Is he expecting them?'

'No, but it's hard to find them anymore. Especially up there. Anybody that does have them won't give them to 'em, because they know what they're going to use them for.'

I took them and put them in my car.

✳

Why did I take the sacks? In hindsight, it was the wrong thing to do. But I was blindsided. I'd agreed to take them before I knew what they were for. Then once I found out, it wasn't exactly too late, but it would have been a little awkward to give them straight back. So I thought I'd say yes for now, and figure out the right thing to do later. There was one other thing. If I'm totally honest, at some level, as a journalist, I was enjoying the irony of his entrusting the sacks to me, figuring it would be 'good material' for the book.

A little later, we went out to a Mexican restaurant called Fiesta Guadalajara. I asked Jerry about Butler. 'I like him but he's getting old. And I think he's going a bit senile. Sometimes when he's speaking he'll be in the middle of a story and he'll forget what he was saying.'

'What if he gets so senile that he forgets who he's supposed to hate?' I said. Jerry ignored this remark.

'I suppose there won't be any Mexican food in the whites-only homeland,' I said.

'Hmmm, I'd never thought of that possibility,' Jerry said. He paused. 'They wouldn't be allowed to vote, but they could cook and clean for us. After all, we're not extremists.' Jerry paused again. He made a Benny Hill face of coy mock-seriousness. Then he giggled: 'Hee hee hee hee.'

I asked about Jerry's kids. Did he see his son, forty-six-year-old Jerry Junior?

'Not very often. Sometimes I run into him at the grocery store.'

'He's not listed, is he?' I knew because Jerry was the only Gruidl in the Idaho phone book.

'No.'

'Why not?'

'Me. He doesn't want anything to do with it. He's got a kid in high school and he doesn't want him getting grief from other kids. We've been fishing a few times but we've got less and less to talk about. He's going left and I'm going right. I feel sorry about it but I gotta do my thing and he's gotta do his thing.'

What about Velma, his eldest daughter? 'I haven't spoken to her in years. She won't let me have her phone number . . . She knows my views on race and she's dead set against it.' Janet, the youngest? 'No, but I've been over at Barbara's house when she's called and I've spoken to her. We get along. She's just distant . . . I'm right and some day they'll understand.'

That evening, I dropped Jerry off at his apartment. The other apartments were dark. 'They're all asleep,' Jerry said. 'I feel like I'm in a mausoleum here.' Then he said, 'Thanks for a great day.'

But it wasn't the end of the day. Back at my motel, I realized my laptop was missing. The last place I'd had it was Jerry's apartment. It was only a few months old. More to the point, it contained numerous irreplaceable photographs and documents. I went back to Jerry's. He was solicitous and concerned. 'First thing to do, file a police report,' he said. An officer named Sergeant Jack Hart came round to Jerry's apartment. I filled out a form, describing the computer in detail. I explained about the photographs and the documents. Sergeant Hart said, 'My wife does little books when we go on vacation, so I know how upsetting that can be.'

One of my first thoughts, oddly, was that it was karma for the sacks. In that self-flagellating mode people sometimes go through after they've made a blunder, I blamed myself for the moral idiocy of toying with the idea of bringing them – flirting with ideological obscenity for the sake of a piquant comical moment. Now that I was experiencing anxiety about my computer, I thought of all the fear and grief cross burnings have caused over the years. Not that I imagined Butler would be burning crosses on anyone's front lawn – not that I would ever have really brought the sacks, for that matter – but still.

If the loss of the computer had given me some moral clarity in one way, it had also thrown Jerry and I together. He now wanted nothing more than to be helpful.

'I've had a couple of ideas,' he said the next morning. He suggested printing up flyers and leafleting door to door. Jerry said locals would be unlikely to call a long-distance number so he said to use his. He also presented me with a brand new microcassette recorder, and some maps of Idaho and neighbouring states for a detour into Yellowstone Park he was encouraging me to take. We asked around his apartment building. One of his neighbours said she'd seen me driving off with a computer bag on top of the car, where I must have absent-mindedly left it. We made a tour of the town, retracing our route from the previous day. Jerry was being so helpful, it crossed my mind that we were getting into a Pastor Butler type of relationship: he was acting as my chief of staff.

Another day passed, and no sign of the computer. By now, Jerry's casual anti-Semitism was routine. Most of the time I ignored it, but I was aware of the unseemliness of having a virulent neo-Nazi as the contact person for my lost computer. I wondered if I could trust him – didn't the monstrousness of his beliefs suggest a fundamental dishonesty? But I was fairly sure I *could* rely on Jerry, and found it all the more odd that, for all his hatefulness, Jerry could also be thoughtful and decent.

On our last morning together, at his apartment, I asked Jerry if he'd ever thought of trying to be less racist.

He looked serious for a moment.

'If I had my choice, my ultimate choice, if I had all power and all immunity, I would exterminate them. Every last one. And anyone that had any traits of it. Because for as long as there are *any left*, they'll grow and multiply and there'll be more discord.'

Jerry looked at me. His tone changed.

'Straight-up question. Are you Jewish?'

'Is that really important to you?'

'Yes.'

'Why?'

'Because if you were, I would feel that all this time you were deceiving me and stringing me along. It never crossed my mind until you asked if it would bother me. But even if you said yes, I'd think you were lying, just to test me. You're not Jewish, I know you're not.'

'I just don't see the big deal. When I think of Jewish people, I think of people like Woody Allen and Bob Dylan and Marcel Proust. People I admire.'

Possibly these weren't the examples most likely to bring Jerry round. 'The Devil is beautiful,' he said. 'Lucifer was an angel of light. So yeah, they're good at *beguiling* you. You've got to understand, Jews have this satanic seed and they *cannot* overcome it.'

'You must see that there's good and bad in all people, so why not try not to be racist?'

'Because I *am* racist.'

It was hopeless. With Jerry, the alleged 'satanic' qualities of Jews was not something that could be proved or disproved. It was simply an article of faith. It was hard to believe he was serious. But he was. I told Jerry I hoped he wouldn't be offended that I didn't want to bring the sacks up to Pastor Butler for the cross burning. 'It's not a cross burning, it's a cross lighting,' he said.

'I'm sorry, Jerry, I know I owe you a favour, but let it be something else, not this.'

'Okay, no problem,' Jerry said. Then he took a stack of flyers advertising the lost computer and said he'd keep handing them out around town.

*

I drove up Highway 95, the same road that had brought me all the way from Las Vegas, and which stretched south from there to Needles, California, past Yuma, Arizona, and into Mexico. I was heading north. On my folding map of Idaho, I was only a few centimetres from Canada. Coeur d'Alene was a genteel tourist town situated on a lake. Population 34,514. Because it was tourist season, rooms were expensive. I booked into a horrible overpriced motel next to a gas station, among a cluster of other corporate motels and chain restaurants. I called Jerry and thanked him for his help. 'I feel so sick about your 'puter,' he said. I'd never heard the word ''puter' before. Its cuteness lodged in my head.

The next morning I shaved off the beard I'd grown, leaving a handlebar moustache. I was hoping to look less Jewish. Though I'm not, I've been told I look Jewish, and tanned and bearded and wearing glasses and my leather flip-flops, I looked like I'd just stepped out of a yeshiva. If nothing else, with the moustache and contact lenses instead of glasses, I looked a little less bookish. But driving to the march from my motel, the contacts started irritating my eyes. The package said they expired in 2001, which may have had something to do with it. I took them out. I checked my mirror. Glasses/handlebar moustache appeared to be the worst of all combinations. I looked like a German paedophile.

The Congress was in two phases, a parade through the heart of Coeur d'Alene followed by speeches at a campground forty miles out of town. Several blocks were cordoned off for the parade. Police officers stood at junctions directing traffic. I parked and walked across the parking lot of a fast-food restaurant called Zip's where I saw twelve or so beefy men in smart-casual clothes having a confab. One was chomping a cigar. Too well fed and smug-looking to be regular people, they'd have been recognizable as federal agents even if they hadn't been having their staff meeting in the parking lot.

I was waiting at the starting point when a van pulled up and Butler hobbled out with four bodyguards, young men in combat boots and dark glasses. Now aged eighty-six, he looked stooped and oblivious, a hearing aid in his ear, as he sat on a bench by the side of the road. It was hard not to feel the customary indulgence that one extends towards the elderly, even the racist elderly. I sat down next to him and said: 'Hi, Pastor Butler, I've been staying with Jerry Gruidl in Payette. I think he may have emailed you about me.' His reaction was hard to read. Could he hear me? I asked him how it was going. 'It's been pretty rough, but we get by,' he croaked.

The route of the parade ran down Coeur d'Alene's main shopping street, with fancy street lights, flower baskets and a parade of smart shops. Later I was told Butler had hoped for 300 marchers, to represent the 300 fighters chosen by Gideon in the Old Testament. (Given that experts put the group's membership at about 200, this was optimistic.) I counted thirty-three marchers. They were spaced three abreast, thirty or so feet behind each other, to take up more room. The permit from the town was for an hour; with only a few blocks to cover, the marchers made frequent stops to fill out the time. Butler, too feeble to walk, was seated on a deckchair on the back of a pickup truck, like a May Queen, looking back on the parade.

The marchers began by taking turns stomping on an Israeli flag. 'Kill! Kill! Die! White race!' The flag was then dragged by the pickup truck. Onlookers and reporters were kept behind the barriers. A talkative old gentleman wearing a neckerchief remarked to no one in particular: 'I'm trying to figure out what type of people are drawn to this.' Then, out of the side of his mouth, he said: 'I think they're a little screwy.'

A dark-haired man with a broad Midwestern accent, aged forty-five or so, herded the marchers. He wore the Aryan Nations uniform, modelled on the old Nazi one: pale blue shirt, twin breast pockets, blue necktie. I was pleased to see he also had a handlebar moustache, so I hadn't misjudged the grooming code too badly.

With a few exceptions, the marchers fell into two main categories: skinheads and religious eccentrics. The eccentrics tended to be older, with beards and/or dirty T-shirts. One, in straw hat, little dark glasses and Nazi armband, looked exactly like the Gestapo villain in *Raiders of the Lost Ark*.

An Old Testament-looking patriarch carried a placard that said: 'Jews will not repent for the cross'. This was Ken Gregg of the 'Knights of Yahweh'. A chubby, geeky guy, who I later found out was Billy Roper, a rising leader in the movement, had a poster that said: 'Keep your brown hands off our white children'.

A bystander shouted: 'God created them that way!'

'He also created yeast infections. You treat those,' Billy Roper shouted back.

With Butler so aged and feeble and the organization bankrupted, anti-racism groups had for the most part elected to stay away. One local spokesman called it the Aryan Nation's 'swansong'. There were a few protesters with their own placards, locals and out-of-towners, with signs saying: 'Jesus is color blind' and 'Hate is a bad lifestyle. Get out now!' The gaggle of protesters shuffled alongside in an impromptu and untidy counter-parade.

'Are you going to reimburse the city for the cost of hiring all these extra police, Butler?' shouted an aging hippy in tie-dye shirt and ponytail.

'Hey, dude, Jesus wasn't white!' a black bystander shouted. 'Give me a break! Get real!'

'He was a direct descendant of Adam, and Adam was a white man!' said the Knight of Yahweh.

'Please do not feed the non-whites,' Billy Roper said.

'Where are your fucking clothes made? Taiwan?' said one protester.

'Get the fuck out of my town!' said another.

'Why don't you come here so I can sock you!' said a third.

One or two onlookers expressed support for the parade. 'God bless ya!' said a woman carrying a Confederate flag. 'Thank you!' A big, strapping, bearded blond-haired guy, who had a young daughter on his shoulders, Sieg-Heiled. 'White Power! Right on, man! Keep this town real!'

The most vocal of the protesters was a middle-aged woman who appeared to be deranged. She denounced the marchers as 'white negroids'. She held two densely worded placards, which were impossible to make out.

'You are filth! You white negroids are subhuman!' she shouted at the Knight of Yahweh. 'Jesus Christ was true God and true man!'

'You don't know your Bible, lady!' the Knight of Yahweh said.

'You shut up and listen like a man!'

'I am,' he said mildly.

'You can go down the free health clinic and get some oestrogen injections,' Billy Roper said.

'The general public calls you nitwits!' she shouted at Billy Roper. 'You call the Jews subhumans! That's what you are, mister! You are white negroid black race! You're no different from animals!'

Even Billy Roper, who'd managed a few light-hearted rejoinders, had no comeback to this observation, demonstrating, perhaps, that the most effective antidote to the racist marchers wasn't rational argument but to be even crazier, to spew gibberish that was even louder, even more vituperative and obscurely bigoted.

It was like a street theatre version of the *Jerry Springer Show*, with the same intrusive, kitchen-sink atmosphere of being granted access to something private, unseemly, and almost trivial. The most surprising thing, in the end, was the heavy presence of burly federal agents, in dark glasses, snapping photographs with big cameras, and riot police crammed into SUVs. Was it really possible that this cavalcade of jackanapes constituted a national-security risk? After the march, fire engines extended their ladders and police snipers climbed down from the roofs.

The last remaining protesters converged on a car with a lone skinhead sitting inside it. 'Would you do this by yourself?' a protester asked.

'You bet.'

＊

That afternoon, using directions I had downloaded from the Internet, I drove forty miles out of Coeur d'Alene for the speeches and post-parade get-together at a campground. I passed a clump of federal officers standing in the woods like birdwatchers with their huge cameras. It may be that I'm now on file as an 'unknown sympathizer' in some FBI office in Washington, DC. At the campground office, I said, 'I'm here for the, ah . . .'

'Church group?' the manager said.

The campground sat in the lap of pine-covered mountains, a beautiful grassy clearing. The Aryan Nations had colonized the near end with a scattering of nylon tents, some cars and vans, a barbeque area, a small marquee with folding chairs for the speeches. By the marquee, books were laid out for sale on tables: copies of *Mein Kampf* in English and German; *The True History of the Holocaust: Did Six Million Realy* [sic] *Die?*; *Might is Right*; *Creed of Iron: Wotansvolk Wisdom*; books on Norse mythology, the Knights Templar, and the Third Reich, especially the Nazis and the occult.

One of the organizers, a young woman, told me all the attendees were supposed to buy raffle tickets. I bought one.

The speeches started. Forty or fifty people sat in the marquee. Butler was sitting in a van off to one side. A generator chuntered in the background. The speeches were amplified, but the speakers were also under instruction from the owner of the campground not to be audible from his veranda. For a rabble-rousing hate group, this was a challenge.

The compère was the guy with a handlebar moustache who'd organized the marchers.

'I'm Mike McQueeny from Wisconsin,' he said. 'I'd like to tell you a little about my story. When my daughter was fifteen years old she started listening to rap music. When she was seventeen years old she was mixing with spics. At eighteen years old, she had a nigger baby. And I disowned her. And I haven't seen her since. She had a boo baby. I haven't seen her in ten years. And I don't care. *You* are my family. I want to introduce you to the greatest man in the world today, Pastor Richard Butler.'

Butler was barely audible over the generator. He said something about National Socialism. Something about America and the Founding Fathers. Something about Christianity.

'I want to thank each and every one of you,' he rasped. 'You are my kindred. You are my family. Hail victory!'

He creakily raised his arm in a Nazi salute. Then he climbed back into the van.

Next up was Tom Metzger, leader of White Aryan Resistance. After frail old Butler, Metzger was loud and vigorous. Too loud and vigorous for one old man near the front who, mindful of the campground owner's instruction, interrupted Metzger mid-flow.

'They'll shut us down,' the old man said.

'You obviously haven't heard me speak before,' Metzger said, with barely disguised irritation.

Metzger's theme was that the white race was being destroyed – not by anti-white racism but by global economics.

'"Make the world safe for democracy." I want to destroy democracy, not make it safe! Democracy is a euphemism for capitalism. Always has been! When they say we're going into a country to give them democracy, that means finance capitalism . . . The only thing you can do now is cheer when there's terrorism. Terrorism is like defending yourself. You know why those guys hit the World Trade Center? I didn't cry over it! The World Trade Center is the New World Order economic headquarters. If it was the ragheads, they knew *exactly* what they were after and I *liked* it!'

Applause.

'Go tell the FBI!' he added, for effect.

Whatever the merits of his position, Metzger at least laid out a consistent world view, and did so with some passion. In spite of myself, I was impressed that he'd taken on the economic question, instead of just putting everything down to Jews and other races. But this would prove the high point of the speeches. A young man dressed in khaki shorts and shirt, looking a little like a scoutmaster, spoke next. He'd brought props: photos of prominent media moguls mounted on small placards. The presentation was so liberally peppered with racial slurs – kike, hebe, Jew-boy, mud person, subhuman ape – that it quickly found favour with the audience. Next to this guy, Metzger had sounded like John Maynard Keynes.

'Our world is sick and Hitler gave us the cure. But the Führer's plans cannot be implemented until America removes these media Jews from their temples of corporate power and gives the mass media back to whites.' His delivery became urgent. 'For blood, for honour, for the glory of the Reich!' he said in the weirdly throttled voice of someone trying to shout without making too much noise. 'We salute thee, oh Aryan martyr Hitler! Offering our lives to your sacred cause, we shall march forth to victory!'

Other speakers followed: Billy Roper; then the Knight of Yahweh; then a man in a baggy ill-fitting T-shirt, with terrible teeth and thick nostril hair: the Aryan Nations state leader for Washington. Much of the chit-chat at the Congress had been about evolution, but the speakers seemed to be devolving into ever more primitive life forms.

I reflected that if I were a white racist, this would be a chastening experience. It's a pretty wacky gathering when a skinhead with a swastika tattoo on his head is one of the more presentable attendees. In its anoraky quality, its hobbyism, the event felt oddly English, like a group campaigning for the preservation of steam locomotives, everyone pretending to have a good time, making the best of it, plodding on with their crusade.

'It's depressing,' said a skinhead in a Support Your Local Klan T-shirt.

The last speaker was possibly the kookiest of the bunch. Named Arch Edwards, he was the one who looked like the baddie in *Raiders*. For a while he'd been promoting an Aryans-only homeland called New Celtica, that would be built in underground hill forts. The prospectus had floor plans that looked as though they'd been done by a child for a school project. It was for northern Europeans only; southern Europeans were allowed if they were 'indistinguishable from an average north European'.

'I encourage everyone to learn Sanskrit,' he began, with a distracted, professorial air. I looked at the skinheads in the audience, who were presumably making a mental note to start those Sanskrit lessons post-haste. 'It looks like a washing line hung with wriggly worms . . . In Sanskrit, the word "human" comes from "hu" meaning "divine". So we're not, in fact, all human.'

The next morning I returned to the campground expecting more speeches, but there was no sign of Butler or any of the luminaries – Roper, Metzger, et al. – who were staying at Butler's house in Hayden. A few skinheads were sitting around a campfire. One of them named Oregon was making a burger on the barbeque. He was twenty-eight; one of his pupils was permanently dilated, giving him an odd look. 'So what's it like in England? You got a Jew problem over there?'

'Not as far as I know,' I said. 'But I've always got on with Jewish people.' I immediately wished I'd answered a little more forthrightly, but there you are – I didn't. Oregon was the Aryan Nations state leader for Oregon. I asked if he'd enjoyed the weekend. 'Not really. This is all fictitional reality. None of this exists.'

'You're getting a little philosophical for me.'

'This doesn't exist,' he said again. 'You go downtown, you don't see Nazis and swastikas. You don't see skinheads out in the streets in New York. It's all fictitional. We're created by the media to scare people. But we don't really exist. First time I went to the Aryan Nations headquarters, I was expecting machine-gun turrets and rifle ranges and guys training and shit. But it was just a bunch of houses. I was disappointed. I liked the Jewsmedia version better.'

'Why don't you leave the movement?'

He rolled up a sleeve to show a swastika tattoo. 'See this? If I ever covered this up I'd be a traitor. Now I know the truth, I can't ever go back. I see everything racial now. Anytime I look at a crowd of people, I'm noticing what race everybody is. I can't even help myself.' Oregon had a friendly manner; a wry distance from his beliefs, as though he himself was a little baffled that he held them.

Jim Ramm, the guy who'd given the speech about Jewish media moguls, wandered up. 'What's your ancestry?' he said.

'Half English, quarter French, quarter Italian,' I said.

'There's a rumour going round that you're Jewish.'

'People tell me I look Jewish.'

Jim squinted at me doubtfully. He had a soft, suspicious demeanour, an oddly sing-song voice, almost as though he was trying to sound like an oddball – or maybe he was just suspicious of *me*. Apropos his 'awakening' in his twenties, he said: 'At first I had a little nagging sense of guilt. Because for so long everyone's been telling me this is wrong.'

'How are your parents with it?' I asked.

'They don't like it. That's pretty much standard in the movement. So you learn to get along, avoiding certain subjects ... Not talking about stuff ... I work with a Mexican and he thinks I'm his *best friend*. And he has no idea I hate his guts. It's called *acting*. Because one day the feds are going to ask him about me and he'll say, *Jeem nice man! He my friend! I like heem!*'

The raffle was held. The prizes were CDs by Nazi bands, copies of *Mein Kampf*, plastic swastikas. I was relieved not to win anything.

✳

A few days later, having made an appointment by phone, I visited Butler at home. His house stood on a quiet suburban lane of single-storey houses with sprinklers and US flags and barking dogs, next to a golf course. A skinhead was sitting on the front porch when I arrived. He was smily and polite, which wouldn't be worth remarking on if he hadn't been a skinhead. He said his name was Jerald. He'd lost his job the day before, when his boss spotted his picture in the *Spokane Spokesman-Review* Sieg-Heiling at the parade. 'It's a moving company. They have a lot of military contracts.'

A pair of Alsatians met me at the door. Inside, the house was doggy-smelling and dishevelled, like a student crash pad but for neo-Nazis. A blanket and pillow were on one arm of the sofa. There was a piano against one wall. A cat padded around, and cat hairs were ground into the carpet. Above the fireplace hung a painting of the four horses of the Apocalypse. A bust of Hitler was on the mantlepiece, next to a picture of Butler's deceased wife. The sense I had, from the young people I'd seen around, was that Butler was an icon and mentor to a certain class of confused white youth. A little like the late Jerry Garcia, the lead singer of the Grateful Dead, who presided over generations of kids passing through their hippy phase, Butler was a 'Captain Trips' for budding racists, a cool old dude who 'totally gets it', an ideological *puer aeternas*.

Butler was seated in an easy chair by the window, wearing a clean white shirt. There, speaking in a dry, faltering monotone, occasionally yawning, he spelled out his beliefs as Jerald the skinhead kept watch from the sofa. With no great show of malice, he outlined the vast religious space opera, of Jews against Gentiles: a final war leading to the total elimination of Jews from the Earth. Matter-of-factly, he croaked: 'The Jew has always been our enemy. He's God's enemy. But he couldn't be our enemy as effectively if we hadn't allowed him to do it . . . The Jew is only the tool of our iniquity. We are the ones that have to straighten up, fly right. And he wouldn't give us any trouble.

'I don't have any animus – you know, personal animus – with them. I know what they are and they know what I am.'

He pointed out the painting of the four horses of the apocalypse. A spectral detail of a pale face was just visible between two of the horses' heads. 'That's the white race,' Butler said. 'The white man was sent to the Earth to conquer the Earth and put God's law into effect.'

'Is there a way of avoiding the war?' I asked.

Butler pointed at a book on his shelf called *You Gentiles* by Maurice Samuel. 'It's by a prominent Jew of the twenties. Read the chapter entitled "We the Destroyers".' I glanced at it. (Later I bought and read this book, a weird little extended essay by a Romanian-born intellectual and translator of Yiddish, full of quirky insights into the differences between Jews and non-Jews, which, boiled down, says that Jews are more interested in God and Gentiles prefer sports, and that this will lead to everlasting conflict.) That it was written by a Jew seemed, for Butler, to make it irrefutable: condemned out of their own mouths! 'So that pretty well answers your question.' Yes, inevitable war.

Butler's other bits and pieces of 'evidence' for his world view were even more shaky: a supposed remark by Ben Franklin that Jews should be excluded from the constitution – a well-established hoax, as I later found out. He cited *The Protocols of the Elders of Zion*, in which prominent Jews reveal their secret plan to take over the world (also a fake created by anti-Semites). 'Jews said it was a forgery. How can you have a forgery unless you have an original?' was Butler's bizarre logic. What good did it do to try to explain? He claimed that the word 'America' came from

German – not from the explorer Amerigo Vespucci, as commonly believed – and means 'heavenly empire'. It was all cobblers.

As a final thought, I asked about Jerry and why he had left. 'I don't know. He had trouble with some of the people. It's a problem with our race. We have too many factions. We always commit . . . fratricide, almost. The so-called right wing is the hardest thing in the world to get together. But I like Jerry. We talked on the phone last night.'

'He didn't say anything about a computer, did he?'

Butler quickened. 'Yes! He said he's got it!'

※

'I – have – your – computer.' Jerry's voice in the message was clear and enunciated. Then he said it again: 'I – have – your – computer.' A couple, a headmaster and his wife, had handed it in. I picked it up from Jerry a couple of days later.

I drove back down to Reno, where I stopped for a few days to get my car fixed. With some downtime, I decided to send Jerry a gift to thank him for his help getting the computer back. What do you give a neo-Nazi? I bought him a humorous anti-Bush quiz book. Then I drove to Las Vegas.

Less than two months after I interviewed him, Butler died at his house in Hayden. It was weird to read an obituary where no one had anything good to say about the deceased. A prominent anti-Nazi hailed his death as the end of the 'big compound era' of white supremacism.

A *New York Times* article noted that Christian Identity

was on its way out as the religion of choice for neo-Nazis. Skinheads and prison racists were now increasingly turning to Odinism, the worship of Norse gods, which had the bonus of not including that whole turn-the-other-cheek business, which was always a little tricky for Nazis to explain. The article ended by saying: 'On Wednesday, after Mr Butler's body was taken away for an autopsy, his relatives moved the belongings of his Aryan Nations roommates out of the house in Hayden Lake and placed them on the doorstep . . . Then they took down an Aryan Nations flag from a window.' The funeral would be a private affair. No new leader was announced.

After I heard the news of Pastor Butler's death, I called Jerry. An answering machine said in a robotic voice: 'I'm sorry but "Hi, this is Jerry Gruidl" is not here to take your call.' It flashed through my head that Jerry might have been so anguished by Butler's passing that he had killed himself.

A short while later, he called back.

'You caught me at home,' he said. He sounded forlorn. 'Oh, I'm not doing too bad, I guess. I'm recovering. I just got out of hospital.'

'What happened?'

'A real act of stupidity.'

But it was nothing to do with Butler's passing, which he regarded with equanimity. He'd had a car accident. He'd been working on his van, checking the reverse lights with the handbrake on. Absent-mindedly, standing outside the van, he'd revved the engine with his hand on the pedal. The door was open and it knocked him down as the van lurched backwards, dragging him along the ground.

'You ran yourself over?' I said.

'Yeah. Dumbest thing I ever did in my life. Do you have any more tapes? I'd sure like some more of your adventures. If you happen to have any around, I sure would appreciate it.'

MELLO T

In a back room of a Memphis-based record distributorship called Select-o-Hits, a pudgy white promotions man named John 'J-Dogg' Shaw was showing me a few of the gangsta rap CDs that had recently passed across his desk. An album called 'In Remembrance of Thug Chuc' showed the epony-mous rapper laid out dead on a gurney. An album by the Skrilla Gettaz, called 'For This Thing Called Skrilla' (skrilla being money) featured the titles 'We Some Gangsta', 'Organized Crime', 'She on This Pole'. Another album, by Birmingham J, had a track called 'Hustlaz and Cap Pellas'.

'What's a "cap pella"?' I asked.

'Cap *pealer*. Pealing a cap is killing you,' J-Dogg said.

Then he said, 'Have you seen the picture of Jeezy with a platinum snowman?'

'No,' I said.

He dug out the most recent issue of the gangsta rap magazine *Murder Dog*. He turned to a full-page photo of the up-and-coming Atlanta rapper Young Jeezy. In the photo, Jeezy was frowning and carrying a very large gun, and wearing a platinum snowman medallion.

'What does it mean?' I asked

'Snow is cocaine. So it means he's a cocaine dealer. Or

was one,' J-Dogg said. 'Isn't that great for the youth? What a great role model!'

J-Dogg is a hip-hop historian and a long-time fan of the music, but he'd grown disenchanted in the last couple of years. 'All these folks can rap about is dope dope dope, shoot shoot shoot, kill kill kill,' he said. 'And then people wonder why youth violence is at an all-time high.'

I looked at the photo again. I wasn't quite sure what I felt about it – whether I thought Jeezy looked faintly ludicrous, holding his gun for a publicity shot, or thrillingly badass, and whether I lamented the direction the music was taking or saw it as a harmless bit of provocation.

This was always the question with gangsta rap. Was it just showbusiness, no different and no more harmful than movies about mobsters or heavy-metal songs about death and mayhem? Or did it represent something bigger? Was it a kind of outlaw code, as much a cause as a symptom of the lifestyle it described?

In 2000, I'd spent two weeks travelling what was then the latest spawning ground for the genre, the so-called 'Dirty South', for a documentary about the music and the lifestyle. Most of the time I'd been in Jackson, Mississippi, following a pimp and gangsta rapper named Mello T. That trip had taken place a couple of years after the killings of two of the most popular gangsta rappers, Notorious BIG and Tupac Shakur, both of them victims of a bizarre musical turf war between the East Coast and the West Coast. Possibly as a result, a mood of restraint had held sway over the industry. But five years later, the period of mourning was over. The most popular style of rap was called 'crunk'. Invented in the South, it was raucous and bass-heavy – 'meant to evoke, and sometimes accompany, drunken nightclub brawls,' according to an article in that premier hip-hop publication the *New York Times*.

Feuding – 'beefing' as it's called – was back, too. Lil' Kim against Foxy Brown. Eminem against Benzino. Lil' Flip against TI, beefing over who could rightfully claim to be the 'King of the South'. Perhaps the most prolific beefer of all was the number-one-selling artist in the country, 50 Cent. The inside sleeve of his latest album, *The Massacre*, contained coded death threats on rival artists, along with mocked-up photographs of 50 himself weighing out quantities of cocaine in his apartment and committing a drive-by shooting with a machine gun. Though there was something amusingly kitsch about it – the idea of a musical performer re-enacting criminal moments from his past – the comedy was somewhat muted by the fact that 50 Cent's entourage had recently got into a real shoot-out with the entourage of another rapper outside a radio station in New York.

Oddly enough, amid all this merchandizing of crime, my old interviewee, Mello T, had moved away from criminal themes. His latest record was an inspirational rap for kids entitled 'If You Try You Can Do It'. Supposedly he was no longer pimping. He'd married his 'boss bitch' Sunshine, and they were raising a baby daughter. From what I knew about Mello – his casual professions of violence and the eerie hold he exercised over his stable of women – this reformation was hard to credit, but it came from a good source, a Jackson-based hip-hop journalist named Charlie Braxton.

And to be fair, Mello had always been ambivalent about his life of crime, lamenting it and celebrating it by turns in true hip-hop style. The first day we were together he told me that the pimping was 'the money behind the music', a way to pay the bills until his career heated up. I expressed surprise that he was a pimp. 'Because in Britain, that would be looked on as maybe immoral,' I said. 'Well, not maybe. Immoral.' The idea of a pimp was so foreign to me that I took the claim with a pinch of salt. I thought perhaps his being a pimp was part of his showbusiness persona rather than his actual job – a character he played, a little like a professional wrestler. Still, I thought it prudent to affect surprise, just in case he really was telling the truth.

I'd met him in the driveway of a mustard-coloured bungalow, the residence of a group he managed, the Children of the Cornbread. He was twenty-seven, wearing a tailored three-piece suit, a bowler hat, Chanel sunglasses. 'This is just Mello style,' he said when I complimented him. 'This is like worldwide international godfather gangsta pimp style.' He spoke in a deep mellifluous voice, with soft consonants, as people do down in Mississippi, saying 'luh' for 'love' and 'cluh' for 'club'. He also sometimes transposed his Ts and Ks. One of his ambitions, he said, was to open Jackson's first black-owned 'skrip club'.

Mello and I drove out to a field where we took shots at a rusty tin can with a gun he kept tucked down his trousers, while an unworried horse off to the side flicked its tail. I told Mello my theory that rap is like wrestling, with rappers exaggerating reality for the purpose of entertaining the public. 'This character I play might just get me killed,' Mello said. 'That's what's so real about it.' He took a few more pot shots, missing the target wildly, and then said, 'When a pistol's up against a woman's head, seem like she listen better.' I didn't really known how to react to this remark. It was so over the top, I had to resist the urge to smile. I suspected he was trying to get a rise out of me. 'That's quite shocking,' I said.

We spent the best part of three days together, me never knowing where the persona ended and the real person began. On our last day Mello offered to introduce me to two female rappers he was working with, Sunshine and Fantasy. We drove over to a nondescript condo on the outskirts of Jackson; it soon became clear that Sunshine and Fantasy were not really rappers but, in Mello's phrase, 'pleasure entrepreneurs'. It was all a little weird and uncomfortable. The women seemed cowed, or possibly they were just being respectful, as they saw it, to Mello for what they must have realized was a big opportunity for him, his international TV debut.

The recital consisted of Mello rapping while Sunshine and Fantasy danced in the raw style of a strip club, bouncing their behinds and pumping their pelvises against the floor. Fantasy looked a little distracted; Sunshine gazed moonily at Mello. The song was called 'Get Your Beg On'. Sunshine said she was working on an album for release the following year. She was also getting married. When I asked to whom, she said, 'My baby over there. My daddy. The number one. My king. My saviour. *My* Jesus Christ.'

*

Five years later, I arrived back in Jackson one Friday in July, having driven across country. From the freeway, Jackson looks like other small American cities – the usual gamut of franchise outlets and, off in the distance, a few small skyscrapers and civic buildings. But once you're on the streets, it's a different story. The downtown is bombed-out and dispossessed. The back roads run past boarded-up

houses strangled with vines, distempered and damp-look-
ing old billboards, nameless gas stations. The roads are
humped, as though the fertility of the land on the banks of
the Pearl River is pushing up from underneath, straining
against the tarmac. The air is damp and everything is
green, but there is something morbid about this abundance
when the buildings are run down and dead.

I'd made a plan to visit a nightclub called the Upper
Level, which was hosting a freestyle competition. I wasn't
sure how to contact Mello and I figured it would be a way
to dip my toe back in the scene. Late in the evening I met
up with one of the club's promoters, Chris 'Big Yayo'
Mabry, at a branch of Red Lobster. Yayo was thirty-three,
in a red lumberjack shirt and jeans, wearing a discreet
diamond earring. He described his style as 'ghetto nerd'.
'I'm cool in the hood, cool in the boardroom, too,' he said.

We reached the club at around eleven thirty when it was
hitting its stride: loud, dark, smoky and packed with two
or three hundred people. Everyone was moving, bouncing,
waving their arms, rapping along to the crunk records.
From time to time, the music would drop out and the crowd
would shout the words.

> Back off bitch!
> Get the fuck out the way!
> Whatchoo lookin' at, nigga?
> Whatchoo lookin' at, nigga?
> Throw it up!
> Throw it up!

I made my way across the dance floor, following Yayo
like a man trekking across a crevasse in a blizzard, wary
of stepping on anyone's feet, spilling any drinks, making

unwanted eye contact. Not that I thought I was in danger of starting any 'static' but I felt self-conscious and slightly foolish: the only white person there, in my western-wear shirt, my scuffed boots, carrying my effeminate satchel and my notebook. I reflected that I couldn't have looked much more out of place if I'd been wearing my old prep school uniform.

Yayo and I arrived at the DJ booth, a walled-off enclosure. He introduced me to the manager of the club, Tonarri, and the DJs Zigzag and Ra-Ra. Tonarri offered me a cognac. I knocked it back and my head quivered. Then Ra-Ra got on the PA and said, 'We got Louis here from London. We gon' show him how we represent right here in the Upper Level. We goin' international tonight, man!'

A little later Yayo and I made our way back out into the storm to meet some of the contestants in the freestyle competition. He rounded up the host, a towering ex-con with gold teeth called Westside Al Capone, and a couple of the amateur rappers, and we went into a quieter VIP area. One of the rappers, a goofy kid with splayed teeth, gave his name as Wamp. He said it stood for 'Whoop Ass Many Places'. He wasn't competing tonight, though. 'I lost my voice,' he said.

'How did you lose it?'

'Rappin'. I rap all the time.'

'What do you do when you're not rapping?'

'Rap. Man, I'm twenty-one. I got over three hundred songs wrote.'

Another rapper, called Charlie Wallace, performed under the name LYLC. 'It just mean 'Lil' C',' he said, when I asked what it stood for. Charlie had won the competition for the last two weeks running. Twenty-three, nice-looking, wearing a baggy red T-shirt with the slain rapper Notorious BIG on it, he was there with his 'manager' (I use the term loosely) Tommy Watts, who was colour-coordinated in beige tracksuit, beige cap and aviator sunglasses.

Charlie said he worked at a supermarket called Sav-A-Lot, stocking shelves and loading trucks. I was grateful to him for telling me his real job, which another, more established rapper might have regarded as damaging to his mystique. Charlie seemed tired of gangsta rap, too. 'I just think there's too much of one concept. Ain't nothing real. Ain't nobody talkin' about anything that can enlighten.'

Then Tommy the manager, seeming to feel he should do some managing, asked me about my project. What kind of book was it? What was it called? Normally I dodged this question but I was starting to feel the effects of the cognac and I mentioned one of the titles I was considering, *May Contain Traces of Nuts*. I could see from Tommy's expression that this was a mistake. 'It's a play on words,' I said. 'Because we all like to go a little nuts every once in a while.'

'You think rappin' is crazy?' Tommy asked.

I changed tack and began saying that my book was a kind of follow-up to a TV show I'd done. I mentioned 'cultures' that are 'outside the mainstream'. Tommy said nothing. I seemed to be digging myself deeper into a hole. Charlie took pity on me, piping up on my behalf, 'Out of the mainstream, like he means Jackson rappers are out of the mainstream compared with a rapper like Ludacris in Atlanta.' Then to me, he said, 'But you got to be careful coming from a Caucasian perspective. People are very sensitive about the meaning of words.'

'Especially, as a member of the quote unquote "dominant culture",' I agreed.

But even this seemed a dangerous phrase, and as though to forestall Tommy's objections, Charlie said, 'Quote unquote! Quote unquote!'

The competition started around one thirty. Two rappers at a time went up on stage and took turns improvising verses that insulted their opponents, using the same beat. At the end, whoever got the loudest cheers won the round. The calibre of the competitors was hard to judge, given that the rapping was so fast and raucous many of the words were incomprehensible. In an early round between Brookhaven Pele and Lil' Tony, Lil' Tony began, 'Well, nigga, first of all, you look like a frog / Long-haired motherfucker, lips hanging down like a dog.' Pele came back with a line about Tony having 'shit-locks' in his hair. In a round between Dirty D and Lord Genius Marcel, Marcel began, 'My nigga, my take on the rap game is serious / You remind me of my bitch when she on her period.'

Overall, the crowd seemed to favour the louder, more aggressive rappers, even when the words themselves weren't clearly tailored to the occasion. A big part of it was intimidation. The rapper whose turn it was would jump around his opponent, bring his face close, getting 'right up in his grill', as the expression has it, while the passive party stared off into the middle distance. In round five, 'Jeru' or possibly 'J-roo' started by shouting, 'Be for real, nigga, you ain't no thug / That shit don't fit you like OJ's glove', before being disqualified. 'I done told you three motherfuckin' times, no touching,' the host said. The final, between Dirty D and Charlie, went to two rounds, but there was no clear winner. By this time, my second cognac was kicking in and I was having trouble following the proceedings. Then suddenly, the competition was over. A draw, apparently. The music came back on: Lil' Jon shouting, 'Get crunk in this bitch.'

I was about ready to leave, but I kept being approached by rappers who'd heard I was a reporter and wanted to give me their phone numbers. In the VIP area, I was interviewing a pair called Two-twelve and Q, both friendly, both looking extremely stoned, when some bouncers dragged a kid outside. Then a little pack of young men chased another man round the corner. I cowered behind the bar, convinced a gunfight was moments away. But the skirmish was over quite quickly and I reflected it was no more violent than the fights one saw in Shepherd's Bush on a Friday night. Just as I was thinking this, my gaze settled on a familiar face.

It was Mello, but a different Mello. Gone were the tailored three-piece suit and bowler hat. Now he had on a boxy tan-coloured shirt, tan trousers, both pressed and pristine, and a backwards baseball cap. I wondered if he'd seen me. Conspicuous as I was, I found it hard to believe he hadn't. I went up to him and said hi.

'Louis, man, I been tryin' to get to you!' he said. 'I been on a righteous pilgrimage. I sponsor after-school programmes, Little League baseball. I'm the George Steinbrenner of Little League. I'm like the Moses of the Ghetto saying "Follow me out of Egypt."'

He was oddly incurious about what I was doing there. I'd thought he might say: 'So what brings you down this way?' Perhaps he assumed I'd been living in Jackson for the past five years and our paths simply hadn't crossed.

It was too loud and chaotic to have much more of a conversation. But I took Mello's numbers, and two days later I visited him at the studio where he was laying down tracks for a new album.

\*

I hadn't actually given too much thought to what I was expecting from the encounter with Mello. I may have been slightly naive, but since I basically liked him – or remembered liking him – I assumed he might like me too and I imagined that the meeting would be unproblematic, like two friends getting together. I wanted to get to know the real person, to see him at home, to meet his stable of women in less artificial conditions, maybe even meet his family. For some reason I didn't ask myself why, given that Mello had stayed in character during my entire first visit, he would suddenly want to reveal himself.

The studio was a smart, custom-built facility, with padded doors and blonde wood, vast boards of knobs and switches and recessed TV screens. The control room resembled the bridge of a spaceship. In the corridors were framed photographs of local gospel singers.

Mello was standing at the mike wearing a Detroit Lions sports shirt and a backwards baseball cap, sipping an energy drink. 'We got a refrigerator full of Red Bull,' he said. 'Y'all drink that up there in London? I got some good herb from Mother Earth, too, if you need some! Ha ha ha!' His two front teeth were gold, his face faintly pock-marked. He was in constant motion, and there was a gracefulness to his conversational gestures, the way he bobbed his head and swept his hands.

The track he was recording was called 'Stop Lyin''.

You bustin' heads to the white meat? Nigga, stop lyin'!
You pimpin' hoes like Mello T? Nigga, stop lyin'!
You movin' keys and you movin' trees? Nigga, stop lyin'!
You say you payin' off the po-lice? Nigga, stop lyin'!

During a break, I told Mello about my reunion visits. I mentioned I'd heard he'd recorded a track for kids called 'If You Try You Can Do It'. Then I asked about the lyrics to this new track which, truth be told, sounded more like the old pimping Mello than the new positive one I'd heard about.

But Mello glossed the lyrics as a plea for rappers to tone down their music: not to rap about selling drugs if they'd never sold drugs. 'I'm tryin' to tell the kids, they might be focusing on, "I wanna be like him." But I'm letting them know he didn't get that car or that video and them girls slangin' no dope. He ain't never shot nobody. I don't want no more thugs or gangstas. I'd rather develop congressmens and doctors.' On a flight of eloquence, Mello went on to decry the system that creates poverty, 'Where ten per cent of the population runs the ninety.' Then, somewhat confusingly, having just called for more black professionals and fewer thugs, he began lambasting black politicians, lawyers and doctors as 'sell-outs'. 'But you know, I'm a honky-tonk killer and I'm comin' to *kill* the sell-out!'

It was too exhausting to take issue with the contradiction, so I ignored it, and asked if he was still pimping. This led to a long disquisition on the nature of pimping, the fact that George Bush was a pimp, that I too was a kind of pimp, that I was pimping every time I went on TV, which culminated in Mello issuing a plea for any women interested in prostitution to give him a call. 'So if they some females out there worldwide who really want to go from zero to a whole lotta zeros, they can holler at me. 'Cause pimpin' and hoin' is the best thing goin'! Ha ha ha!'

I seemed to be back at square one with Mello – a place of high-flown rhetoric and boasts that might or might not hide some reality underneath.

Three other rappers arrived: an ex-crack dealer named Donnie Money; another pimp named J-Mack; and Ice Cold, a family man who laid epoxy floors for a living. Donnie put down a verse for 'Stop Lyin''. Then Ice Cold recorded a hook for a new track, about friends who become envious when drunk. A few hours later, their parts done, they left – and then something strange happened. Now that it was just me and Mello, his tone softened. His posturing melted away and he spoke lovingly about his two daughters, aged two and eight – the younger one by Sunshine, the older from a previous relationship with a schoolteacher. He mentioned he'd had run-ins with the law since I'd last seen him, been charged with homicide and making pornography. He spoke vaguely about it all, but I sensed it had scared him. Oddly, the legal problems had come at a time when he was straightening out, he said. His father had died, which had prompted him to think about his life. He'd started coaching Little League, teaching after-school reading programmes. 'Yeah, baby, I been tryin' to be a hundred per cent square. I just want to be a good father.'

And like that, we began making plans for the coming week. He offered to show me his house, his neighbourhood, introduce me to his friends. He said he had a little poster-board he brings when he speaks at high schools showing the names and photos of all his friends who died before they reached twenty-one. 'I tell them "*He* died at sixteen, *he* died at eighteen, *he* died at nineteen. But *all* of them dropped out of school."' I could meet Sunshine again, too. She was in Chicago but would be back on Tuesday. Only his two daughters were off-limits. 'For security reasons.'

❋

Then he disappeared. I tried his mobile, left messages. No reply. 'This is Mello T,' his message went. 'You know I'm out there tryin' to chase that cheddar, 'cause cheddar sho 'nuff make it better. So just leave your name at the tone and I'll get right back to ya.'

After a day and a half lounging at my motel, writing up my notes, waiting for him to call back, I made other plans. I arranged with a rapper named Coup Dada to visit one of Jackson's bad areas, a neighbourhood called Wood Street. I'd recently met Coup Dada as part of a musical collective called US From Dirrt. Interestingly, their latest release, *I'm a Hater*, was a beef record. It contained a dis of the one Jackson rapper to make it big internationally, David Banner. 'Mississippi superstar / You know just who you are,' they rapped. They threatened to vandalize Banner's luxurious Jackson house, specifying that they would send a goon squad to piss on Banner's couch, then shit in his fridge, before finishing him off 'execution-style with a dirty twenty-two'.

And yet US From Dirrt had seemed a modest and obliging bunch, thoughtful, unflashily dressed, just grateful for an opportunity to sound off to a visiting journalist. Coup in particular had struck me as sparky and playful. Dark-skinned and almond-eyed, twenty-something, his hair in a do-rag, he'd acknowledged that much rap was self-destructive. He'd admitted that some rappers became more out-of-control and lawless as they became more successful, seeming to want to imitate their lyrics to buttress their credibility. But then he had added, with a note of ironical indignation in his voice, 'But even if what you're implying is true, that rap is self-destructive, these guys get filthy rich before they self-destruct! So it's still there for us! This the last great movement for us. This is *our* political party. It's a hip-hop party, but it's *our* party.'

Coup seemed a sensible choice as a guide round Wood Street since he'd grown up there. The journalist Charlie Braxton tried to dissuade me from going. 'Wood Street?' Charlie said. 'No, no, no, Louis. No, Louis. No. They shoot cops. You don't want to go, Louis. They'll smell tourist on you. You know what they call Wood Street? *The area of terror!*' But I went anyway, meeting Coup late one morning at his mother's house.

Though she'd raised him in Wood Street, Coup's mother had recently moved to a nicer area, where the only sign of poverty was the age of the cars. A battered Buick with a smashed tail light was in her garage. Inside he introduced her to me as 'Ma-Bay', a tough-looking forty-three-year-old, in grey sweat shorts and sweat top, hair straightened and pulled back severely. She had a gold tooth, which looked odd on an older person. She was a security officer at a local college. Coup said she also used to own a bar in Wood Street.

The house was tidy and sparsely furnished. Candles, inspirational posters on the walls; the lyrics of 'Amazing Grace' and a prose poem called 'The Miracle of Friendship'. We stood by her dining table, next to the kitchen. She called me 'sir' and didn't ask me to sit down or offer me water. As a white person and a journalist, I realized

I represented something. I must have seemed like a social worker or a government inspector.

Ma-Bay downplayed the dangerousness of Wood Street. 'It was a good area twenty years ago,' she said. 'It's getting back where it started from. If you not in no gang or anything, you don't represent anything, you not going to have any problem.'

'I heard they shoot cops.'

'They never shot no police there,' Ma-Bay said.

'That's ridiculous,' Coup said.

But once we were outside the house, Coup said, 'My mom said we could go anywhere in the neighbourhood, but that ain't strictly true. She doesn't like it when people speak bad about where she from, because that like speaking bad about her, her family.' Then, apropos his mother, he commented mysteriously, 'Maybe we just been speaking to one of the biggest players in the area, *no one would tell you.*'

This remark set the tone for the afternoon, which turned into a kind of litany of coded answers and circumspection. He wouldn't tell me his age, though that may have been for the usual showbusiness reasons. He was wearing a T-shirt with a picture of one of his dead homies on it, but he didn't want to talk about it. Then, speaking about his wife and their four kids, who were living in Kansas City, he said, 'She felt it would be better to shield them completely away from it by living in another area than the one I was brought up in. Because I might have made a lot of enemies along the way. Not saying that I *have.* But I don't have any of those in Kansas City.

'This is Wood Street. This is the end I can take you to.'

We'd driven onto a rutted road. The only houses I could see were abandoned shotgun shacks with metal chainlink fences round them, and vacant lots where houses had been torn down, overgrown with vines, tall grass, saplings. We parked next to Coup's uncle's house and got out.

Wood Street itself ran parallel to a railroad track on one side and a creek on the other. At one end, it was bounded by a road bridge. Cut off on three sides, the neighbourhood felt abandoned and stagnant. The houses, or at least the ones that remained, were wooden shacks on brick pilings, leaning and peeling and dilapidated, so broken down they looked art-directed, like the set of a horror film. Mailboxes on posts at crazy angles; patched-up mesh over the porches; sofas on porches. Still, in the heat, there was a pleasant lazy mood. The only noise was the buzz of insects in the long grass.

As we walked, Coup said again and again, 'That's another street I can't take you to. I can go there, I just can't take *you* up there . . . All these streets lead to Wood Street. These niggas gon' call me and ask who I was with.'

As vivacious as he'd been before, his mother's caginess seemed to have unsettled him. He worried about what it was appropriate to say, feeling it was disrespectful to his neighbourhood to talk about the crime and the desperation. 'I never seen any drugs in the hood,' he said, bizarrely. 'The white man has taught me about hypocrisy. I learned what true mafia-ism is.' For me it was frustrating, since I'd been expecting a kind of ghetto safari. But it was laudable, too, his unwillingness to merchandise affliction. His sense that rap, for all its pitfalls, was a black movement seemed to extend to the hood and its lawlessness too. He felt protective.

On the way back to the car, we bumped into Coup's uncle, a skinny, haunted-looking man in jeans and T-shirt.

I told him I was a journalist interviewing Coup about his music. 'My uncle thought I was serving you,' Coup said later, meaning selling me drugs. 'Did you see how shocked my uncle was? See how he was smilin'? "You rappin'?"'

As we were driving out of the neighbourhood, an expensive-looking four-by-four appeared behind us. 'Shit, we bein' tailed,' Coup said. He seemed nervous. I wondered if he was being melodramatic, but I was a little nervous too. There was no question the vehicle was following us. Then it slowed down, stopped and turned around. Coup's confidence returned and he said, 'Nobody gon' question Ma-Bay's son. When the boys realized who it was in the car, now they think I'm serving you.'

Finally, almost out of exasperation about everything he felt he couldn't say, Coup broke out, 'For bling bling, every bling that was on my neck and on my homie's neck, somebody died for that. Blood was shed for that. And I'm not going to glorify it . . . What you hear in gangsta rap? Our lives is *worse than that.*' He spat out the 't' of 'that'. 'So it's nothing to be glorified.'

It had been a frustrating encounter. I found in my own journalistic attitude and hunger for war stories an echo of the suburban appetite for gangsta rap itself. That ghetto kids should get caught up in the drama of being gangsta seemed eminently understandable when I myself found it so involving, even at third-hand.

Back at my motel, I checked my messages, and found that Mello had called.

＊

I met him down at the studio again, where Ice Cold was recording more tracks for his debut album. We sat at the back while Ice did his vocals. I didn't like to confront Mello about his disappearance. Something in his manner discouraged direct approaches – a quiet authority which I imagined was one of the things that qualified him as a pimp.

Unbidden, he mentioned he'd been down in Mobile, Alabama, pushing various records he and his 'circle' were working on. I took this as a partial explanation for his unavailablity. He expanded on some of the themes of our encounter earlier in the week, talking about the tribulations that had been visited on him. 'I'm still blessed to be here in the flesh. Hell came to me on Earth the last four years. It's been a test. It's like what Job went through in the Bible.' He said he was still 'twenty per cent' into pimping but he was trying to go straight. 'I been playing it under the radar,' he said. 'Really my whole thing lately has been surviving. As soon as I get my first record deal, I'm out of everything.' He sounded one other note, to do with our documentary, seeming to say that he felt it hadn't helped him. He implied that since his career hadn't been advanced by the show we made, what advantage was there to being in a book? But his manner was so indirect, I didn't fully understand what he meant until later. We made another arrangement to see his neighbourhood.

Then he went quiet again.

By now, I was getting used to Mello's disappearances, so I didn't wait around. I made arrangements to go to Atlanta, reasoning I could use the time to meet some of the new stars of the crunk scene.

In particular I was curious to meet David Banner, the subject of US from Dirrt's dis record. His real name is Lavell Crump, and rather embarrassingly, I'd passed up a chance of an interview in 2000 in favour of Mello. When I found Banner at the music studio, he brought it up, in a spirit of good-natured badinage. 'Five years ago, y'all wasn't interested in me, I remember *that*,' he said. A big beefy man, maybe six feet three or four, with an unruly beard, he was putting the finishing touches to his new album *Certified*. The track he was working on, which he listened to at deafening volume, went, 'This is for the thug niggas / All the pimps and the drug dealers / Thieves and the motherfucking killers.'

Unlike Mello, Banner is someone with whom it is relatively easy to draw the line between persona and real person. On his albums he raps about pimping and stomping bitches, but he is in fact highly educated, a former school teacher and student-body president, who is, as he put it, 'a semester and a thesis away' from his master's degree. In between making tweaks on a track where the phrase 'that's why we get crunk in this bitch' was fractionally too low in the mix, Banner lamented the double standard that dictated that rappers should have experienced first-hand the episodes they describe in their raps. 'You don't go to Will Smith and see if he really can fly a flying saucer before he does *Independence Day*. And besides, the person who really did those things may not be the best story-teller.' And yet even Banner, with his studious bent, wasn't immune to hip-hop machismo. He hinted that he might have a criminal background that he couldn't reveal ('I would never tell about the things I really did') and was a little sheepish about having been a teacher.

I asked whether he'd seen the photo of Young Jeezy with a snowman medallion. Banner hemmed and hawed, presumably not wishing to criticize a peer. Then, moments later, Banner said, 'Speak of!' and who should walk in but

Young Jeezy himself, wearing a long baggy sports jersey with his name on it – though no snowman medallion. He was accompanied by a tall, older man, his manager, Coach K. He'd come to talk to Banner about a track he was producing for his forthcoming debut album, *Let's Get It: Thug Motivation 101.*

This was an unexpected opportunity: a chance to interview the gangsta of the hour. By now, I was a little exasperated with Banner. I had the sense he wasn't too sure who he was supposed to be, that he felt a responsibility to enact certain gangsta poses and express solidarity with the streets, but that they didn't fit him that well. I was starting to remember why I hadn't wanted to interview him in 2000. So I took Coach K's number and a little later we rendezvoused in the lobby of another recording studio. Young Jeezy was indisposed, working in the studio, so I chatted to Coach instead. He seemed proud that Jeezy had done many of the things he described on record. He said the forthcoming album would include a 'book' by Jeezy on the 'rules of thugging'.

'They makin' so much money,' Coach went on. 'Jeezy does four or five shows a week. That's $40,000 a week, just from shows.'

As we chatted, a very dark-skinned young man with a brooding, suspicious air passed back and forth through the lobby. Coach introduced him as Kinky, the co-owner of Jeezy's label, Corporate Thugs Entertainment. He was twenty-four, wearing a plain white T-shirt, baggy jean shorts, and a watch that cost $28,000. Finding out I was journalist, he relaxed a little – I think he'd assumed I was a policeman. I asked how he'd met Jeezy and he said 'boot camp'.

'The army?' I asked.

'Jail.'

'What were you in for?'

'Shit I had no business doing.'

Kinky welcomed the resurgence of gangsta rap. 'Jeezy doesn't talk about the glamour,' he said. 'He talks about the struggle. People tired of hearing the fake.'

'Do you ever worry it could go too gangsta?'

'Be no such thing as too gangsta,' Kinky said. 'Fuck a nigga! When it come to my money, fuck another nigga! If it ain't got to do with me or my click, fuck a nigga!'

'That seems a little mean-spirited,' I observed.

'It's not mean-spirited,' Coach said. 'When you come from nothing, you've got to look out for your own. Beefs in the hip-hop community are just the same as corporate beefs. Coke beefing with Pepsi.'

It seemed superfluous to point out that as yet no CEOs had been iced in executive drive-bys.

The paradoxes of the gangsta rap world were enough to make my head hurt. As a fan of the music, it was especially frustrating that of all the subjects I'd covered this was the one I had most sympathy for, and yet it was here that I felt the most distance and suspicion. I saw the love of gangsta poses as an understandable response to the feeling of disenfranchisement. But to them, I was an outsider. In no other story did I sense so much closing of ranks against me, so much reluctance to criticize any of their own. I compared it with the porn world, where directors, actors and ex-actors had no problem sounding off on the excesses of the business. Here it was different. Even though I was sympathetic, skin colour still got in the way. It was that simple. The trust wasn't there, because I was white and they were black.

＊

I drove back to Jackson, and two days later, Mello called. He was down at a strip club called Babe's, celebrating his thirty-first birthday. I felt flattered to be invited. I bought some champagne as a gift and headed down. But there was no party. I found him sitting on a stool in a quiet corner, working his way through a bottle of cognac. He was half-drunk, and any misgivings about talking about pimping had vanished. Now his manner was swaggering and unabashed. He gestured at a young blonde stripper named Kay, who he said wanted to join his stable of women. 'She call me all the time but she got to prove she worthy to know me. She fascinated with me. She want to be with me. But if she gon' be with me, then she got to love money a little bit mo'. Heh heh.' Kay seemed drunk and oblivious to these claims.

'She about to be my number four,' he went on. 'I remember at one time I had five living with me and Sunshine. Now I got Sunshine plus two others. I want seven hundred, like Solomon. It ain't about force with me, it about choice. If she choose me, cool. If she don't choose me, that's cool too.'

As the evening wore on, Mello became drunker and more grandiose. 'They can't lock me up right now because God won't let 'em,' he said. 'Anybody that could talk was lined in chalk.' He took a sip of his Hennessy. 'I'd love to have a place like this. I got some politicians, I'm going to have to either pay 'em or kill 'em. I'd rather pay 'em, but I don't have no problem with killing 'em.' Blown back and forth by crosswinds of rhetoric, he alternately celebrated and lamented his lifestyle. Having just announced that he lived to make his stable of women greater, he said, 'This shit is boring to me. This life is boring to me. I want your life, man.'

'I went to bed last night at eleven thirty and did a crossword puzzle,' I said.

'I would love to go to bed at eleven thirty and do a crossword puzzle, man. I would *love* that. I want to be square and do crossword puzzles, all that kind of shit. But I'm in love with the game.'

I was as confused as ever by Mello, but in a moment of clarity my confusion crystalized into a single, simple question. 'Do you hate the game or do you love it?' I asked.

'I hate the game, but I love to do it.'

It was either a profound comment on human psychology and the contradictory impulses we all feel or it was nonsense, I wasn't sure which. But I reflected that whether someone is being hypocritical or not is, in some instances, a question of style – by other names, it can be called irony or role-playing. Mello was capable of taking up a variety of opposed positions without shame or guilt because it was never clear how serious he was being. His personas came and went like songs on a jukebox, the theme depending on the occasion. But as long as I found him entertaining, I had to some degree surrendered my right to judge him.

I thought about the frustrations of seeing him again. In the end, he had no interest in revealing his real life. For him, our relationship was strictly showbusiness. Given that he was a pimp, someone willing to subject the most intimate parts of human life to the marketplace, I wondered how I could have expected otherwise. The Mello he might have been willing to show me – the swaggering fancy man of the first visit – was cowed by his run-ins with the law. The Mello I wanted to meet – the behind-the-scenes man, the husband and father, whose life was presumably domestic and unglamorous – would have undermined his mystique and maybe hurt his career.

And so I was conceding defeat. He might be a bully or a criminal or a model citizen or someone deprived of other choices in life – but I wasn't going to find out.

The next day, I began my long journey back west. As I drove, I thought of Coup's remark, 'This is the last great movement for us. This is our political party.' Raised in an environment without money or opportunity, gangsta rappers have created a ruthless code of honour. Observing the code means showing no weakness; being prepared to fight for yourself and your circle; never saying too much. That the lifestyle is seductive is shown by the popularity of the records describing it: whether it's lived or listened to, at root the appeal is the same. Only the stakes differ. And so we keep on, hating it, loving it.

# OSCODY

One of the frustrations of Mello being so elusive was that it had robbed me of an opportunity to test an idea I had, that the mysterious power a pimp holds over his women is essentially the same as the power of a cult leader or guru over his flock.

Several months earlier, in Los Angeles, around the time I'd been visiting porn sets and scrutinizing male genitals, I'd met up with the reverse side of this equation – an ex-member of a well-known cult – and seeing Mello again put me in mind of his story.

He called himself Rio, and he was one of the last survivors of Heaven's Gate, a group that made the headlines in March 1997 when its thirty-nine members were found dead in the house they shared, having apparently committed ritual mass suicide.

A striking detail that emerged in the news coverage was that eight of the male 'students' had had themselves castrated, and toward the end of our meeting I asked Rio about this aspect of the group.

It was, he said, simply a way of making it easier to 'control our vehicles', meaning their bodies. Class members were supposed to be celibate and pure of mind. Some took pills to keep their hormones in check but they had side effects, so a couple of them researched the procedure, drove down to Mexico and got snipped. 'The ones that did get neutered, were so . . .' – Rio began laughing – '. . . happy after that. They were almost giddy as children!'

The cult leader, Do, went next. He was in his mid-sixties at that time, a former music teacher whose real name was Marshall Herff Applewhite. Do's procedure was botched and it took him a long time to heal. But heal he did, and after that several others followed suit.

I asked Rio if he'd thought about getting castrated.

'Oh,' he said, 'I had control of my vehicle, I didn't have to.'

We'd met at an organic coffee shop called the Urth Caffe in Beverly Hills, near where Rio lives. He was smooth and poised, wearing an expensive watch and shoes, with a shaved head and neatly trimmed beard. He said he'd just turned fifty but he looked much younger. 'I look like you!' he said. Then, crediting the Heaven's Gate beliefs he still holds, he added, 'It's a higher mind, man!' He cut a rather stylish, urbane figure, but I also had the sense of his having made an effort for me. There was touch of calcula-tion behind it, and I wondered how well life was going for him, as one of the last of the Heaven's Gate cult survivors.

'It was the most wonderful thing that ever happened to me,' he said of his time in the group – the 'monastery', as he called it. He joined in 1994, having attended one of their lectures at Marina Del Rey, Los Angeles. At first they wouldn't have him. This was one of the misconceptions about 'predatory cults' – they could actually be quite hard to join. Rio attended another meeting. They showed him a video of Do. 'He seemed like the messenger to me. And that's what I told them. They got a kick out of that.' The elders phoned Do that night. Then they told Rio the good news. Bring clothes, some camping equipment. That's all you need. Rio was divorced; he had an eleven-year-old son who lived with his mother. He drove out to Phoenix two weeks later and joined the monastery.

When he arrived, they trimmed his hair, shaved off his beard, and disinfected his whole body. He spent a couple of weeks watching videos of Do's teachings, getting up to speed. To Rio, Do was the reincarnation of Jesus. 'You don't realize what this was . . . this was undoubtedly a visit from another place. No doubt. Everybody knew.' His voice was breaking with emotion. 'It's, uh, it's miraculous. Just for me to think that, somehow I was involved with the one that came again . . .' Now he was crying lightly. 'That, and the love everybody had. They were like all of my best friends.'

He left a month or so before the 'exit' – because of an 'irresistible feeling'. It wasn't that he had any fear of leaving the planet, he said. He was happy about the exit, as was everybody. He just had an urge to do something else. 'So I asked Do if I could talk to him and I told him, I'm having feelings like there's something else for me to do. And it was a very emotional conversation, 'cause I loved Do. So he said, "Well, let's sleep on it."' Do went and spoke to 'Ti', his dead partner, once known as Bonnie Lu Nettles, who'd either died of cancer in 1985 or ascended on to a spaceship or both. 'About an hour later, he asked to meet with me again, and he had talked to Ti. He said, "according to Ti, you leaving seems to be part of the plan" . . . So he announced it to everybody in the room . . .'

It struck me that the 'something else' Rio felt the urge to do was perhaps simply *to stay alive*. Some of the other Heaven's Gate members had been in more than twenty years. Rio had been in three, so he still had a sense of life on the outside. Before meeting him, I'd wondered if he might be more distanced from the group now – that he might have 'woken up' and seen Do as a false prophet. But his continuing attachment made sense, too. To go through all that, then realize that it was meaningless, would be hard to bear. After the 'exit', Rio went on to become the most media-friendly of the Heaven's Gate cult survivors, selling film rights to his story to ABC, appearing on the cover of *Newsweek*, being interviewed by Diane Sawyer.

The year after the suicides, another ex-member killed himself in the prescribed style. And the year after that, another. Do's 'brainwashing', if that's what it was, reached beyond the grave. Rio said he had no plans to exit his vehicle. Indeed, he was full of projects. A film script, a book proposal about his experiences in Heaven's Gate. 'Right now I'm working on a consumer product for animals,' he said. 'Petsmart really wants it bad . . . It's for cats, dogs and reptiles. I don't want to tell you the name because I don't want it to get out. I'll just tell you: it's something that goes on the window.'

*

They were found lying on bunk beds, each of them wearing Nike trainers, with a little arm patch saying 'Heaven's Gate Away Team', under diamond-shaped purple shrouds, having poisoned themselves with a mixture of apple sauce, phenobarbital and vodka. For several days, the news was filled with accounts of the group, interviews with ex-members. It was the worst mass suicide on US soil (the worst in US history was the 900-plus suicides of Jim Jones' church in Jonestown, Guyana).

In the office where my production team had been researching a documentary on UFO believers, there was a mild sense of surprise at the coincidence that our subject matter, which had felt, truth be told, a little passé when we started looking into it, was now suddenly breaking news again. Then on day three or day four of the media frenzy, we found a FedEx package on the desk of one of the producers, where it had been lying unnoticed. It contained videotapes from the cult, their 'exit videos', press releases, a 'Heaven's Gate Away Team' arm patch, and maps and directions for finding their house.

It seemed one of the cult's dying wishes had been that we should be the ones to find their cast-off vehicles and break the story to the world.

There was a letter that said: 'Hopefully, you will be able to get a team to the physical location detailed in the accompanying location document ASAP . . . We are also hoping that this letter could act as a pass on to our premises or as an entrée to the site. We are hereby giving you our permission to enter – if in fact our desires have any bearing on this matter. Perhaps you can present this note to the security guard as authorization. It is our desire that you have first priority to the story.'

It was news to me that we'd even been in touch with the group, but so it was. My colleague Simon had stumbled upon their website, and exchanged emails. Initially they were keen to be involved in our documentary. Then they changed their minds – they said they needed to focus on other matters. In hindsight, this had an ominous tone.

The writer had even been thoughtful enough to highlight the best route to the house, and included details about being courteous to the landlord ('His wife is named Fifi and she has also been extremely nice to us; she has some idea that we are "angels".') and how to break into the building – 'You'll likely need to hop the fence and enter the house to open the gate. The entry door between the two garage doors on the SW side of the house will be left unlocked.'

I felt a little chagrin at missing such a big scoop. At the same time, I was aware there wasn't much I could have done with the information. After all, the documentary was supposed to be a light-hearted look at UFO belief. How we would have used footage of me stumbling on to the scene of a mass suicide was far from clear.

Still, it was too intriguing a lead to pass up, so we arranged to interview one of the handful of survivors, a man named Wayne Parker, or 'Oscody', who lived in Phoenix, Arizona. Oscody was far from ideal interview material; he spoke slowly and deliberately, and he wasn't very enthusiastic about the project, but he was the best we had.

As the interview drew near, Oscody said he was no longer sure he wanted to appear on camera at all. Thinking I might be able to finesse the situation, I called him up. I affected a jaunty manner and attempted to have a jovial conversation. He mentioned there was a swimming pool at his apartment building. I suggested we might go swimming together, an idea he didn't really take to. 'Well, there's certain things about, um, exposing the vehicle that just don't feel comfortable to me,' he explained.

'You don't mind if I expose my vehicle?' I asked.

'Well, um, you know, I'd like to be hospitable. The pool hasn't been cleaned. I'll tell you that much. It has some palm fronds at the bottom. It's not very enticing.'

'Well, my vehicle hasn't been cleaned. And it isn't very enticing either.'

Fortunately, the borderline offensiveness of my attempts at repartee failed to penetrate his thick fog of grief.

※

Oscody's apartment was in a building fairly typical of those you find in the West – two storeys, stuccoed, around a small kidney-shaped swimming pool. Except for a computer in the corner with a flying toaster screen saver, it was totally bare. He looked a lot like the cult members I'd seen on the Heaven's Gate farewell videotape. Balding, with his hair cut short. Beard. Round face. His manner was so calm and even, he seemed like someone under heavy sedation.

Since he was no longer camera-friendly, we'd left the crew to wait in the van, while my director Debbie, my producer Simon and I tried to coax Oscody into (as I put it) 'showing his vehicle'. We explained that we were interested in his story, that we were a documentary team rather than news and so could afford to be a little more in-depth. We reminded him that we were the preferred media. Oscody absorbed all this without saying a word. Then we pulled out our trump card: the letter that came with the package; the 'preferred media' validation.

As Oscody read it, his eyes watered.

'Excuse me,' he said. 'The, ahem, vehicle sometimes responds.'

Two other former cult members, Mark and Sarah, arrived soon afterwards. Mark was friendly and animated. Sarah was low-key and seemed a little wary.

It soon became clear that all three were against showing their faces on camera, so we spent what was left of the evening driving round Phoenix forlornly looking for a backdrop against which we could silhouette them – a view overlooking the city; a starry desert landscape. There were eight of us in the van, including crew; we made awkward chit-chat – me scrupulously using all their terminology about 'graduating' and 'class members' and 'the next level' and worrying all the time that Debbie or Simon or one of the crew was going to make an off-colour remark.

At one point, Mark said, 'This whole idea about it being a cult is so off-base. I mean, these were brilliant people. The intelligence . . . We're talking about doctors, lawyers. One of them was the person who did all the programming for ATM machines.'

We ended up stumbling around a rutted track in the pitch dark in a park somewhere on the outskirts of Phoenix. Mark had thought we'd get a nice view of the city but we hadn't banked on the noise of about thirty teenagers drinking and playing eighties hits. 'Mickey' by Toni Basil had just come on when we called it a night.

My abiding memory of the whole encounter is how bare Oscody's apartment was, with nothing in it but that computer and its flying toaster screen saver.

＊

Seven years later, in the Las Vegas university library, I browsed articles on the history of Heaven's Gate. Marshall Herff Applewhite, or 'Herff', as people called him, had been a music teacher in Texas. Married with two children, he struggled with homosexual impulses. He divorced. In 1970, he lost his job at St Thomas's University amid a scandal over an affair with a student. He became depressed; heard voices.

In one version of the story, Herff met Bonnie Lu Nettles in a psychiatric hospital in Houston, where he was attempting to 'cure' himself of homosexuality. For a while, they ran a New Age centre together. They hit the road in 1973, convinced that they were the two witnesses spoken of in the book of Revelation.

Starting in 1975, they began recruiting. For years, they toured the country, giving presentations, answering questions, winning converts. The dropout rate was high; at no time did they number more than a hundred. They taught that Earth was a 'garden' for growing souls, which would be picked up by a spaceship when they were ready. The worst mistake one could make was to identify one's self with one's body or 'vehicle'. All sensuality was shunned. They abstained from sex or even lustful thoughts, wore baggy clothing, cut their hair short.

The kitchen was called the 'nutrilab'. Cooking was 'fuel preparation'. They could watch certain TV shows: *Star Trek* and the *X Files* were okay; news shows about natural disasters were encouraged, because they fed into the group's apocalyptic thinking. *Little House on the Prairie* was not, because it was about a family and therefore it 'vibrated on the human level'. Students had to close their eyes during scenes that were arousing.

Posted on the Heaven's Gate website was a list of offences: 'Trusting my own judgment – or using my own mind'; 'Staying in my own head, having private thoughts'; 'Having likes or dislikes'.

In 1985, Ti died of liver cancer. She'd been expecting to be picked up by a spaceship, physically, and taken to

Heaven. When that didn't happen Do adapted the theology. Now, instead of needing an actual spaceship to land, their souls could migrate over a distance. Thus the groundwork for their suicidal exit eleven years later was laid.

One academic article gave this account of their final years: 'The group's efforts to get its message out were hitting a dead end. Among the few who clicked on to the Heaven's Gate website, the main response was ridicule . . . Hardly anyone joined . . . A dropout claimed that members "resented the fact that the world wrote them off as another kooky cult."' I thought guiltily of my own contact with the group and their faith in my good intentions.

In late 1996, speculation appeared on the Internet that there was a spaceship in the tail of the comet Hale-Bopp. The comet would be closest to Earth on the first day of spring 1997. Do had predicted UFO landings many times in the group's twenty-one-year history, but this time there would be no landing. They were going out to meet the craft a hundred million miles from Earth.

Having made money designing websites, the group splurged in its last few months on outings to San Diego Wild Animal Park and Sea World and a UFO conference in Laughlin, Nevada. They kept itemized ledgers of all their expenditures. They travelled to Las Vegas, saw Cirque du Soleil ($2,661), gambled (winning $58.91), and ascended the Stratosphere, the tallest building west of the Mississippi. Among their last acts, three days before the suicides began, was a group outing to see the Mike Leigh film, *Secrets and Lies*.

*

One night in May 2004, I climbed the Stratosphere. 1,149 feet high, it looks, from the outside, a little like a flying saucer on stilts, ungainly but beautiful. The observation deck has raked windows so you can look down as well as out, down on to the lights of Las Vegas and out on to the ring of dark mountains which holds the city in its arms. It feels the way being lifted slowly into space on a flying saucer might feel. Outside Las Vegas the landscape is lifeless; the city is like a Moonbase; it is easy to imagine there is no other life on Earth.

At my motel, I watched the videotape in which the Heaven's Gate members deliver their 'exit statements'. On camera, they are shy and gentle, all of them aware of how they are likely to be perceived – as brainwashed dupes, weirdos, cultists – and doing what they can to forestall that impression.

They sit outside, two women with a sunny garden stretching out behind them. 'I'm so happy.' 'We're looking forward to being in our next-level bodies.' Modest, humble, nervous, with their hands folded, in baggy shirts with their top buttons all done up. 'This vehicle isn't much of a communicator and especially it's not comfortable in front of a camera.' One starts crying.

A middle-aged black man, Thomas Nichols, the brother of Nichelle Nichols who played Lieutenant Uhura in *Star Trek*, says: 'I'm the happiest person in the world.' One younger member ends her statement by slapping her chest in the style of Captain Picard in *Star Trek* and saying: 'Thirty-nine to beam up!' Laughter in the background.

Two women, sitting erect, in their thirties and fifties respectively, say: 'Hideousness has become the norm.'

A young guy wearing spectacles says: 'When we leave, I know the media will treat this as a sort of weird bizarre cult, whatever you want to call it. But look deeper . . . look for what we've taught people and the message we've left behind. We know that it's difficult to understand but the next level requires a commitment, a kind of final ingredient of leaving the body and giving it up until you can actually graduate.'

A skinny woman with sticking-out ears says: 'I know y'all can get the impression that there's some kind of charismatic people that may have had a strong influence on a lot of weak-minded people. Well, there are a lot of people that we've worked with over the years that might be able to push through that impression.' She refers to Do as Jesus; starts weeping; talks about 'demons'. Demons meaning – unwanted desires? Sexual urges? The impulse to quit the cult and reunite with her friends and family in the outside world?

I'm struck watching it by how many of them there are. I start to think this must be the last, then another comes on, then two more . . .

A man, fiftyish, short hair: 'We know that the spin doctors, the people that make a profession of debunking everybody, putting down everybody, are going to attack what we're doing, just like they attacked the Solar Temple, Waco, what have you. They'll say these people are crazy. They were mesmerized, whatever. We know it isn't true, but how can you know that?' Then a man in his forties: 'We know the media will do a hatchet job on us.'

In his video, Do looks a kindly man. He speaks slowly. He has the air of the music teacher he once was. I imagine myself among them, a fellow member of the cult. It would be very peaceful and gentle, and probably quite boring. Several newspaper accounts commented how tidy the house was, how neatly they all died.

It is hard as a non-believer to know what value to attach to the suicides. What does it mean? Their awareness of how they are perceived makes it difficult to view them as brainwashed. Only when they speak about the hatefulness of the world am I brought up short. Only then do they seem disconnected. I find a lot to feel sad about in their deaths, and also a little to admire. Whatever else you say about the suicides, they were done out of a kind of love. They wanted to do it. Or thought they wanted to. If there's a difference . . .

*

I'd asked Rio when I met him if he knew what became of Oscody. 'He's in Phoenix,' he said. 'So are Mark and Sarah.' But Rio was wrong. Oscody had 'exited' back in July of 2001, without fanfare, unknown to the world at large, bringing the Heaven's Gate suicides to a grand total of forty-two. I found this out when I spoke to Mark on the phone.

'It's kind of difficult, an awkward thing to talk to people about,' Mark said. 'Rio didn't know about it, because we hadn't really talked much in the last year or so.'

I met up with Mark and Sarah in the suburbs of Phoenix at a New Orleans theme restaurant called Lafite's, inside an Embassy Suites hotel. We were the only customers. Instead of rings, the napkins were bound with strings of shiny beads of the kind they wear in New Orleans at Mardi Gras. Dixieland jazz played incongruously.

Sarah had long dark hair, earrings and a pendant; she

looked vaguely Persian. Mark was red-haired, geeky, in black trousers and grey polo shirt. They were intelligent and friendly. Sarah was, once again, a little wary.

I bought them lunch, and they seemed pleased to have a chance to relive their days in the community, as the waiter eavesdropped on our conversation. They were in the group for twelve years, from 1975 to 1987. Like Rio, they regarded their time in Heaven's Gate as the greatest of their lives. 'If you could find an apostle who would say what it was like being in the presence of Jesus,' Sarah said, 'it was just fabulous.'

'It was *hard*,' Mark said. 'But there's nothing in the human experience that matches it. Nothing.' It was like 'unconditional love' between all the members, Mark said.

'So why did you leave?' I asked.

'Good question,' Sarah said.

'Yeah, good question,' Mark said.

'Still wrestle with that today,' Sarah said.

The answer, I suspected, was because they loved each other. Their love trumped the love of the group. Now, in addition to their workaday jobs, they run the Heaven's Gate website and distribute videos and books to anyone who's curious. Mark answers emails. Once a week, he'll get an enquiry about whether it's too late to join the rest of the class in space by committing suicide. 'We tell them! We say the class is over . . . The best thing to be is good for the rest of your life and always strive to be closer to God.'

I was impressed with how thoughtful and considerate Mark and Sarah were. Mark spoke eloquently about how hard it was to weather the onslaught of media coverage: 'That very rough one-to-two-week period when the public was saying "Please! Explain this to us! Make them *less* so that we can go on with our lives!" You know? "Ridicule them! Do something with them!"'

Later, reading over a transcript of my conversation with them, I was struck by a passage where Mark talked about Oscody's 'exit' and how it was to break the news to Rio:

> M: Rio and I for some reason hadn't talked for a long time and it never came up and he went kind of like real sad: 'Really?' I said, 'I thought I told you.' . . . And he understood the context. He understood what it meant.
>
> L: Why was he sad?
>
> M: No, he wasn't sad.
>
> L: Oh, I thought you just said he was sad.
>
> M: No, he wasn't sad.
>
> L: What did you say?
>
> M: He was like surprised. Like, [brightly] 'Really? I didn't know that.' And so I explained the context and the circumstances. And he said, it was a very noble thing. [voice breaking]

# MARSHALL SYLVER

Looking around the crowd that was gathering outside the conference room at the Golden Nugget hotel casino, it was hard to believe they were all there to see Marshall Sylver.

He'd endured a high-profile trial for fraud, numerous lawsuits, a scalding magazine exposé – enough disgrace, you would think, to derail the career of a supposed success coach. But still they came, young, old, all races, maybe two hundred or more, hoping to learn the secrets of Passion, Profit and Power, at the knee of the master.

I'd made a documentary about him five years earlier. Now I was back, hoping to catch him unawares at his seminar, the guest of one Gene Puffer. As a repeat student, in theory Gene could get himself and a friend in for free. It had crossed my mind to pay for the seminar, but Dena, the friendly woman on the phone at Sylver HQ, had told me it cost $1,495.

Right now, Gene was downstairs getting a coffee. He said he might get thrown out if he was spotted by anyone on Marshall's staff. Gene had been among several ex-Sylverites that had testified against Marshall and there was bad blood. Dena had asked me to confirm his name when I'd called, to make sure he qualified as a 'reattend'.

'I'll call back,' I said. There was a chance that if his name were entered into Dena's computer, sirens would sound and flashing red lights go off throughout the building.

The idea of seeing Marshall again had been making me anxious for a month, even infiltrating my subconscious. A few weeks earlier, having arrived back in Vegas, and realizing a surprise visit to his seminar was my only hope of contact, I'd had a dream in which he physically threw me out of his class, dragging me along by the arm as I fired questions. He looked different in my imagination. Instead of slicked-back hair and suit, he had a blazer-cut leather jacket and his hair was fashionably tousled.

I was surprised by the strength of my animus against Marshall, but the truth is I'd never really warmed to him. In 2000, I'd attended a couple of his events, and even then I'd been troubled by the high-pressure sales practices. In the years afterwards, the Millionaire Mentorship Program had attracted so many complaints that the State of Nevada ended up prosecuting him for fraud. Among the details that came out: the so-called 'elite course' available only to 'qualified pre-interviewed students' had signed up a mentally handicapped man, offered money-back guarantees which it refused to honour under any circumstances, and employed a near-destitute 'millionaire mentor' who moved in with one of his 'students,' then made off with his car and $10,000.

Two months before the seminar, in July, I'd spent several days at the county clerk's office in downtown Las Vegas, reading the transcripts of case C19/451, the State of Nevada vs M. Sylwestrzak. Among the details were the names of two witnesses who testified against Marshall: Art Eagle and Gene Puffer. Both were graduates of the

Millionaire Mentorship Program, a ten-week get-rich-quick scheme. Three and a half days learning 'wealth creation', followed by ten weeks of daily calls from one of Marshall's elite cadre of 'millionaire mentors'. If you didn't double your money, you got a full refund. It sounded too good to be true, and it was.

I met up with Gene and Art at a gourmet coffee chain. Gene was tall, with a moustache, and a chunky technical watch. An out of work airline pilot, he was doing substitute teaching to pay the bills. Art was a struggling entrepreneur, paunchy, with thinning hair. He was wearing a short-sleeved shirt and tie and a dainty, thin watch. He was the picture of a downtrodden salesman. He told me his story.

❈

He'd been an actual millionaire at one time, he said, with $5,000,000 in his bank account. He was vague about where the money had come from. For a while, he'd had it in a bank account in Grenada, where he was getting insane rates of return, 40, 50 per cent. He convinced his mother and his sister to put their money in the same bank. But there were problems with the withdrawals. Then the head of the bank fled to Uganda. Art and his family lost everything.

He heard Marshall's commercial on Christian radio. Learn the skills necessary to become a millionaire. It mentioned a 'mixer', a social event where you could learn more, taking place at Marshall's 'mansion'. Art was intrigued.

The mansion turned out be a conference room at a hotel, but Art liked what he heard. His only concern was that he might not have what it took to make it in the Program. 'I need to believe that I can help you,' Marshall said in his leaflet. Art was a slow reader and writer since suffering a brain injury as a teenager.

He approached Marshall. 'I told him a little about my personal situation. I have a couple of hindrances that sometimes put me behind other people a little bit. He said don't worry about it, you're going to do fine, and that's why we have this guarantee.' Reassured, he signed up. He put the course on his credit card. A total of $6,600.

The classes in 'wealth creation' came first. They role-played, pretending to speak and act like millionaires. They were told to pick an 'income vehicle'. They could sign up under Marshall as part of a 'network marketing company' – something like a pyramid scheme – or they could come up with their own idea. Art was so impressed he decided he wanted to work for Marshall himself.

Marshall told Art he'd need to sign up for another course. Art plonked down another $5,000 for a place at 'Mentorship University'. Marshall told Art he'd need to see a résumé, too. Art took him at his word. If he wanted a résumé, he'd get one, but not any old résumé. He'd get the *à la recherche du temps perdu* of résumés, an obsessive, painstaking work of art, a love letter of sorts. He began spending up to six hours a day on his computer polishing it, adding subsections, logos, fonts. When finished, it ran to 133 pages, complete with a table of contents, an introduction and a conclusion. Meanwhile, he was volunteering his time to Marshall's company, doing odd jobs like helping to clear up after seminars.

In the time left over, Art did his assignments for the Millionaire Mentorship Program. But he was struggling with some of the definitions in his workbook for the Program. He kept a journal of his progress which, in its confused good faith, reads like satire: 'Week 4: VISION TRAINING. Subjects such as "Focus on Focus" and "Potentializing" are mentioned in the Week 4 section, but for the most part I don't know what they exactly mean . . . I tried to figure out what "Future Pacing" was and do some Vision Training for that.'

Art needed help from his 'millionaire mentor', Mark Connolly. Mark had claimed to be a millionaire. But he was elusive. He was late with his calls. 'I found out later it was because he had no phone and no car,' Art said. Halfway through his mentorship, having invested about $12,000 in Marshall's seminars, Art became desperate for money. He was still holding out for a job with Marshall. Mark Connolly was fired as a mentor. A man called Michael Yee took over. 'And that's when Michael Yee told me, No, you're not going to work with Marshall or anything.' Art discovered that, according to the small print of a personal release for an outward-bound self-esteem-building event for the Mentorship University, he'd also waived any guarantee of being hired.

'Michael Yee's advice was essentially, Well, go get a minimum-wage job! Just get some work! And I thought, I don't need to pay $6,000 for someone to tell me to get a minimum-wage job.' So Art pursued his dream of running his own business seminars, called 'Biz-Masters'.

Towards the end of the Program, Art got a call from Mark Connolly. 'He said, "We're working on these ideas together, Art, do you mind if I come over and stay at your place, and that'll give us some close proximity while we work?" So he moved in with me and began sleeping on the floor. I didn't know at that time that he didn't have a vehicle, and I had a Mercedes Benz that I was letting him use.

'Even though he was only going to stay a couple of weeks, he ended up staying a couple of months. I was carrying his food and rent and everything, so it was draining me pretty heavily. I didn't realize he'd worked as a male prostitute, and one of his old tricks, a lady, had come into town and wanted to meet up, and he said, "Can I borrow your car?" I thought it was a regular date, and he just never came back.' In addition to the car, Mark made off with $10,000 Art had raised on his credit card.

'And this was supposed to be his mentor!' Gene said.

Shortly after completing the Millionaire Mentorship Program, Art lost his apartment and had his other car (the one that hadn't been stolen by his former mentor) repossessed. His credit by now was ruined, too. Until he made some of his money back, he said he felt he couldn't go back to Texas and see his family. 'I'd like to be at least somewhere on the rebound.'

He'd brought his 133-page résumé in a white ring binder. It had a logo on the front and it said: 'You need The Eagle now!' He was still out of work.

*

My own experience of Marshall began in 1995. I was up late channel-surfing, in Hawaii for my dad's wedding. 'If you're watching this infomercial you're probably not where you want to be,' Marshall said. There was something not quite human about his delivery. Every gesture and inflection seemed practised. He explained that the mind is like a tape recorder, and that by using the power of hypnosis you can change your mental cassette, become a new person. It wasn't so implausible when Marshall himself seemed half machine. He was selling a set of tapes to help people take control of their lives. His technique was called 'subconscious reprogramming'.

In 2000, curious about this reprogrammer of human beings, I travelled to Las Vegas to make a documentary. I arrived at an auditorium where he was due to give a presentation. There was no sign of Marshall, so I spoke to one of his employees as he helped set up. The employee was Michael Yee, the young man who would later become Art's mentor.

As we talked, I saw Marshall walk past. He strode purposefully. His hair was combed back, and he was powerfully built. I expected him to come up and say hello; he knew who we were; we were there at his invitation. But he kept walking.

I asked Michael to speak to Marshall backstage and see if I could introduce myself. Michael went off still wearing his microphone, and without meaning to, my sound recordist picked up the conversation through his headphones.

'The BBC was wondering if they could have a minute.'

'No,' Marshall said. 'And do me a favour. It's very bad to step in on another guy's gig. I heard you talking about your other businesses. "I work for Marshall. That's what I do." Because you just made us both look like idiots. You look like you're trying to worm in on my territory.'

Michael re-emerged looking subdued. 'Unfortunately, Marshall is in his trance session,' he said.

For the presentation, Marshall came out on stage wearing a microphone headset. 'Stand up! Make yourself feel good! If you want more money, stand up, say "Oh yeah!" If you're still seated, you're *not going to get it*! I got a question for ya! Who wants to be a millionaire? What if I told you exactly how to become a millionaire? How many of you would be willing to do it? Okay, I got ninety-five per cent of you are *liars* . . .

'Ninety-five per cent of the population is led around by their noses by the other five per cent. Ninety-five per cent of the money on this planet is controlled by five per cent. Half of all the money on the planet is controlled by one per cent of the population. Pretty scary, huh?'

As weird and controlling as he appeared behind the scenes, Marshall was masterful in front of an audience. He showed video clips of his beautiful mansion and his appearances on David Letterman. All this success could be ours, if we only did what Marshall told us to. The hallmark of the Sylver style was a mildly contradictory message: you need to do this to change your life; but you probably won't do it because you lack faith. He was both gung-ho and discouraging. The paradoxical nature of this combination was surprisingly compelling. We were like kittens being teased with string. It goes without saying that not everyone can be part of the 5 per cent; someone has to be in the 95 per cent. In fact, 95 per cent of the people do. But there we all were secretly thinking: I'm a 5 per-center! Not those others, but me! It was in exaggerated form the regnant myth of the American Dream.

'How many of you would like to programme your mind to automatically go to the gym? Put your hands up. How many of you believe that if someone else believes in you it's almost easier to believe in yourself?'

Marshall brought a woman on stage. He hypnotized her into thinking she was 'as rigid as a steel bar'; laid her, face up, between two struts; then stood on her like a plank. If he could hypnotize someone into being a plank, the thinking went, then why shouldn't he be able to hypnotize me into stopping smoking, being 'permanently slender', acquiring the habits of a multimillionaire? 'How many of you would be willing to trust me to see if together we can't make your life better and get rid of that bondage that's been holding you back?'

The atmosphere was like a church revival, but instead of rebirth through Christ, the climax of Marshall's presentation was the moment when, for a limited time, he offered discounts on his two major courses. Geed up from the presentation and the image of a woman hypnotized into being a plank, we scurried into the lobby where sales staff were standing by with credit-card machines. My fellow attendees looked for the most part to be struggling business people. They handed me their business cards which had the names of network marketing companies. 'Prepaid Legal' was one, a subscription legal service which cost twenty dollars a month. Another, 'Renaissance', taught people how to incorporate themselves as companies and save money on taxes.

When the frenzy had subsided, Marshall had sold twenty-two Millionaire Mentorship Programs at about $5,000 each, and seventy places on the Turning Point seminar for $500 each. A gross of $145,000.

'I'm so glad you're here. Welcome to Vegas,' Marshall said when I finally got to meet him backstage. He was swigging Pepsi from a bottle, still wearing his microphone headset. He had a deep melodious voice, like a DJ, and an unnerving way of holding my gaze. It's only when someone really holds your gaze that you realize how little we do it as human beings. I asked him if he was doing it on purpose.

'Well, you know what I've discovered, Louis, is that highly intelligent people are always extremely responsive. And as I speak to you and you hear the sound of my voice; as your eyelids start to close – close your eyelids . . .'

'No, Marshall, I'm going to resist being hypnotized.'

I've seen this conversation a few times on tape. At this moment, his face hardens. He really seems to think that, having waited several hours for the interview, I am just going to conk out at his bidding without asking any questions. From this point on, the conversation became more awkward. 'What was today in relation to your total programme, the Marshall Sylver system? Today represented how much?'

'A day,' Marshall said. Then we sat in silence for a few seconds.

'A day?' I said.

At the end of the conversation, Marshall said: 'You're loved. Welcome. Glad you're here! Thanks so much for having an interest.'

A few hours after telling me I was loved, I got word that Marshall had been so unimpressed with my interview that he was having second thoughts about cooperating with the documentary. The exact nature of the problem wasn't clear, or possibly I've blocked it out. I don't think it could have been lack of deference on my part; perhaps he was offended by my not being better dressed; maybe he didn't like that it was a documentary, rather than a well-lit sit-down interview. Maybe it really was my unwillingness to be hypnotized. Who knows? But he wasn't happy.

With no access to our main character, I visited Michael Yee. Though he worked for Marshall as a salesman, Michael was something closer to a disciple. His faith in Marshall was absolute. He slicked his hair back like Marshall. He said he'd spent tens of thousands of dollars on Marshall's seminars. He used to be an introvert; through Marshall's system he'd created a whole new personality for himself. Confident. Outgoing. Successful. And, it has to be said, a little robotic. Marshall wasn't running a business. It was a 'moral mission,' he said. 'People helping people. Money just comes naturally.'

Michael lived in a house in a pristine new development rolled out like carpet on the south side of Las Vegas. Upstairs, amid his *Star Wars* memorabilia, he told me to try to lift a figurine of Yoda out of his hand. I lifted it out. 'No, I said "try to lift it."' The point was, you can't 'try' to do something that it's in your power to do. So you shouldn't 'try' to do anything. It was a word that implied possible failure. 'Do or do not, there is no try,' Michael said, quoting Yoda.

Changing one's language, as Michael explained it, was a big component of changing one's outlook. Don't say you've got a problem, say you've got a 'challenge'. Don't say you're 'fine', say you're 'awesome'. Then you'll start to feel awesome. He said he'd feel awesome even if he just found out he had cancer.

'If you just had an accident and you lost several limbs, you're bleeding profusely, how would you be doing then?'

'Awesome. I'm alive. I'm breathing. I'm doing awesome.'

He outlined his theory, learned from Marshall, that there are two types of people in the world: wolves and sheep.

'See, the sheep are all penned up. And one sheep goes to the left, they all go to the left. Well, that's the masses. Now the wolves have all the freedom. They have all the woods, they have everything out there. They can come and play when they want and leave when they want.'

'But the wolves actually eat the sheep,' I observed.

'They come and go when they want to.'

'They actually kill and eat the sheep.'

Later, one of the other salesmen suggested I come along to Marshall's thirty-eighth birthday party as a way of getting back in his good books. I bought him a cigar trimmer, trailed after him during a tour of his palatial home, marvelling dutifully at his collection of historic magic posters. I concentrated on not speaking too much, nervous that anything I said might queer the deal. But the next day I found myself back on for the Turning Point Seminar.

\*

There were about sixty of us at the seminar: working people, a range of ages. Fairly typical was Mark, a hotel custodian, who wanted to get married but felt he lacked money to support a wife. His confidence was holding him back. 'What has attacked your self-esteem so much?' Marshall asked him in front of the class. 'What is it that brings the tears up inside of your heart? What is it that makes you emotional right now? Almost feeling that you can't be real in front of people that love ya?' Marshall seemed intent on trying to make Mark cry. 'One of the things I want you to get, Mark, is that you *are* a multimillionaire. How would a multimillionaire address another multimillionaire? How would a multimillionaire look at another multimillionaire?

**The Call of the Weird**

. . . A multimillionaire does not look down when he speaks to another multimillionaire. A multimillionaire smiles, holds himself open.'

The main message of the class was to have faith in Marshall. Unless we believed in him and followed his instructions, he wouldn't be able to help us become millionaires. He told us to stand up and turn around when he snapped his fingers. It felt pretty silly. It also felt a lot more like being a sheep than a wolf. Wasn't there a bit of a contradiction in Marshall's assertion that we could become wolves if we just did as he said? 'Even if you think we're only telling you to do it for our personal gain, how many of you are willing to trust us and follow through and do what we tell you to do? Put your hand up nice and high.'

I wasn't sure what to do. On one hand, having just been to his house the day before and cosied up to him, it felt rude not to stand up and twirl around, or put my hand up when he asked if we trusted him. But then, I *didn't* trust him. I kept my hand down.

We role-played with partners, pretending they were our parents. We took turns saying: 'Father, I have something I want to release,' and sharing intimate details of our lives. Volunteers walked up and down with boxes of Kleenex. We lined up and ate fire. Emotions ran high and it felt churlish to begrudge the forum that had allowed people to experience something; but I felt goaded and coaxed and I didn't like it.

The biggest trust we could put in Marshall was to splash $5,000 on a place in the Millionaire Mentorship Program.

At the end of the class, I approached Marshall. I still felt cowed and influenced from eight hours of turning in circles and being exhorted to be positive, to believe in Marshall and his system. I was hemmed in by politesse. It felt somehow destructive to voice dissent. I said that I'd seen real emotion among the participants, but that I wondered if the commitment lasted with people. Marshall mentioned the Millionaire Mentorship Program and the daily calls designed to hold students to their commitment. I asked Marshall how many millionaires he'd created.

'I've got ten that I've created right now. I've got a plan to create a hundred over the course of the next four or five years. But I think we're going to be way ahead of that, actually.'

'I may have an unhealthy sceptical mind, but it would help me if you could bring out some of the millionaires onstage for testimonials. Is that something you've thought about doing?'

'Yeah, we have.'

Pause.

'So why don't you do it?'

'Because the sceptics won't do the programme anyway . . . What you can do, Louis, is let go of the scepticism. It doesn't serve you. You're not being helped by it.'

I was running out of questions, and didn't feel I was getting anywhere.

'Does the Millionaire Mentorship Program really work?'

'No,' Marshall said, sharply. 'Not for you. It would never work for you. Because you have to have the faith of a mustard seed and you have none.'

Not long after I left, the investigation started.

*

First came the Attorney General's raid on Marshall's house. Then the following year, an exposé on Marshall appeared in *Las Vegas Life* magazine. Among the revelations: he'd served six months in a federal prison for counterfeiting fifty-dollar bills; part of the sentencing had been four years in drug rehab; in 1990 he was convicted of misdemeanour battery for assaulting a police officer; he was being sued for sexual harassment by a former employee, a one-time model, who said Marshall had told her she had a 'luscious butt' and claimed he could give her a one-hour orgasm, among other lewd comments; he was being sued by several casinos for unpaid gambling debts. The man who'd 'subconsciously reprogrammed' himself as an Übermensch of discipline and focus was bouncing $20,000 cheques at the Luxor.

The state's prosecution began in December 2003. The trial was for nine counts of theft by obtaining money on false pretences.

Marshall was represented by Dominic Gentile, a high-powered criminal defence lawyer, described in a profile in the *New York Times* as 'the devil's own advocate'. In the eighties, he'd specialized in defending cocaine dealers. Possibly on Gentile's advice, Marshall opted not to take the stand. The responsibility of testifying on behalf of the Sylver System fell instead on the shoulders of Michael Yee, now no longer working for Marshall, but still every inch the believer. In fact, the Sylver trial became a de facto trial of Michael Yee's 'subconsciously reprogrammed' personality: his blithe assertion that success is a state of mind and that to admit that there might be other factors involved is automatically self-sabotaging.

The trial hinged on the Millionaire Mentorship Program

specifically Marshall's failure to make good on his money-back guarantees. Marshall's defence was that his money-back guarantee was conditional on the students having completed 'all assignments and daily commitments'. And the disgruntled graduates hadn't done that. They hadn't chosen the right 'income vehicle'. Or they'd missed one of their mentor's phone calls. The reasons varied, but there was always a reason.

In his testimony, Michael resorted to cheese-paring answers. He said the programme wasn't really about making money but about 'the four cornerstones of well-being'.

The prosecution asked Michael about Mark Connolly sleeping on Art's floor.

*Prosecution:* Would that suggest a financial problem to you?

*Michael:* It may, it may not. People become friends. People stay at their friends' for whatever reason.

*Prosecution:* Okay, would that indicate a problem with success?

*Michael:* I might be hurting for money right now. It doesn't mean I'm not successful.

*Prosecution:* Are you a millionaire?

*Michael:* The Program wasn't designed for get rich quick. It's not.

*Prosecution:* Are you a millionaire?

*Michael:* No. That doesn't mean I won't be one.

*Prosecution:* What are you doing for work right now?

*Michael:* What am I doing for work?

*Prosecution:* Yeah.

*Michael:* I work at Towbin Dodge.

*Prosecution:* And what do you do there?

*Michael:* I sell cars.

*Prosecution:* Okay. Thank you, sir.

Talking about losing money in a business venture, Michael struck up a greatest hits medley of self-empowerment clichés: 'You've got to eat chicken while you're hunting elephants, and go back to the drawing board, but just because I've had a bad meal doesn't mean I'm going to quit eating.' He put dissatisfaction with the course down to a small group of agitators whose belief wasn't strong enough. 'During that time frame, we had disgruntled individuals that were interrupting many of our seminars and, in effect, were affecting what other people were thinking . . . Everybody was thinking and talking and being together with people. Just the number and the volume of people requesting refunds came from a small cell of individuals that was collaborating and growing.'

The truth, in Michael's world as in Marshall's, was that there was no reason ever to refund any money. The Program worked. Therefore failure to make money on the Program was ipso facto evidence of 'failure to complete the assignments'.

In his summing up, the prosecutor said of Michael: 'He's clearly a Marshall Sylver follower to this day. He recites Marshall Sylver speak as well as anybody and whether he knows it or not, he's indoctrinated. He still is.' He reminded jurors that Michael Yee could not say whether a single one of his students had doubled their money. 'Marshall Sylver is a professional seminar dealer. That's what he does. He sells no actual goods through his programmes other than the seminars themselves and some of these multi-level marketing memberships that fall below it.'

Marshall's attorney pointed out that the Program was still running. He said the promotional brochure which listed the money-back guarantee was no longer being used, 'as a result of some problems that some people were having understanding' it. The crux of his argument was that Marshall had operated 'in good faith', and therefore he could not have had an 'intent to defraud'. He mentioned Art's résumé. 'Which I'm sure anybody who is an employer is just going to be thrilled to receive, okay? 'Cause God knows if you're a successful businessman you got nothing but time, okay, to read a hundred and thirty-three-page résumé.'

It ended, after three weeks, in a mistrial. The jury was deadlocked – on some counts ten to two, on some nine to three. The prosecutors said they intended to retry the case.

✳

Back in Vegas, and having finished reading the trial transcripts, I called Michael. He wasn't listed in the phone book, so I tried him at Towbin Dodge. I was put straight through. I reminded him who I was; asked if he could spare any time to catch up. He sounded surprised to hear from me.

'How did you get my number?'

'From the trial transcripts.'

'Hmmm, this week's real busy. And this weekend's not good. I got a birthday on Saturday and a wedding on Sunday.'

I could feel I was being brushed off. 'What about next week?'

'Well, you could try me early next week.'

'Great, shall we say Monday lunchtime?'

'Better if you just call me on Monday so I can see how I'm fixed.'

At the end, he said, 'Not a challenge, bro!' But the signs weren't good.

Killing time, I spent a morning with Art, drinking expensive coffees at the same popular gourmet coffee chain. He was wearing a green Hawaiian shirt, and shorts with pale chunky legs sticking out of them. He had a folder of material from Marshall, including a photo, seemingly mocked-up, of Marshall standing on a woman whom he'd hypnotized into believing she was a plank, a steaming mug of coffee in his hand.

'That woman there, I knew her. She was kind of a groupie for Marshall,' Art said. 'I was a little like a groupie for a while, I guess you could say. Because I wanted to work for him. He was doing a show in Salt Lake, so I drove all the way to Salt Lake just to see the show' – more than 400 miles – 'because I had never seen one of his hypnosis shows before . . . I was surprised. I thought hypnosis was like putting someone into a trance.' Art closed his eyes and put his arms out like a zombie. 'And they kinda follow you around, but basically all it is is just suggestion. Some people are open to it and they do it, and you tell them to quack like a duck, and they do it just 'cause you suggested it, I guess.'

I asked about his injury. He said he'd run his car into a telephone pole at low speed, fifteen miles an hour or so, aged sixteen or seventeen. He didn't realize it but he had an abscess on his brain. Three days later he lost his sight, and the ability to walk, talk, read and write. 'I was president of the class, captain of the football team. I'd been nominated for class favourite. I was real thin, no acne, full head of hair. When I got out of hospital, I had to start over with Dick and Jane books. Great big pencils and the paper with wide lines. They had to give me steroids to heal the brain damage and the steroids gave me acne and hair loss and changed my whole metabolism.

'Did you see the magazine article about Marshall?' Art asked. 'He was convicted of counterfeiting money.'

'It said something about sexual harassment, too,' I said. 'He told a woman who worked for him he could give her a one-hour orgasm.'

'That's a little sad,' Art said. 'Having to resort to cheesy lines like that.'

He thought he might have Michael Yee's address on a card at home, so we climbed in his beaten-up 1989 Plymouth Sundance with 125,000 miles on it and no AC and drove to his rented room. His two-storey apartment complex was built round a shady courtyard with a swimming pool. Pale beige stucco with brown trim, mildewed and warped. Run-down but pleasant. Art's room was cluttered with folders and tapes and books, all about succeeding at business. *Successful Selling. You Can Choose to be Rich. Millionaire Mindset. Superstar Selling* by Bob and Zonnya Harrington – six audio cassettes. 'I got that one at the Salvation Army for two dollars. I'm gathering stuff like that for Biz-Masters.' His dream was still to run seminars helping people with business and finance.

There was no sign of Michael's address. On the way out, Art pointed up to a towering brown mirror-building, the latest shiny megaresort, with three cranes on top, still incomplete. 'That's Steve Wynn's new hotel,' Art said. 'It's the most expensive hotel in the world, so they say. That's why I like this town. There's a lot of things happening. A lot of industry. It's visionary.'

*

I wrote Michael Yee a letter. Under the influence of a leaflet Marshall had written to promote the Millionaire Mentorship Program, I struck a similar overheated tone, using words like 'challenge' and 'adventure' and lots of exclamation marks. A few days later, having heard nothing back, I drove out to the car dealership where he worked, on a horrible little stretch of road called Auto Showroom Drive. The receptionist paged him: 'Michael, your friend Louis is here to see you.'

He was eating lunch, he said, but wouldn't mind chatting while he ate. We went back to his office, which he shares with two other salesmen, both of them, like him, wearing name tags and company shirts. I sat in front of his desk and he sat behind it and he ate his two beef tacos out of a folding polystyrene container.

'If you think about it, if one person can take a system and it works, then is the system working? Sure! The question is: are people working the system? If one person climbs Mount Everest, everybody can, if they do the exact same thing.'

'You don't think there are people who aren't capable of doing it?'

'If you put your mind to it, you can do anything you want.'

Since I'd seen him, he'd helped to launch a network marketing company. 'Our slogan was "Macy's quality at Walmart prices."' But Michael was working for free while the company was getting started and the co-founder backed out of an agreement to pay him for his work. Eventually, Michael ran out of money. He put his things in storage and drove back to Vegas late the previous year. 'I had nine hundred dollars and everything I could get in my car.'

Michael had seen Marshall the previous day. 'We talk maybe once a month. He's not somebody I go out and socialize with on a daily or weekly basis.'

'Do you think Marshall takes advantage of people?'

Michael paused. 'What's your definition of taking advantage?'

'Just by your standard.'

Michael paused again. 'Nope. Probably does the same thing I do. He's very persuasive. Absolutely. But that's why people take the Program. To learn how to be that. This stuff does work. It is real. See, what you perceive to be true is your reality.'

Michael finished his tacos.

'I'd like to maybe see you at home,' I said.

'I don't have a challenge with that.'

❋

I called Michael a couple of times to see about visiting him at home. He'd be busy and ask me to call back, then I'd find his phone was switched off.

Weeks passed. I tried Sylver Enterprises again. 'It's a fantastic day at corporate offices, this is Donnell, how may I serve you?' I tried emailing the website.

I had lunch with Art, now down to his last $100. He'd been making up prospectuses for his latest business concepts, one for a seminar company called Wealthwerks with an 'e'. 'I wanted to register it as a domain name. Wealthworks was already taken. But the guy said in Europe they sometimes spell "werk" with an "e".' He had a treatment for a TV show about finance called 'Biz Buzz'.

I tried nudging him towards thinking about getting a job. I was becoming concerned that Art viewed me as a successful person, a good person to be around and talk ideas with, and that this faith he had in me brought with it a kind of responsibility – a responsibility I wasn't sure how to discharge. We went to a sandwich shop. I ordered a veggie sub. 'I'll get that, too,' Art said. 'That sounds good.' I was his new millionaire mentor.

By now I'd resigned myself to hearing nothing back from Marshall or his people. I asked Art if he would chaperone me, as a former attendee, to one of Marshall's events. He declined. So the morning of the seminar, one Saturday in September, I met for coffee with Gene Puffer. We were in downtown Vegas, on the ground floor of the Golden Nugget hotel casino.

Gene had brought another disgruntled Sylver graduate. Daniel Braisted was forty-five or so, clean shaven, wearing a short-sleeved shirt and glasses. 'Marshall's a brilliant man. He's achieved a lot, and he didn't do what he said he was going to do . . . He sends me an email inviting me whenever he's speaking here in Vegas, and then when I show up he throws me out.' Now Daniel was working for a company founded by a controversial heath guru, Dr Robert O. Young. 'He believes there's only one disease in the world. Overacidity of the body.'

'What, even causing things like autism?' I asked.

'Yeah! I've seen the blood!'

'Is it network marketing?'

'It has to be that, because that's the only way to explain it. And *he's* international. He'd be great for your book. For me, I don't see the interest in Marshall. He overstepped himself, he promised something he couldn't deliver. I thought the mentors would be successful people. Instead they were just caring people who were willing to make a few calls every day for three hundred dollars a week. I still respect him.'

'Why?'

'Because he's *good*.'

'Good at *what*?'

'He knows how to present. He's a good presenter. At Turning Point, there are people who make major break-throughs. They eat fire! I ate fire! . . . The challenge I have is when people overextend themselves. But Marshall has people who did the same seminar I did and they *love* him.'

'*Who* is he *helping*?' I said, surprising myself with my own ardour. 'He hasn't helped *anyone*!'

I was irritated with Daniel. Here he was taking Marshall's side, and he was the one who'd lost out.

At eight thirty, I walked up to the conference room where the seminar was being held. Daniel didn't want to come up, scared, I think. Gene said he'd come up at five to nine. He thought he'd be thrown out as soon as he was spotted.

*

'Good morning! Welcome back!' a camp little attendant said. 'You're in for an exciting day.'

A long line snaked round the registration room. Everyone was wearing name tags. There was an atmosphere of excited anticipation, and so many people it seemed safe for Gene to come up. I paged him.

'Do you recognize anyone?' I asked.

He looked around. 'No.'

We went up to the desk, and just like that we were signed up: a 'reattend' and his guest. By coincidence, it was Dena that took our names, the same young woman I had spoken to on the phone. I couldn't quite believe it. We were in.

We signed release forms promising to keep confidential

anything that happened during the session and indemnifying Marshall against lawsuits for accidents during the fire-eating or whatever it was. Another volunteer made up name tags for us. Gene and I walked to the back of another line, this one for people waiting to go into the conference room. Now I was in, I had a weird feeling of disappointment. Two days in a Marshall Sylver seminar! Gene needed the men's room.

'Gene!' It was Dena, walking out from the registration area, looking agitated. 'You will not be able to reattend. I need your name tags back.'

'May I ask why?' Gene said.

'You know why.' And as easily as it had arrived, our opportunity turned on its heels and left.

We were walking towards the lifts when we saw the man himself, Marshall, striding towards us. Rock-faced. Barrel-chested. Hair, as ever, slicked back.

'Marshall,' I said. 'Could I come to the seminar?'

Without stopping, he looked at me, then at Gene, then back at me. He stiffened, as though he'd seen an apparition.

'No, you cannot. Don't even come near me. I'll have security throw you out.'

'Could I grab an interview with you?'

He was disappearing up the corridor. Without slowing down, he said again, in the same tone of voice, 'Don't even come near me. I'll have security throw you out.'

It made a change from, 'You're loved.'

＊

Deflated, Gene and I traipsed back to the coffee shop. Gene queued up for coffee, I jotted down some notes from the encounter. Gene came over, having decided he'd had enough coffee. Then he changed his mind again, and joined the back of the line.

We drove round to see Art. After moving apartments several times, he was staying with a friend, paying nominal rent. He had the top half of a huge airy New York-style loft on the far western perimeter of Las Vegas where the city literally runs out into desert.

Art and his landlady Liz were eating sausage and egg McMuffins. I told them about the run-in with Marshall. Art didn't seem too interested. To his credit, I suppose, he regarded Marshall and the Millionaire Mentorship Program as old news. We chatted a little about George Bush, whom they were both supporting in the election. Art said he was training as a tech support guy for DirecTV, a cable company.

'You've really landed on your feet, Art,' I said.

Later, I reproached myself for not being smarter in my approach to Marshall. I wondered what would have happened if I'd gone in with someone who wasn't blacklisted. I would have got into the seminar and then what? Well, probably some underling would have asked me to leave during the lunch break. The truth was, he was never going to sit down and speak to me. He never granted interviews these days, especially not to reporters who had made doubting documentaries about him. But still, I felt a little ashamed that I hadn't made more of an effort to at least appear impartial.

On rereading my notes, I understood more about how Marshall worked. The main commodity he was selling was belief. Believe you can do it. Believe Marshall can help you. That was the first prerequisite of success. But you couldn't go through the motions. You had to be sincere. And they were sincere, the seminar attendees. And having once believed, even though many of them didn't double their money, it was hard for them to recant their belief. They couldn't retract their sincerity. Having committed so much time and money, it would have felt foolish, and disloyal. It was a much-magnified version of the hemmed-in feeling I'd had at the Turning Point seminar. This was the corner-stone of Marshall's success. People were paying to be indoctrinated in 'success', but he was also training them to love him.

One day, a possible interpretation of my dream came to me, the dream in which Marshall's hair was tousled and he wore a leather jacket and he'd dragged me out of the seminar. He was dressed that way *because that was how I dressed*. My subconscious was warning me that Marshall and I were more alike than I realized. Like Marshall, I influenced people, I practised forms of journalistic persua-sion, ultimately for my own ends. By what right could I rule that Marshall's techniques were exploitative? It was like passing judgment on a love affair.

Months passed, and I heard nothing about the promised retrial. The prosecutor who'd brought the original case moved to a different department. Then in December the case was closed. Sylver Enterprises Inc. pleaded guilty to one count of deceptive trade practices. A misdemeanour. The court imposed restitution of $11,882.69 and a fine of one dollar.

When I watch the documentary about Marshall now, the moment that strikes me isn't Marshall's anger with Michael, but what happens next. Michael's called back in to see Marshall and we hear Marshall's voice again, recorded by my sound recordist.

'Please forgive me for kinda biting your head off just now,' Marshall says. 'I grabbed you and I just thought about that and my heart was heavy. That wasn't handled well. I love you.'

'I love you, too,' Michael says. 'I'm here to support and – I'm learning!'

'Okay! Back again!' Michael says when he reappears, beaming from ear to ear, like a fool in love. 'Everything's fine! We're going to have some fun!'

# APRIL, LAMB AND LYNX

It was mid October, and I was riding through the hot, flat farmland of California's San Joaquin Valley, on a family outing. At the wheel of my car was April Gaede. April is in her late thirties and she has light brown hair. She grew up on a ranch and she looks a healthy, outdoorsy type of person. Sitting in the back were Lamb and Lynx, April's twelve-year-old twins, pixie-faced little girls with blonde hair and blue eyes.

April was telling me about the twins' debut CD which they had finished recording a few months earlier.

'We've been making sure there are no National Socialist emblems on it so it can be sold in Germany,' April said. 'It's okay to have the word "Aryan", which is good because one of the song titles has Aryan in it. "Aryan Man, Awake". But, like, we won't have pictures of Grandpa's [swastika] cattle brand in there. And then there's a really cute picture of Lamb and Lynx saluting. We'll take that out.'

'Sieg-Heiling?'

'*Saluting.* "Sieg Heil" is what you say. Saluting. It's a Roman salute.'

The name of the twin's band is Prussian Blue. A folk band, but no ordinary folk band, Prussian Blue specialize in White Power music. They play a repertoire of cover versions of songs by skinhead groups, some traditional German songs, including the 'Panzerlied' (the anthem of the German panzers), and a few original compositions by Lamb, 'Aryan Man, Awake' being one of them, another called 'Skinhead Boy'.

I'd spent several days filming April and the twins the previous year and been struck by the intensity of April's beliefs and her readiness to recruit her daughters into the cause. In the months afterwards, I'd stayed in touch with the family, curious how the girls were growing up, how fully they were absorbing their mother's message, and how they were enjoying their growing status as White Power celebrities. I was also keen to meet the newest addition to the Gaede clan, little Dresden, named in honour of the city in Germany that was firebombed by the Allies during the Second World War.

Earlier in the day, on the way back from the restaurant where we'd had lunch, I'd asked about Dresden.

'It's not like we named her Aryana or something,' April said. 'To me that would be more extreme.'

'Yeah, but at least Aryana is a name,' I said.

'Well, Dresden's a name. What about Paris? Paris Hilton?'

'If someone says, "Oh, that's an interesting name," what do you say?'

'I say it's a city in Germany. And then they'll say, "Oh, okay. And you've been there?" And I'll say, "No, they make fine china and porcelain and stuff." And we'll leave it at that. Unless I'm in a particularly ornery mood and then I'll say, "It's where the real holocaust happened."'

Naming a baby Dresden was a little weird even to some

The Call of the Weird

other members of the white racist community. 'It would be kind of the same thing if I had named one of my sons Adolf,' one concerned fellow racist had posted on a White Power discussion forum. 'All young people – and especially girls – want nothing so much as to fit in and be accepted by their peers and friends . . . I worry that something like that could have the opposite effect and make her reject your beliefs, simply because they had been thrust without question upon her so completely in the form of her own name.'

'I don't think it carries anywhere near the load that "Adolf" does,' April had replied, 'though I wouldn't mind naming a son that either. My husband said no when I suggested it for a boy and we settled on Wolfgang.'

***

My road back into their lives had not been easy. I'd called after I touched down in Vegas, months earlier. I'd called again in July, after I'd been to the Aryan Nations World Congress. But April had taken issue with aspects of the finished documentary. It had bothered her when I asked if she ever considered going into therapy to help overcome her powerful racial antipathies. 'I had several emails from people in Britain saying they would kick your ass if they saw you because of that remark. They thought that was waaaay out of line.' She'd seen discussion on the Internet to the effect that social services should intervene and take the kids away from her. Not surprisingly, this had given her pause.

In September, I'd spent several days trying to negotiate my way into a 'Pro-White' festival which April and the twins were attending, and where Prussian Blue were due to perform. It was called Folk the System. The website promised 'a variety of folk-building and cameraderie-enhancing activities.' Sack races, axe-throwing, and caber-tossing were mentioned.

I wondered what a 'Pro-White' festival might look like. I couldn't help admiring the quirky idealism of taking a creed linked in most people's mind with hate and trying to make it the basis for light-hearted social intercourse.

But April had not been won over by my numerous pleas and phone calls. Folk the System had come and gone and I'd more or less given up hope of seeing April and the twins again. My suggestion, via email, of an outing to a theme park had been a last throw of the dice. April said she would think about it, but I was not optimistic. I told myself that her unwillingness to expose the twins to further publicity was a good thing. I'd always felt the twins were too young to be held responsible for ideas their mother had imposed on them. Though I was keen to see how they were changing, it was more important that they should have their anonymity. As a journalist, I was no less a symptom of their being used for the ends of White Power than any of their other media activities. Better that they should be allowed to lead a normal life.

I settled into an apartment in Hollywood and began writing up my notes from the other re-encounters from the trip. And then, having resigned myself to not seeing them, I received a message from April saying she liked my idea of an outing. She had a place in mind. A Halloween theme park. I wasn't clear on the details but it took place every October, with a large cast of ghosts and ghouls. Whatever twinges of conscience I had suddenly evaporated in the heat of opportunity. I bought Lamb and Lynx a couple of small Halloween gifts and drove up from Los Angeles one Saturday morning.

*

I'd first met April at a skinhead music festival in Riverside County, southern California. The event was called the Gathering of the Gods and featured six or seven 'hatecore' groups. Brutal Attack, Final War and Extreme Hatred were all on the bill. There were maybe 300 skinheads in attendance, dressed mostly in white vests, with tattoos. I'd hoped I might be able to interview one or two of the skinheads and I gamely tried to engage them in conversation. 'Hi, are you media-friendly?' I would ask. The reaction was not favourable. 'What's the point?' asked one. 'You'll just kike it up.'

Myself, my director Stuart (who is Jewish) and our two-man crew, had consulted with a pair of 'security experts' from Pinkertons earlier in the day. The experts had explained that the skinheads would probably be members of the Aryan Brotherhood, a prison gang that would think nothing of attacking a couple of supposed 'Jew journalists'. Unfortunately, the experts from Pinkertons couldn't come with us into the event – that would have meant giving up their weapons at the gate, which they refused to do. They remained in a van down the block from the festival. In the meantime, we were to stay alert at all times and make sure we had a clear route to the exit.

As a result, the whole time I was at the festival I was in a state of anxiety, afraid one of the skinheads might try to 'Jew-bash' me, looking about, like a driving-test candidate checking his mirrors. At first I didn't notice when Prussian Blue took the stage.

Dressed in tartan skirts and boots, the two girls played a version of 'Road to Valhalla', a ballad by the British skinhead Ian Stuart about white racists in the afterlife. They accompanied themselves on the guitar and the violin. The audience of skinheads, who until this point had been moshing and giving Nazi salutes, stood still and listened. One or two wiped tears from their eyes. The girls beamed, and Lynx did a little jig in excitement.

I approached April, not realizing she was the twins' mother, merely because, with no tattoos, and in her late thirties, she seemed one of the less intimidating people there. She said she would be happy to be in a documentary, and mentioned she was the mother of the two girls. Several days later, I drove four or five hours north to the small city in central California where they lived.

I arrived on a beautiful, cloudless day. Most of the days are beautiful and cloudless in that part of California. The only evidence of anything unusual about their house was a row of three pairs of skinhead boots by the front door, two small, one big. Had I been more observant, I might have noticed the bumper stickers on the battered white pickup truck parked in front: 'Stop Hating My Heritage', 'Member Of The Ladies Sewing Circle And Terrorist Society' and 'My Boss Is An Austrian Painter'.

The house itself was part of a new development on the outskirts of the small city where they live. It was a single-storey, stuccoed building, with a tidy little front lawn and shrubbery (April was working part-time at a garden cen-tre). April answered the door wearing jeans and a black T-shirt with 'Resistance' on it, the name of the skinhead record label which would be putting out the Prussian Blue CD. She introduced me to Lamb and Lynx.

The house was sparsely decorated. It had pale beige carpets and off-white walls and Ikea furniture made with blonde wood (even in matters of home decor April favours Nordic looks).

We agreed we might as well start with a recital, and so in the front room, Lamb and Lynx sang an a cappella version of a song by the British skinhead group Skrewdriver:

> I wanna tell you 'bout South Africa
> And the so-called fight for freedom
> The much-praised black resistance
> And the communists who lead them . . .
> Strikeforce! White survival!
> Strikeforce! Yeah!
> Strikeforce! Gonna kill our rivals!
> Strikeforce! Into the Devil's lair!

Each time they said 'strikeforce' the girls gave a Nazi salute. When the song ended, I clapped, a little uncertainly.

'They don't seem old enough to really know what that's about,' I said.

'Well, I've explained it to them,' April said. 'What's the ANC?'

'It's, um, African . . .' Lamb began, 'National . . .'

'Congress,' April said. 'And what's happening in South Africa?'

'The blacks are killing whites,' Lamb said.

'And in Zimbabwe?'

'And in . . . Bim-zah-bwe,' Lamb said, and looked out of the the window.

'They seem a little young to get into politics and racial issues,' I said, adding 'maybe' when I noticed April glowering at me.

'Yeah, but they've got to start sometime,' she said.

✳

They had given their first performance aged eight, singing a White Power song called 'Ocean of Warriors' at a 'Eurofest' organized by the National Alliance, the neo-Nazi organization that April and her fiancé both belonged to.

In April's version of the story, Lamb and Lynx had wanted to go onstage and sing a White Power song, having seen a woman perform 'Tomorrow Belongs to Me' and figuring they could do just as well. The National Alliance leaders had been so impressed with the vision of the two little blonde girls singing racially charged songs, they'd offered to pay for the recording of a CD. How two little eight-year-old girls had happened to know all the words to a White Power song was another question. 'I think they learned "Ocean of Warriors" because I'd given my brother a copy and he just loved it,' April said, 'and they wanted to sing it for him.'

Lynx gave a marginally different account: 'My uncle liked it and mom suggested learning it and we were okay with it. So she wrote out the lyrics and when we were driving somewhere we'd have a little singing session.'

Either way, the band was born. The name Prussian Blue came a couple of years later. The girls read the name of the colour in a magazine, April said – 'and since their eyes are blue and my dad's side of the family are Prussian Germans they thought it would be a good name for the group. Prussian Blue is also a compound that should be present in the residue left over from Zyklon-B and which is not present – get this – *not* present at the so-called "gas chambers" in Auschwitz. It's kind of tongue-in-cheek.'

They would promote racial pride among young white teenagers, an alternative to mainstream pop music, which April views as propaganda for the Jewish-dominated Establishment. 'They're going to show how being proud of your race is something that would be very appealing to young teenage girls,' she said, as Lamb flopped over the back of the sofa and Lynx giggled. 'Especially as they get a little bit older. I mean what red-blooded American boy isn't going to find two blonde twins, sixteen years old, singing about pride in your race . . . very few of them are not going to find that very appealing.'

The girls did not go to school. April educated them herself at home, according to a syllabus of her own devising. She used text books from the fifties. In her study, April showed me an ABC book she was working on for toddlers, entitled *A is for Aryan*. 'Every letter has a word that is important to the white race or represents the white race,' she said. 'So B is for blood, C is for creativity, D is for dixie, E is for eugenic . . .' The artwork was being drawn by white prisoners, some of them incarcerated for hate crimes against non-white victims.

Lynx and Lamb were in the same room playing on the computer. I asked Lynx what she thought of April's ABC book.

'It's cool,' she said and smiled politely.

※

I spent two days with April and her daughters on that first visit. In those two days, she barely stopped talking about race. She inhabited a world in which every action was assessed according to how it would either help or hurt the cause of white nationalism.

A handful of times, I found a topic that might divert her for fifteen minutes or so into a race-neutral zone: the Beatles and Monty Python, Thomas Hardy (*The Mayor of Casterbridge* and *The Return of the Native* are her favourite books). The rest of the time, April was a one-woman White Power radio station, finding a racist dimension in the most innocent topics: *The Lord of the Rings* ('For me, it was totally racial'), *Young Frankenstein* ('by Mel what's-his-name – that Jew'), the Harry Potter films ('When the goblins in the bank came on, Lamb turned to me and said, "They look just like Jews!"'). It struck me that she is not only a racist, she is a racial fundamentalist.

April said she had been racist all her life. Her parents had raised her that way – though she allowed that she'd passed through a 'brainwashed lemming' phase in her late teens and early twenties. She studied journalism in college, but dropped out and worked as a horse trainer. She only got serious about White Power politics around 2000, when her second marriage was breaking down (her first, the one that produced the twins, ended after her husband, a musician, got hooked on crack and crystal meth; now clean, he was totally supportive of her beliefs, she said). In 2001, having shopped around and compared a few different racist groups, including a visit to the Aryan Nations in Idaho, April joined the National Alliance. Since then, she had been a tireless and dedicated white activist, leafleting local schools, writing letters, recruiting any white people she thought might be sympathetic.

We spent our second morning driving up to see April's father, Bill, a farrier and cattle rancher who lives a few hours north. Bill grazes 500 head of cattle, every one of them branded with the official registered ranch brand – a swastika. I had been struggling to understand how April had become the way she is, and I was hoping Bill might provide some context.

Bill was seventy years old. He was wearing thick dark glasses, a cowboy hat and a torn Wrangler shirt. 'Right now, all the people are so politically correct that they wouldn't say shit if they had a mouth full of it,' he said, standing by his truck which had a big black swastika on the side of it. I told him I was a multiculturalist. 'Are you? When you get married, are you going to marry a white person or a nigger?'

This took me by surprise and all I said was, 'Ugh.'

'What do you usually date? Do you usually date white women?' April asked.

I paused, and sighed, and said in a small voice: 'Do Jewish women count as white?'

'No,' Bill and April said together.

'Not in our books,' Bill said.

'I think we should hope he marries some Jewess,' April said. 'Won't that be funny? A Jewish princess. She's gonna have you right *there*.'

'Twisted right down,' Bill said. Then adopting a strange high voice he said: 'Louis! I want a new ring, Louis! Flush the toilet for me, Louis! I can't push the handle down!'

Bill went some way toward explaining April. But still, for single-mindedness, she was way beyond him. 'My whole family agree with all my beliefs,' April said, 'but whereas they're just believers, I'm an activist. They're racialists. They're nationalists. But they haven't taken it to the next level.'

I wondered what it must be like for Lamb and Lynx, being exposed to April's beliefs every day. To be fair, they seemed, much of the time, charming and well adjusted. But their mother's skewed world view would occasionally peep out. 'Did you know Martin Luther King was a plagiarist and he liked to sleep with white prostitutes?' Lamb remarked on our first morning together.

Over lunch one day, Lynx told me how, though forbidden to have a Gameboy, she was allowed to play *Ethnic Cleansing*, a shoot-em-up computer game put out by the National Alliance in which a skinhead goes through a ghetto shooting blacks and Mexicans. 'They hide in bushes and they're perched on basketball hoops and they make gorilla sounds,' Lynx said. 'Ooh! Ooh! Ooh!'

Once or twice, I heard them using racial slurs – muttering 'jungle bunnies' as we passed some black people in the car. Introduced to a man from New Mexico, Lynx said, 'You don't look like a spic.'

But I also sensed a wistfulness in the twins, a desire to be like other girls – to be normal.

＊

In August 2004, a month before the conversation about Folk the System and the sack races, and despairing of ever seeing April or the twins for my 'follow-up', I made arrangements to visit the headquarters of the National Alliance in West Virginia.

Anti-racism watchdog groups say the National Alliance is now the largest neo-Nazi group in America. They put its dues-paying membership at between 800 and 1,500. Unlike the Aryan Nations, the National Alliance is secular. They don't field candidates for elections, they consider their function to 'educate the public'. Its website speaks about its goal of achieving 'White Living Space'. 'We will not be deterred by the difficulty or temporary unpleasantness involved,' it says, going on to describe the racial utopia it envisions, a place where young women will waltz, reel and jig but never 'undulate or jerk to negroid jazz or rock rhythms'. Marc Chagall is singled out for special opprobrium as a Jewish artist, along with Barry Manilow – the surreality of this pairing rather serving to undermine the supposed value of racial categories.

Oddly enough given its stand on 'rock rhythms', the National Alliance raises most of its money selling Nazi skinhead music on its label, Resistance. It also puts out a quarterly skinhead music magazine of the same name. But in its broader character, the National Alliance is at the intellectual, elitist end of the White Power spectrum. It is the Grey Poupon of hate groups. It publishes a bimonthly current affairs magazine, *National Vanguard*, and a monthly newsletter, *Free Speech*. Both contain articles on supposed Jewish world domination that are largely free of racial slurs but no less hateful for it. In a recent issue of *Free Speech*, a review of a book called *Blood Ritual* contained the line: 'Naturally, the Jews aren't the only group who have practised (and might still practice) ritual murder,' going on to mention the Carthaginians and the Aztecs. This combination of a seemingly reasonable tone with a flat-out bizarre racial message, tossed in casually in parentheses, is typical of the National Alliance.

I drove up from Mississippi, where I'd been chasing

gangsta rappers, through Tennessee, into West Virginia. The poorest state in the Union, poorer even than Mississippi, West Virginia is shaped like a stain on the map. Landlocked, bounded by rivers and mountains, it felt a little like the land that time forgot. I passed rickety old barns; elegant white shuttered houses with porches; a general store that stocked 'lye soap' and 'Amish cheese'. The countryside reminded me of England. Rolling hills and leafy trees looked down on fields and white wooden fences.

The headquarters themselves were a few miles outside the tiny town of Hillsboro, in the foothills of the Allegheny Mountains which run like a spine up the border between Virginia and West Virginia and flow into the Appalachians. I drove up a rutted dirt track, past farm buildings and a mobile home, into the woods. There was a sign saying 'No Hunting or Trespassing – Keep Out' and a small 'life rune', the logo of the NA, which looked like a capital Y with three forks. But no swastikas, no signs saying 'Whites Only' as there were at Aryan Nations.

I was met by Shaun Walker. An ex-marine and ex-skinhead and now the chief operating officer of the National Alliance, Shaun was a beefy man. He looked to be in his mid-thirties. He had a punctilious military manner. His hair was clipped at the sides. He was wearing a white shirt, button-down collar, a tie with a tie clip. He mispronounced words. President Putin was 'Pootnin'. He said 'amalgation' for 'amalgamation' and coined the word 'sheerly', a synonym of 'purely'. I might not stoop to mentioning this were the National Alliance not so fixated on notions of superiority and excellence. It seemed a failing that its personnel did not seem to fit the description of members of the master race.

Shaun took me on a tour of the headquarters, crunching up a gravel road to the 'quonset hut', a hangar-like auditorium with 200 or more seats where they hold their biannual 'leadership conferences'. The road was overhung with trees and crowded with bushes. Shaun cut an incongruous figure, deep in the wilderness, in his shirt and tie, as insects chirped loudly. He looked like some minister of a government in exile, biding his time, dreaming of the downfall of the occupying power.

'We want a white, sovereign homeland,' he said. 'We'd like to use the existing borders. If we can expand the borders, that would be okay. If it's a portion of the existing United States, that would be okay. There would be no permanent residence of non-whites. You'd have to keep interracial mating away. If they want to come as tourists, okay, that's not a problem. There's only a problem if they want to move permanently or mix racially.'

When the National Alliance founder, William Pierce, bought the acreage in West Virginia in 1984, he'd envisioned it as a kind of proto-homeland, a first step on the road to an American Reich. 'There was a prevalent idea of buying an area and selling parcels and starting a little whites-only community,' Shaun said. 'That was the original intent. But communes don't work. They never have.' By 1990, they had abandoned that idea.

We crunched up another gravel road to the warehouse for Resistance Records. Its shelves were stacked with boxes of racist CDs. Angry Aryans. Celtic Warrior. Blue-Eyed Devils.

'1993 is when the first American White Power CD was pressed,' Shaun said. 'And eleven years later, we have around seven hundred, eight hundred, so the whole thing is geometrically expanding . . . We believe we're the largest distributor.'

In a striplit back office was a store of other merchandise. Stickers saying 'Earth's Most Endangered Species – The White Race – Help Preserve It'; copies of *The Jews and Their Lies* by Martin Luther and *White Power* by George Lincoln Rockwell (the late American Nazi Party leader) alongside editions of Dickens, the Hornblower series by C. S. Forester and Seamus Heaney's translation of *Beowulf*. Two or three young men were stuffing envelopes, answering phones and filling orders. Shaun said they have eight full-time staff at the headquarters and another eight around the country.

'When are you going to put Lamb and Lynx on the cover of the magazine?' I asked.

'This month!' Shaun said. 'We're actually making their CD right now. Oh, the little kids love it. In fact, there are little kids around the country that write 'em letters and stuff.'

Shaun handed me the latest issue of *Resistance*, which showed a severe-looking Lamb and Lynx, in short tartan skirts and white shirts, leaning against a brick wall, hugging their instruments. Indeed, Lamb's skirt looked hiked up – most of her thigh was exposed – and she was almost scowling. It was hard to judge, but the overall effect was somehow a little off-key. But it was a delicate point and I wasn't sure how to broach it.

'Why aren't they smiling?'

'I don't know. April showed the twins a bunch of photos they had taken and that's the one they picked!'

'Because they're being, ah, how do you read that?'

'Uh, I read that as that's the picture April sent us! Ha ha!'

'Hmmm.'

On the way out of the warehouse, walking back towards the main office, Shaun shared his opinion of the Aryan Nations. Butler, then still alive, was a good person, he said. 'But the organization is just slap full of crackpots. And it has been infiltrated by the federal government since time immortal [sic].'

'They did seem like they were marching, uh, goose-stepping to the beat of a different drum,' I said.

'When you go and you meet people, and their media spokespeople that come to you, and if they strike you as weird or oddballs, that's *bad*. People aren't supposed to be *oddballs*.'

I felt Shaun and I were getting on quite well at this point, so I lowered my voice and confided: 'But being a Nazi is pretty weird.'

'Well, maybe. George Lincoln Rockwell was quite charming!'

'I'm speaking as someone who likes weird people,' I said, backpedalling.

'Adolf Hitler had *so much* personality and charisma.'

'I'm talking about nowadays. To be a Nazi sympathizer in this day and age. It's odd, because it goes against what so many people feel, and what I feel, which is just that we should get along with people.'

'Yeah, but the problem is, Mother Nature says other-wise. Why does "white flight" exist? Why in America has fifty per cent of the white population moved in the last forty years? Why do areas like Detroit and Camden, New

Jersey, exist? Why did all the white people leave? Biology is the reason! You can't change it! They could buy a house for ten per cent of what they paid in the white area.'

'That's what I did.'

'But most whites will not. You, I guess, get along better with them.'

※

Later, back at my motel, I read the interview with Lamb and Lynx in the new issue of *Resistance*. Maybe because they were speaking to a white racist publication the tone was different to the one they'd taken with me:

*Res:* What do you say to those people who think the only reason you are playing and singing pro-white music is because your mom pushes it on you?

*Lamb:* Our mom introduced us to racial music and she asked us if we wanted to learn an instrument . . . I don't think she pushes it on us . . .

*Lynx:* We are hooked on playing WP [White Power] music and even if our mom all of a sudden stopped being racial, we would follow through with racial music.

*Res:* What kind of music do you like? Do you have a favorite artist?

*Lamb:* I like everything except nigger music. I don't like rap, jazz, blues, or hip hop. Final War is a good example of the type of music I like best. I also like Youngland and Max Resist. I also like the Saga version of Skrewdriver songs.

*Res:* Being so young, aware, and proud of your heritage, is it hard to relate to other kids your age?

*Lynx:* Yes, it is sometimes, because they don't understand what is going on and even if their parents are closet racists, they don't teach their kids the facts . . .

*Lamb:* It is hard to relate to some kids who are mainstream,

like my friend who lives down the street. She has black
dolls. She makes them kiss with the white dolls. Yuck!
We told her that doll was ugly and that it was wrong. Her
parents are closet racists but they are afraid to teach her
to be racist, too. I guess they just think she will figure it
out. But there could be a time when she might come home
with a black boyfriend and think that is okay. Then what
will they do?

The use of a racial epithet surprised me. Likewise, the
description of the non-white doll as ugly. There's a kind of
decorum practiced among certain white racists, that dic-
tates that they don't put down other races. Their beliefs,
they maintain, have to do with pride in one's own race.
Hence, they style themselves 'white separatists' rather than
'white supremacists'. This was how they talked when their
guard was down.

And was Final War really Lamb's favourite kind of
music?

※

The photo of Lamb and Lynx in short skirts on the cover of
*Resistance* spawned a lively discussion on White Power
message forums on the Internet.

'Breaking News: National Alliance using kiddie porn
now,' ran one post, with a copy of the cover pasted into the
message.

'Who is running *Resistance*?' asked another. 'Aryans?
Or *filthy kike pimps in Tel Aviv*?'

'Do you think Hitler would have allowed his little girl
out dressed like that?' asked a third.

Using her online name SheWolfoftheNA, April
responded: 'I would like you to understand exactly the

aim of the cover of *Resistance* magazine this time. We are hoping to get the attention of young girls who are being bombarded with images like Britney Spears and the like. We are competing against the Hilary Duff/Mary Kate and Ashley Olsen phenomenon and girls dressed like *Little House on the Prairie* won't cut it. We need to be able to attract young women to our way of thinking in a way that will be timely as well as maintain our cultural and racial identification. The one thing that we lack more than anything, are women in our white nationalist community. I believe that we need to attract them as young as possible and to do it in any way that works.'

It was true, I reflected, that teen idols on the Disney Channel dressed in a grown-up way and wore make-up; but as a rule, they also smiled in their photographs. The girls hadn't smiled, I think probably because they wanted to look tough. But the combined effect of the short skirts and the not smiling gave them a kind of come hither look which on twelve-year-old girls was, to say the least, disquieting.

When I saw them again the following year, on the way to the Halloween theme park, I asked April about the *Resistance* cover. I put it to April that she'd dressed the twins provocatively on purpose.

'But there's no flesh showing!' she said. 'I mean, they're wearing leotards . . . At the very most, you could have said okay, maybe their skirts were a little short. But for them to claim it was kiddie porn? Did you see that? Isn't that bizarre?'

'Well, I think they were trying to make a point by exaggerating.'

'Well, yeah, but that's stupid. That's like what the Jews

do. That's what we accuse the Jews of doing all the time, exaggerating figures and stuff to make a point.'

'They said *you* were acting like a Jew,' I pointed out.

✳

The Halloween theme park, when we got there, turned out to be a kind of epic version of the haunted houses they have at funfairs. There were walks through dark woods, a large spooky house, and a 'hayride', all of them staffed with people dressed up as ghouls and ghosts, looming out of the shadows, cackling, howling and hooting.

I'm unusually sensitive to sudden loud noises, and I found the only way I could make it through the haunted zones without completely jangling my nerves was if I put my fingers in my ears and squinted. The idea of the outing, of course, had been to give me a chance to chat to Lamb and Lynx about the changes in their lives and about their beliefs. We'd done a little of that in the car. Lynx talked about the need for 'real' diversity. What if lions and tigers interbred until there were none left, just a mixed-up species of half-and-halfs? Listening back to the tape of my conversation with the girls, I was surprised to hear me say to Lynx, 'Good answer.' Then I mentioned that 'lygers' were real animals but that they, apparently, suffer from weight problems, as I'd learned on a Channel 5 documentary. I said this in the spirit of making a concession to her argument.

The truth was, I felt odd soliciting incendiary remarks from Lamb and Lynx. Their comments about White Power had a rehearsed quality – they didn't seem quite real. I had a feeling they would rather be listening to their Sony Discmans.

I was looking out for changes in them. They had both grown a couple of inches while I was away. They were a little more ladylike, wearing tiny amounts of make-up. Lamb had earrings. They had braces on their teeth.

'We have tickets to go to a Green Day concert on November 20,' Lynx said. 'We know they're not racial. They're probably a communist band. But it doesn't matter because it's still good music and stuff. And it's kind of upbeat and they're talented musicians.'

April's mother had been waiting for us at the park. Her name was Dianne. She wore glasses, and had short white hair. She grew up in Devon and came to America when she was fourteen. She babysat Dresden while we explored the park. After we'd done the walks and the hayride, we sat round in the concourse eating hot dogs while a rock band played and people dressed as zombies and ghouls mingled with the paying public.

'Are there still gaps where the buildings were bombed out in the Blitz?' Dianne asked.

'Not really,' I said.

'I was in Bristol. It was bad. So many derelict buildings. You'd see a bathtub two storeys up, just sticking out of the wall. They bombed Bristol pretty badly.'

'April likes him,' I said, meaning Hitler. It seemed rather an important point – destruction of Europe by April's dear leader – but Dianne didn't hear. 'What do you think of April's views?'

'I think the races should be separate. I'm not a fighter the way my husband is. You don't want a khaki nation do you? I had a friend over in England. He said everyone was khaki!' She squeezed Lamb's cheeks. 'Look at that face.

Isn't it beautiful? Blonde hair. Peachy complexion. Why would you want to go and ruin it?

✳

The following morning, dandling baby Dresden on her lap, April played me a song from the new CD that Lamb and April had written together called 'Sacrifice' about martyrs to the cause of white nationalism. 'Sacrifice, they gave their lives, all those ones who died.' It mentioned Rudolph Hess and William Pierce, the founder of the National Alliance. There was also another cover of a song by Ian Stuart, called 'The Snow Fell'.

'I can't wait to do the video on this,' April said.

'You're doing a video?'

'Yeah! And a DVD!'

There were microphone stands in the front room. The girls sang 'Green Fields of France', a song about the First World War, which had also been covered by Ian Stuart. It had been drizzling, and when they finished Lynx went to the window and said, 'I like the smell after it rains.'

'Do you think you might be a stage mom?' I said to April.

'Do *you* think I'm a stage mom?' April said, with a sudden surge of intensity. 'What is a stage mom? Is a stage mom someone who buys their kids musical instruments and hauls them off to lessons every goddamn week when she has laundry and a thousand other things to do? And gets them to an open mike night so they can perform and books them into a recording studio? Isn't it someone that's overwhelmingly controlling and overbearing? I don't think you could accuse me of that.'

Lamb, who had been strumming chords on her guitar, suddenly announced: 'I just wrote two new songs.' She played a set of chord changes. Then another. 'That's the second one,' she said.

'We could get some lyrics that someone sent us,' April said.

'Who sends you lyrics?' I asked.

'Racial people,' April said. 'People in the movement. Prisoners.'

'No, Mom. I want this song mainstream,' Lamb said. Then her tone softened: 'So we can have some mainstream songs for shows.'

'Would you like Prussian Blue to be a mainstream band?' I asked Lamb.

'Somewhat, yeah. Um, we could also make a mainstream band, and that would be completely different.'

'What would you sing about in your mainstream band?'

Lamb was sitting on the sofa with her knees up inside her baggy T-shirt, like a big tent. 'Well, I'm writing a song about how you don't have to do stuff just because other people say it's cool. Like smoking and drinking. It's called "You Don't Have To".'

＊

There was one other big change in the twins' life. They would be going to school the following year. April had found one that she was happy with. It was 70 per cent white. She seemed excited at the prospect of sending Lamb and Lynx to school full of white racial propaganda. She had an idea that the diary of Anne Frank, which is part of the curriculum in California, had been written in ballpoint pen, which wasn't widely available until after the war, and that therefore it was probably a forgery. 'I'm certainly going to support them if they want to challenge their teachers, and if they want to write a paper about the Anne Frank diary being questionable or Martin Luther King being a degenerate,' April said. 'I'll go speak to their teachers and if they get downgraded for including stuff that's factually accurate, I'll go in and call 'em on it.'

'What if they don't want to do that?'

'How do you mean?'

'What if they don't want to challenge their teachers. Would you support them then?'

'Yeah! Whatever they want to do.'

My own sense was that they'd probably want to make friends with classmates and get good grades, rather than offer a National Socialist-influenced critique of the school curriculum, but I was no longer surprised that April might think otherwise. It reminded me a little of a fantasy I sometimes used to have myself of going back to school as a grown-up and knowing more than everyone else, putting the teachers in their place, except hers was a White Power version and she was living it through her kids.

I wondered how the baby would grow up. Lamb and Lynx were already eight years old when their mom became a 'racial activist'. But Dresden would never know anything else. From her very conception, she was a kind of breeding experiment. A test case of racist child-rearing.

The twins were watching Green Day, whose videos they had on TiVo. April was holding Dresden in her lap and moving her like a puppet in time to the music. 'Yeah!' she said in a baby voice. 'Hopefoowy, she will get some musical tawent fwom somewhere!' Dresden danced around, seeming to enjoy it. Her hair was wispy, strawberry blonde. Her arms and legs were like marshmallow. She poked her tongue out and gurgled.

Lamb and Lynx said they were hungry. 'What are we going to eat?'

'We could always stick a Jew in the oven!' April said. 'Ha ha ha!' But she was still thinking about Dresden and her musical future. 'You know what would be fun? You could have a bluescreen and make her dance and make her play all the different instruments and make it look like she was doing it all on her own.'

# EPILOGUE

Late in the year, still staying in my rented apartment in Hollywood, I began writing.

Within days of moving in it had become clear that, from a creative perspective, the apartment couldn't have been worse. I'd been in a rush when I viewed it, and I'd failed to notice that it overlooked a motorcycle dealership and an alleyway favoured by the drivers of heavy lorries. It was possibly the noisiest apartment anywhere in the city, a kind of ongoing chamber concert of urban noise. During the lulls between the revving of the motorbikes, the trundling of the heavy trucks, the drone of the police helicopters overhead, the whoop of the car alarms in the parking lot of Sizzler, and the tintinnabulation of the bottles and cans in the shopping carts of passing street people, I worked through the winter.

But even as I wrote I kept phoning my old subjects, updating my notes, interviewing new people, attempting to disclose some secret that lay at the bottom of my ever mounting heap of material.

I checked in with Art, the hapless Marshall Sylver follower, finding he'd lost his job at DirecTV and was now selling Las Vegas timeshares. I chatted to Pat, the pro-stoning patriot I'd seen up at Almost Heaven, and was surprised to hear he'd relaxed his scruples about remarriage and shacked up with a woman he met on the Internet – raising the question of whether he might have to stone himself.

I spoke to April, still hoping I might attend a Folk the System event or a 'Eurofest'. And so it went on, with calls to Hayley, JJ, Mello T, Ike and others.

As the months passed, some of the stories I'd been covering made headlines again. In January, a federal judge threw out the obscenity indictment against the 'horror porn' director Rob Black. In March, after a court ruled that the husband of a woman who'd been in a 'persistent vegetative state' for fifteen years was within his rights to remove her feeding tube, Colonel Bo Gritz was arrested in a quixotic act of protest, attempting to bring bread and water to the invalid, who naturally was in no position to consume them.

The following month, a nationwide manhunt was launched to capture the neo-Nazi hitman who'd killed the family of a judge in Milwaukee. I called April for her thoughts and learned she was among those caught up in the investigation – four SWAT-type federal agents had arrived on her doorstep, she said. I began to wonder whether I'd underestimated the threat posed by the White Power movement when I'd written them off as jackanapes. A few days later, the real culprit was caught: an out-of-work electrician with an obsession about his failed medical malpractice claim.

By now my return date to Britain was past due, but though I missed my friends and family and my house, I still didn't feel ready to go back.

One of the last calls I made was to Harold Camping, the Oakland-based Bible scholar who'd been the subject of my first ever TV interview in 1994, back when he was predicting with 99.9 per cent certainty that the world was about to end later in the year. He'd based his conclusion on a painstaking analysis of the 'jubilees' mentioned in the Old Testament, and publicized it in a book entitled *1994?* (the question mark being an acknowledgement of the 0.1 per cent possibility that everything would be fine). Though his scholarship was emphatically non-mainstream, Camping actually had a large following. His radio ministry, Family Radio, owned stations across the US, with listeners in the millions.

For that first interview, I'd visited him a few months before the predicted apocalypse at his headquarters in Oakland. In the flesh, he had seemed a kindly man. He was in his seventies, with a deep voice and a craggy face. It being my first assignment, I was nervous. I still wasn't quite sure what I was doing there and so I was relieved when he did most of the talking. I recall him saying that the end, when it came, would be 'super-terrible'. He went through some of the events mentioned in the book of Revelation, marking them on a calendar . . . last chance for salvation is on Wednesday the ninth . . . a third of the waters turn to bitter wormwood on Thursday . . . Jesus returns on Saturday . . . and so on. Among the questions I asked was, 'Let's say I worship the Devil. Should I be worried?'

What I was expecting when I called him again, I don't know – I wasn't even sure whether he was still alive. I suppose I just hoped that, since my book was about following up old stories, I might learn something by checking-in with my oldest story of all.

I found his offices in the phone book and reached a doubtful-sounding receptionist, who went off the line and then put me through rather grudgingly. He sounded much as I remembered – warm and friendly and indulgent of my ignorant questioning, with the one difference that, at eighty-three, his hearing seemed to be going. Naturally, he didn't remember our interview; nor was I keen to remind him, since the show in which I'd done the segment had been satirical in tone. 'It was for the BBC,' I said, breezily, and changed the subject.

If I'd been expecting him to be apologetic or defensive on the small matter of Jesus's non-appearance and the failure of the waters to turn to bitter wormwood, I was disappointed. It was possible, he said, that he'd rushed the printing of *1994?*. There was a verse in the Bible he thought he might have misread. But to be fair, he said: 'I didn't make a *prediction*. I said there's a high likelihood that 1994 *could* be the end.'

We chatted about his ministry. He said it was lucky I'd called. He'd been studying the Bible ever more diligently since our last conversation, and his latest scholarship indicated that we were at the end of the 'church age'. I wasn't sure what this meant, except, apparently, that we no longer needed to go to church – a liberty that I'd been allowing myself for some time. He had one other piece of news, however. He said that while he'd been wrong to predict the apocalypse in 1994, all the evidence now pointed to the end coming in 2011. He'd just finished writing a book on this very topic, and it was important that as many people as possible should be forewarned.

'Aha!' I said.

'It's based *entirely* on a very careful reading of the Bible

. . . The last twelve years I've been working *very very* hard on this and I have a whole lot greater information today than I did first time around.'

'So what advice are you giving to people?' I asked.

'Oh, the advice I give to people is to get ready to meet God. It's a super-terrible future that awaits mankind unless they become saved.'

'And you don't see it as an obstacle that you said the end would happen in 1994?'

'Well,' he said, 'it's like when you first try to ride a bicycle. You fall off the first time and then you get back on and you ride again.'

When I embarked on my Reunion Tour, it was with the idea of seeing how the lives of my ex-subjects had changed and how they were faring in their various strange commitments. Weirdness, as I understand the word, is a form of belief or a practice that isn't merely outside the mainstream but is also in some way self-sabotaging. Having sex on camera for a living violates the most intimate sphere of life; to pay someone money to hypnotize you into being a millionaire is foolishness; preparing for an apocalypse that never comes is, among other things, a distraction from the more important business of life. To me these things are axiomatic. And so, I went back, in a spirit of curiosity, inflected, perhaps, with a little Schadenfreude, to see whether the disappointments of age, the censure of the straight world, might have forced them to rethink their outlook. I thought it was possible that with time they might see the light; they might shake off their beliefs and start to become more normal.

The months that followed threw me up against a cast of people, all with different visions of the world and different ideas of self-fulfilment, but all of them energetically pursuing their destiny. A few, in the overheated worlds of rap and porn, had found some measure of success. Many had faced challenges and setbacks, especially those true believers, like the pioneers of Almost Heaven and the racist empire-builders of the Aryan Nations, whose uncompromising faith-based vision had set them at odds with reality.

But people don't change their beliefs easily. Even when their deepest convictions are challenged – by the failure of the world to end, for example – they continue on their way, sticking to the old routine: they get back on their Weird bikes and ride again.

The same applies to me. I'd hoped the trip might be an opportunity for me to get in touch with my own weirdness. Without a camera, I wondered if I might become more immersed in my stories and therefore more open – forced to acknowledge my shadow side. But if anything, I found myself *less* susceptible to the call of the weird the second time round. The Nazis seemed more lamentable; the gangsta rappers more irresponsible; the gurus more manipulative. Instead of an inner weirdo, I was surprised to find an inner curmudgeon. Perhaps it's understandable to be more jaded on one's second exposure to something strange. I also suspect the protection of the camera and crew on my first TV-making sorties had allowed me, in a dilettante-ish way, to imagine I had more in common with my subjects than was really the case. In going back, unarmed, as it were, I was forced to be more realistic. As Mello T himself said, when it comes to pimping I'd rather go to bed early and do a crossword puzzle.

And yet in one important respect I *did* start to recognize

a kind of weirdness in myself. Occasionally, I saw ꞵ
between the seductions of some of the strange wo. ·
was covering and my own journalism. In reporting the.
stories over the years, maintaining relationships partly
out of genuine affection and partly out of the vanity of
wanting to generate 'material' for a programme or a book,
I realized I too had created a tiny off-beat subculture, with
its own sincerity and its own evasions. A little like a cult
leader or a prostitute, I had been working in a grey area
somewhere south of absolute candour . . . but like the other
cults and subcultures contained in these pages, I have also
been pleased to find a depth of feeling in our group.
Though occasionally I'd been rebuffed by my old subjects,
or shocked by their beliefs, and though I'd sometimes
questioned my own motivations, in general, I was more
amazed by their willingness to put up with me a second
time, and surprised by my affection for them. I'd been
moved at times, and irritated, and upset, but the emotions
had been real.

This is my Weirdness. If the lesson of Harold Camping
is any guide, it is my destiny to live it to the end. 'Have you
ever argued with a member of the Flat Earth Society?'
a self-help guru named Ross Jeffries once asked me. 'It's
completely futile, because fundamentally they don't care
if something is true or false. To them, the measure
of truth is how important it makes them feel. If telling the
truth makes them feel important, then it's true. If telling
the truth makes them feel ashamed and small, then it's
false.' My experience on my trip has borne this out. On the
list of qualities necessary to humans trying to make our
way through life, truth scores fairly low. Why do people
believe and do weird things? Because in the end, feeling

alive is more important than telling the truth. We have evolved as living creatures to express ourselves, to be creative, to tell stories. We are instruments for feeling, faith, energy, emotion, significance, belief, but not really truth.

As noted by both Shakespeare and Elvis, the world is a stage we walk upon. We are all, in a way, fictional characters who write ourselves with our beliefs.

As I worked away in the cacophonous apartment, with the noise of the passing trucks and the motorcycles shaking the walls, I realized that this might be the secret I was hoping to disclose. I would never stop phoning round my old subjects. I would never stop musing over cups of tea, and wondering what became of the people I met; the journey was ongoing and endless. And I became aware of that vast continent of human stories that lay at my back, stretched out under the overarching sky: the UFO believers and porn performers, and cult leaders and rappers, and somewhere a neo-Nazi playing mah-jong on his computer in a room he shared with fifteen-cent fish. And for now, I put down my pen.

and Alison Clevenger, for finding my laptop computer by the side of the road in Idaho and returning it safely to me. Thanks most of all to Nancy. Without her valuable insights and her constant support and encouragement there would be no book. I owe her more than words can say.

# ACKNOWLEDGEMENTS

Everything in this book is faithful to the way it was, except for a few elisions of time, for the sake of the narrative, and two names: Dave Roach and Art Eagle.

Though I wrote the book on my own, the TV shows that inspired it were made collaboratively. In the interest of economy, throughout the text I have referred to 'my documentaries', but the hard work was done by a host of producers, directors, editors and APs. Special thanks to Michael Moore, for giving me my break, David Mortimer, for giving me my own show, and to Kevin Sutcliffe, Ed Robbins, Geoffrey O'Connor, Kate Townsend, Will Yapp, Simon Boyce, Jim Margolis, Maria Silver, Karen Morton, Alicia Kerr, Stuart Cabb, and a host of other production personnel, for making sure the show stayed on the air. In going back, I was helped enormously by Charlie Braxton, Luke Ford, Rob Balch, Rick Ross, and Ron Faulk. I was also helped, of course, by the many contributors whose stories are the subject of this book. Thanks also to Mike Oehler and Ken Kurson, for their hospitality, Majestik Magnificent, for helping me find a car, my editor Richard Milner, for his patience, Philippa Brewster, for her editorial notes, Scott Galloway, for his advice, and Brett